In Defense of Dolphins

Blackwell Public Philosophy
Edited by *Michael Boylan*, Marymount University

In a world of 24-hour news cycles and increasingly specialized knowledge, the Blackwell Public Philosophy series takes seriously the idea that there is a need and demand for engaging and thoughtful discussion of topics of broad public importance. Philosophy itself is historically grounded in the public square, bringing people together to try to understand the various issues that shape their lives and give them meaning. This "love of wisdom" – the essence of philosophy – lies at the heart of the series. Written in an accessible, jargon-free manner by internationally renowned authors, each book is an invitation to the world beyond newsflashes and soundbites and into public wisdom.

Permission to Steal: Revealing the Roots of Corporate Scandal by Lisa H. Newton
Doubting Darwin? Creationist Designs on Evolution by Sahotra Sarkar
The Extinction of Desire: A Tale of Enlightenment by Michael Boylan
Torture and the Ticking Bomb by Bob Brecher
In Defense of Dolphins: The New Moral Frontier by Thomas I. White

Forthcoming:
Terrorism and Counter-Terrorism: An Applied Philosophical Approach by Seumas Miller
Spiritual but Not Religious: The Evolving Science of the Soul by Christian Erickson
Evil On-Line: Explorations of Evil and Wickedness on the Web by Dean Cocking and Jeroen van den Hoven

IN DEFENSE OF DOLPHINS

The New Moral Frontier

Thomas I. White

17. X. 2008 Friday Harbor

To Cindy —
Friend of the oceans and
all who live there.
Best wishes,
Tom White

Blackwell
Publishing

© 2007 by Thomas I. White

BLACKWELL PUBLISHING
350 Main Street, Malden, MA 02148-5020, USA
9600 Garsington Road, Oxford OX4 2DQ, UK
550 Swanston Street, Carlton, Victoria 3053, Australia

The right of Thomas I. White to be identified as the Author of this
Work has been asserted in accordance with the UK Copyright, Designs,
and Patents Act 1988.

First published 2007 by Blackwell Publishing Ltd

1   2007

Library of Congress Cataloging-in-Publication Data

White, Thomas I.
In defense of dolphins : the new moral frontier / Thomas I. White.
      p.   cm.
Includes bibliographical references.
ISBN 978-1-4051-5778-0 (hardcover : alk. paper) – ISBN 978-1-4051-5779-7
(pbk. : alk. paper)   1. Dolphins–Philosophy.   2. Animal welfare–Moral and
   ethical aspects.   3. Human-animal relationships–Philosophy.   I. Title.

QL737.C432W48 2007
599.53–dc22
2007014522

A catalogue record for this title is available from the British Library.

Set in 10.5/13pt Minion by Graphicraft Typesetters Ltd, Hong Kong
Printed in Singapore by COS Printers Pte Ltd

The publisher's policy is to use permanent paper from mills that operate
a sustainable forestry policy, and which has been manufactured from
pulp processed using acid-free and elementary chlorine-free practices.
Furthermore, the publisher ensures that the text paper and cover board
used have met acceptable environmental accreditation standards.

For further information on
Blackwell Publishing, visit our website:
www.blackwellpublishing.com

To the happy memory of

Paul Oskar Kristeller
Richard Curry Marius
Margaret Mann Phillips

Teachers and friends

And

To Lisa

Contents

Preface

This book provides an account of the conclusions I've reached about two questions that I've pondered for nearly 20 years: What kind of beings are dolphins? What does the answer to this question say about the ethical character of human/dolphin interaction? This is a wide-ranging book that combines philosophy and science, research and anecdotes. It is written for a general audience with the aim of encouraging our species to reconsider our current relationship not only with cetaceans, but also with the other nonhumans with whom we share this planet.

As a discussion aimed at a general audience—not a technical readership of philosophers or scientists—this book has a specific plan and goal.

- I begin by surveying the major scientific research on dolphin intelligence and social behavior, and I claim that this research reveals that dolphins possess sophisticated intellectual and emotional abilities. Using a traditional definition of "personhood," I then argue that dolphins are nonhuman persons and, therefore, are entitled to moral standing as individuals. Finally, I conclude by arguing that the deaths, injury and captivity of dolphins connected with a variety of human practices are ethically indefensible.
- The ultimate aim of the book, then, is practical—to argue for an end to certain ways that humans treat dolphins.

This book advances a specific point of view. I believe that an impartial and objective examination of the relevant scientific evidence supports the idea that dolphins are a "who," not a "what," and that most of the current treatment of dolphins by humans is wrong. I also believe that even the most skeptical reading of the research concludes that certain practices must be stopped. Even a skeptic would have to concede that there is a reasonable possibility that dolphins are nonhuman persons and that current practices may, therefore, do considerable harm to beings with moral standing as individuals. Even a commonsense approach to ethics recognizes that if there's a reasonable possibility that our actions will hurt someone, then we have a duty to avoid doing them. That is, at the very least, serious doubts can be raised about the ethical acceptability of certain practices in the fishing and entertainment industries. Accordingly, even the most skeptical and anthropocentric analysis of the data must recognize that the only ethically appropriate course of action is to suspend such practices as fishing "on dolphin" and captive breeding programs. In a questionable situation, the "benefit of the doubt" goes to the individual who would be harmed.

In light of the book's intended audience, goal, and legitimate editorial issues regarding the size of this book, my discussion has specific limitations.

- I am aware that using the concept of "personhood" and placing so much emphasis on the capacities and vulnerabilities of a sophisticated consciousness puts us dangerously close to anthropocentrism, and I have tried to address this issue at different points in the discussion. However, I do try to argue in a way that even the most skeptical reader will find convincing. I think that in the case of dolphins, the fact that there is so much scientific research about the character of their consciousness gives us firm, uncontroversial grounds for making a judgment about whether certain kinds of human/dolphin contact are ethically defensible. I believe that even humans who see the world in a thoroughly anthropocentric way would have to concede that the scientific evidence creates enough doubt about the ethical acceptability of current practices to warrant stopping them.

- This book discusses only dolphins, not other nonhumans. It does not address the general issue of "animal rights." The strategy I use in this book should not be taken as implying that personhood, consciousness and sophisticated cognitive and affective capacities are the only, or even the best, philosophical grounds on which to make judgments about the ethical acceptability of human/nonhuman interaction.

- This book does not lobby for a single tradition in moral philosophy or environmental ethics. Because the book is aimed at a general audience, I use a very basic philosophical approach to ethics that mainly explores issues of *harm* and *appropriate treatment*.

- I do not discuss debates about such technical philosophical issues as the nature of the self, the nature of self-consciousness and whether there is a legitimate distinction between rational and emotional aspects of consciousness.

- Similarly, I do not discuss debates about such technical scientific issues as the "initial brain hypothesis" as it relates to the evolution of the dolphin brain.

This book would have been impossible without the assistance of many people over the years. Each of the following individuals provided a unique contribution for which I am deeply grateful (although I hasten to add that my thanks should not suggest that any of these people necessarily agrees with my conclusions): Kristin Andrews, Karen Bell, Sam Bleecker, Lisa Cavallaro, Paola Cavielieri, Fabienne Delfour, Christoph Demmerling, Laura Engleby, Will Engleby, John Gorey, Joy Hammp, Denise Herzing, W. Michael Hoffman, Carol Howard, Deb Huckabee, Stan Kuczaj, Nicole Mader, Lori Marino, Herbert Medina, Jessica Miles, Kelly Moewe, Lisa Newton, Ken Norris, David Ozar, Adam Pack, Marilyn Paul, Diana Reiss, Peter Roberts, Cindy Rogers, Dan Sammis, Ro Sammis, Della Schuler, Susan Shane, Suchi Psarakos and Bernd Würsig. Logistical support was provided at different times by Upsala College, Rider University, Loyola Marymount University and, most especially, by Peter Mosinskis, Michael Reiner, Justin Goodkind and Kirsten Nordblom. I am also indebted to my agent, Jeff Herman, my editor, Jeff Dean, and to a variety of people at Blackwell Publishing—Linda Auld, Susan Dunsmore, Rebecca du Plessis, Lisa Eaton, Jamie Harlan, Leanda Shrimpton and the anonymous reviewers of the book's first draft.

Thomas I. White
Redondo Beach, California

Prologue
Why does a philosopher study dolphins?

One of the curiosities of the group of people who become interested in dolphins is that many arrive there via fairly circuitous paths. My own story is no exception. I received my PhD in philosophy from Columbia University, and for the next 15 years I specialized in sixteenth-century Renaissance humanism. By the mid-1980s, however, I was beginning to think about more contemporary issues (questions of business ethics, and the debate whether men and women approach ethical dilemmas differently). I was also trying my hand at writing college textbooks. So when Prentice Hall asked me to write a large, introductory philosophy textbook in 1987, I regarded this as an interesting challenge.

Probably the most difficult part about writing such a textbook would be to make the more arcane issues in philosophy come alive to students. Undergraduates have no shortage of enthusiasm for moral, social and political philosophy. But students typically get much less excited over the basic questions of metaphysics: the nature of reality, the self, and personhood, for example. Fortunately, the publisher wanted me to approach a few topics from some nonphilosophical disciplines. As I was mulling over the structure of the book, a friend who had just vacationed in Florida returned with some literature about "dolphin swim" programs in the Florida Keys. Having grown up by the sea in Massachusetts and then living near the ocean in New Jersey, I'd heard many stories about the intelligence of whales and dolphins. So it occurred to me that a description of the advanced traits of the nonhuman dolphin would be an ideal way to introduce students to the metaphysical concept of *personhood*. I would write a chapter that would define what a person is and then ask the question: "Is a dolphin a *nonhuman person*?"

I'd decided that the best way to begin studying dolphins was to talk to people who work with them. If luck was on my side, I might even get the chance to spend some time in the water with them myself. I'd heard good things about the Dolphin Research Center (DRC) in the Florida Keys, one of the handful of places that offers "dolphin swims." DRC is unusual for a captive facility. It is home to a community of about 15 bottlenose dolphins, but the dolphins do not live in concrete tanks. The Center is located on the Gulf side of the Keys, and while the dolphins live in pens separated by fencing, this is more to keep other things out than to keep the dolphins in. The fences are so low that dolphins can easily come and go, although most never do.

One of the most impressive things about virtually everyone I've met in the dolphin world is just how willing they've been to help someone like myself new to the field. And this generous spirit was apparent in my first contact with people at DRC. Some of the staff agreed to be interviewed. I was given permission to spend as much time as I wanted observing the dolphins. Best of all, I was even able to arrange for a couple of swims.

The first day I saw humans and dolphins together remains one of the most unforgettable.

My visit to DRC began with a quick tour of the facility, during which I was invited to watch an upcoming swim. Anxious to observe how the dolphins would interact with their human visitors, I watched as a family of three made its way to the dolphins' dock. The parents entered first and then helped their young son into the water. The boy was clearly apprehensive – and he became even more nervous when a dolphin named Little Bit swam up and parked herself right beside him. Encouraged by the trainer to reach out and touch the dolphin, the boy responded. Unfortunately, he responded somewhat too enthusiastically. He reached out and slapped his hand directly onto Little Bit's blowhole – the opening on the top of a dolphin's head through which these cetaceans breathe. Little Bit slowly backed up, allowing the boy's hand to slide down her rostrum. And she remained near the boy, remarkably attentive throughout the remainder of the swim.

To the untrained eye, the encounter was simply interesting. It wasn't until I discussed it later with one of the DRC staff that I understood the full significance of what had happened.

Little Bit had a reputation for taking a special interest in children, but her behavior when the boy put his hand over her blowhole was most unusual. Ordinarily, one of the quickest ways to "spook" a dolphin is to move your hand towards the top of its head. Dolphins' eyes have great mobility, but this is one of their few blind spots. And unlike humans, who can breathe through either our noses or mouths, dolphins have only one opening to their lungs. If you move your hand towards a dolphin's blowhole, he or she will usually jerk its head away. But the boy's hand didn't simply move out of Little Bit's view towards a sensitive area, it fell squarely on top of her blowhole – the equivalent of clamping your hand over a human's nose and mouth. The fact that Little Bit responded to this by slowly backing up – and then staying patiently with the boy for the rest of the swim – was extraordinary.

However, I was then told about an even more remarkable encounter – this time involving a blind boy and a dolphin named Tursi.

Since the child was unable to see the dolphins in the pool, he was trying to orient on them by following the directions of his parents and the trainer in charge of the swim. But then Tursi – a dolphin who typically had no interest in swimmers – swam up to the boy and whistled to let him know she was there. And she remained by him for the whole encounter, vocalizing the whole time.

Remarkably, Tursi had determined that the boy was sightless, and she adjusted her behavior appropriately. Dolphins generally recognize the difference between human adults and children, and they tend to be more patient and gentle with children. But the fact that Tursi also adapted her behavior to the boy's sightlessness was quite impressive.

However, perhaps the most interesting fact is that Tursi herself was blind in one eye. Could this have had anything to do with the way she related to the boy?

These episodes with Little Bit and Tursi were a particularly good place for a philosopher like myself to begin. The incidents were so rich that they are as engaging now as the day I saw the one and heard about the other. And they raise a number of important questions:

- Why did Little Bit and Tursi behave as they did? Did Tursi really understand that the boy was blind? How would she have determined that? Why did she take so much interest in him? Is it possible that seeing a child with a disability that she shared prompted a compassionate and patient response? Humans have for centuries claimed that only our species has thoughts and emotions. Does it turn out that we're wrong? Tursi's brain is bigger than yours or mine. What went on inside it that led her to act the way she did with the boy? Did Tursi's actions stem from thinking and feeling?
- And what does Tursi's and Little Bit's behavior say about other dolphins? If these dolphins' actions come from thoughts and emotions, the same

must be true of other dolphins. So what does this say about what type of being all dolphins are – Little Bit, Tursi, the other dolphins in the pool with them, and the millions of other dolphins who inhabit the planet's oceans? What is it like to be a dolphin? What intellectual and emotional abilities do they have? What is their "inner world" like? Do they all have different personalities, as we do?

- These encounters certainly seem to suggest that a dolphin is a "some *one*" not a "some *thing*" – indeed, a someone who perceives the world and makes decisions in a way similar to how we humans do. At the same time, these incidents remind us that dolphins are also fundamentally different from us. They live in the water. They look more like fish than primates. Their famous "smile" is no such thing. It's the fixed design of their head – a hydrodynamic feature, not a facial expression. The sounds they make don't seem anything like our words. In fact, we don't even hear many of their sounds because they're above the range of human hearing. What's the philosophical significance of all of this? If the similarities suggest that we're no longer alone at the top of the biological hierarchy, what do the differences say?

- But how can we be sure that we've correctly interpreted what happened between the dolphins and the boys? Are we really reading the facts in an objective and unbiased way? Or are we committing the cardinal sin in studying nonhumans and "anthropomorphizing" dolphins? Have our fantasies and imagination gotten the best of us so that we're just attributing human characteristics and intentions to dolphins when there's no good reason to do so?

- And, ultimately, if dolphins really are aware, intelligent, even compassionate beings, what does this say about how we treat them? Tursi and Little Bit may live in a facility that gives them the freedom to leave, but what about the hundreds of dolphins who live in concrete tanks and spend their lives entertaining us with acrobatics? And are Tursi and Little Bit themselves even free? After years of living in captivity, forming bonds with the other DRC dolphins, and depending on humans for food, is staying put truly an expression of their freedom? Or is it a combination of "learned dependency," loss of the social and hunting skills necessary to survive in the wild, and a predictable source of food? Is their decision a sign of happiness and contentment with the situation or a pragmatic trade-off?

The questions that my visit to DRC stimulated were fascinating enough in themselves. However, they took on new importance when I learned a few months later that hundreds of dolphins were dying at the hands of humans each day in the nets of tuna boats. If this were the death of humans, we'd surely all condemn it. Was this situation acceptable just because it involved nonhumans? Didn't the apparent intelligence of dolphins count for anything?

I first heard about the massive number of dolphin deaths in an unexpected way. Shortly after my visit to DRC, I participated in a post-doctoral seminar at the University of California at Berkeley on the philosopher Socrates. Since I was actively writing the dolphin chapters for my textbook at the time, I decided to take advantage of the fact that a number of prominent dolphin researchers lived in northern California. Before leaving New Jersey, I wrote to Diana Reiss, Berndt Würsig and Ken Norris; I described what I was working on; and I asked if they'd be willing to talk to me. All graciously accepted and were unfailingly generous in directing me towards scientific research that I should familiarize myself with. Then, shortly after my first conversation with Diana Reiss, I received a call from her about a lecture to be given by David Phillips from Earth Island Institute, the San Francisco-based environmental organization. When I'd originally met with Diana, I had outlined to her the ethical implications of nonhuman personhood in theory. But she said that Phillips was going to be speaking about something that captured the matter in practice – the deaths of dolphins in the nets of tuna boats.

The concept of "dolphin-safe" tuna didn't exist in the late 1980s. Indeed, the fact that dolphins were dying as a result of a particular way of fishing for tuna in the eastern tropical Pacific was virtually unknown to the general public on the East Coast of the United States. American tuna boats sailed out of San Diego, however, so the issue was better known in California. Phillips described the situation in depressing detail during his talk. But as an environmentalist, he emphasized the impact of such a large number of deaths on the overall viability of the dolphin populations in the eastern tropical Pacific. If it turned out that dolphins had all the traits of *persons*, however, the matter was much more serious. The deaths of *individual* dolphins would matter as well.

Being in California that summer also made me aware of another ethical issue – the use of captive dolphins for a variety of human purposes. Environmental issues received prominent coverage in the San Francisco papers, and the captivity of marine mammals was becoming increasingly controversial. Marineland Africa USA ran a facility north of San Francisco, and SeaWorld has a west coast operation in San Diego. And at bases in Hawaii and San Diego, the U.S. Navy reportedly trained a group of captive dolphins for military purposes.

Although less dramatic than the deaths of dolphins in tuna nets, captivity had important ethical implications. Some animal rights activists were campaigning against captivity, and there had already been some controversial attempts to free some captive dolphins. Claims and counterclaims were made about the health and lifespan of dolphins in captivity, the quality of the water in their tanks, their social lives, and the like.

At that point, I didn't know enough about dolphins, tuna fishing, the military or the entertainment industry even to hazard a guess about who was right or wrong on these issues. But if dolphins were actually nonhuman persons, the various types of captivity would require serious justification.

By the end of my summer in Berkeley, then, what had started simply as an interesting strategy for keeping undergraduates awake during a chapter on metaphysics had taken on a much more serious dimension. The trip to California helped me with my immediate problem of learning enough marine biology to write the personhood chapter. But the trip also revealed the scope of the ethical issues. Even so, while I learned enough to write the chapter that had originally set me on this path, I didn't feel that I knew enough to be especially definitive.

My attempt to find some kind of answer to the questions involved took me on a 15-year odyssey. I pored over scientific books and research papers on cetaceans. I interviewed marine scientists and dolphin trainers. I visited a variety of facilities where dolphins live and perform. And, most importantly, nearly every summer from 1990 to 2004, I ended up on a research boat in the Atlantic for anywhere from a week to a month.

This book will describe both the conclusions that I reached at the end of my journey as well as something of the process by which I got there. But this book will also ask *you* to reflect deeply on the subjects discussed here so that you too confront what must surely be some of the most important questions our species could face: Have humans actually been sharing the planet with other intelligent – but nonhuman – beings for millions of years without realizing it? And what does this say about our species' current treatment of dolphins?

CHAPTER 1

Dolphins
The philosophical questions

Tales that go back to ancient Crete tell of a band of unusual beings that inhabit a mysterious world far from human habitation. Little is known of them, but the fact that they would appear out of the dark to help lost travelers and even save drowning sailors led some ancients to believe that they were gods. These beings are curious about humans and seek contact with us, but we still do not understand the strange sounds they make as they communicate with each other. They can do things with their biological senses that we cannot achieve with our most advanced technology. Some say they have the ability to heal. Some claim these beings are telepathic. Others go further and say they are highly advanced spiritually and have a wide range of psychic abilities. Whatever they are, they remain enigmatic subjects of human fascination.

Who are these exceptional entities? Buddhist monks living in the farthest reaches of Nepal? A tribe of Native Americans who practice the ancient wisdom of their forebears? A colony of aliens transplanted from the cosmos? Hardly. They are dolphins – beings who are related more to Flipper than to the Buddha and whom we can meet daily at aquaria and theme parks.

While dolphins are neither divine nor extraterrestrial, they are very different from humans and surprisingly complex. And, most important, the fact that dolphins have such advanced traits raises a number of philosophical – and especially ethical – questions. Are dolphins so advanced that they should be considered nonhuman "persons"? If so, what does this say about our behavior towards them? Dolphins die daily as a result of human fishing practices, and hundreds are held in captivity. Is this morally justifiable, given their unusual nature?

———————————— "Human" Versus "Person" ————————————

You might be surprised to read the question, "Are dolphins persons?" because in everyday language, most of us use "human" and "person" interchangeably. But philosophers distinguish between the two, seeing "human" as a *scientific* concept and "person" as a *philosophical* concept. *Human* refers to any member of the biological category *homo sapiens*. *Person* refers more to the combination of advanced traits by which we define ourselves – things like self-consciousness, intelligence and free will.

A variety of complicated theoretical issues are connected with personhood, but it has one especially practical implication: persons get better treatment than nonpersons do. It's acceptable to hit a punching bag, but not your spouse. Persons are seen as having rights – to life, liberty, equality, and the like – that nonpersons like chairs, tables, trees or amoeba lack. And most of us think that if we treat persons no better than we treat nonpersons, or if we violate a person's rights, we've done something *wrong*. In other words, what starts as a theoretical discussion in metaphysics quickly migrates to the applied world of ethics – the part of philosophy concerned with matters of right and wrong.[1]

———————————— Human, Person and Ethics ————————————

The ethical significance of the human/person distinction surfaces first in the question: *Is every human also a person?* This question regularly comes up in the world of medicine, when we find situations in which it's not always clear that a human is also a person. For example, someone who is irreversibly "brain dead," but being kept alive by a life-support system, is still a human life. But what made that individual unique is no longer present in that body. Accordingly, if we ended life-support for that patient, most of us wouldn't call it murder because, in essence, the *person* was already dead.

---

[1]   I want to make it clear from the outset that I am not claiming that personhood is the sole, or necessarily the most important ground for nonhumans to have moral standing. However, if it is possible to establish that dolphins are nonhuman persons, I believe that even the most anthropocentric humans would have difficulty defending the way humans currently treat dolphins. I have chosen to stress the concept of personhood in this inquiry, then, primarily for strategic reasons.

The human/person distinction also surfaces in the abortion debate. Many defenders of abortion claim that, particularly in the early stages of pregnancy, only one person exists – the mother. Even though they concede that abortion ends some sort of human life, they contend that it isn't murder. The only *person* involved is exercising her right to choose what happens to her body. And so the abortion isn't wrong. Many opponents of abortion take the opposite tack. They argue that a fetus is, at the very least, a potential person. And this means, they say, that it has a basic right to life that must be respected no matter what the circumstances. The situation, then, involves a clash between one person's right to choose and another person's right to life. And since a right to life is seen as being primary, abortion is denounced as wrong.

However, the human/person distinction also implies another question: *Are there persons who are not human?* After all, in theory, any being with self-consciousness, intelligence and free will, for example – no matter what the species – would qualify as a person. It's this question that led me to study dolphins, because many of the stories we hear about them suggests that we've come upon a person who isn't human.

The existence of nonhuman persons would fly in the face of everything our species has believed about its uniqueness for thousands of years. Indeed, we've gotten so used to thinking that humans are the only beings with advanced intellectual and emotional traits that we use "human" and "person" as synonyms in everyday speech. This attitude is also reflected in how we refer in ordinary conversation to "people" versus "animals" – conveniently ignoring the fact that humans are as much a part of the animal kingdom as lions and tigers and bears. But if an "animal" like a dolphin actually has all of the traits of a "person," it would call for as fundamental, dramatic and unsettling a shift in how we see ourselves as abandoning a geocentric view of the heavens did. In the same way that Earth no longer occupied the center of the universe, neither would humans. It would also call for a shift in how humans treat dolphins – and, very likely, many other nonhumans.

Philosophical Ethics

The ultimate question we're investigating in this book is: *Does our species currently treat dolphins in a way that's ethically justifiable?* We all know from everyday conversations that as soon as we start saying that something's "right" or "wrong," it's easy to be misunderstood. So let's be clear about what's involved in a philosophical approach to ethics.

Even in ordinary conversation, ethics is actually simpler than it seems. Despite the different meanings each of us may give to words like "right," "wrong," "moral," "immoral," "ethical" and "unethical," in the end, all we're saying is that something is, more or less, either *acceptable* or *not*. That is, when we use words like "right" and "wrong," we're saying how well something (usually an action, but sometimes a belief, idea or intention) measures up against some sort of "ethical yardstick."

Much of the disagreement and confusion in everyday discussions about ethics comes from the fact that people use so many different yardsticks. For some, it is the laws of a society. For others, it's the norms and traditions of a culture. A large number of people use religious teachings. Many individuals prefer a more personal yardstick – the fact that they deeply and sincerely believe that something's right or wrong. And some people put together a yardstick from so many different sources that it's a veritable patchwork.

A *philosophical* approach to ethics takes the one element we have in common – our humanity – as the basis of its yardstick. Philosophers take the position that – just because of the nature of the cloth from which we're cut – there are two things that all humans need in order to have a rudimentary sense of satisfaction in life, and to be able to grow, develop in a healthy way and flourish. First, our basic physical requirements must be met – food, shelter, safety, health and the like. Second, we need to be treated in certain ways. That is, there's something about the way that human beings are constituted that, no matter what, being treated unfairly, being discriminated against, being manipulated, being lied to and the like go against our grain and are deeply troubling. We may be able to handle bad treatment and deprivation. But we'll never find it truly satisfying. To say that an action is *right* from a philosophical perspective, then, is just a shorthand way of saying that it makes it more likely that we'll get these needs met. To say that something's *wrong* means that the action in question is going to get in the way of our getting these needs met.[2]

---

[2] The idea that human beings have these general types of needs (basic material needs of life and appropriate treatment) is a common notion that surfaces in discussions of "basic human rights." From this perspective, we have a *right* to something because we *need* it. Virtually every description of "human rights" – the United Nations' Universal Declaration of Human Rights, for example – is based on the assumption that what makes something a basic human right is that humans *need* it in order to experience a sense of basic satisfaction with our lives and to grow and develop in a healthy fashion.

Ethics and Nonhumans

But what does any of this have to do with dolphins? Many people believe that only humans can think and feel. Scientific research in the last few decades, however, has shown that many more nonhumans than most of us are aware of have sophisticated nervous systems and some level of intellectual and emotional abilities. This means that a variety of nonhumans feel more pain at our hands than scientists had originally thought. And this raises the question of whether it is unethical for us to cause such pain in these beings and to use them for our convenience when there are other ways that we could achieve the same ends.

A full discussion of the "animal rights" controversy and the central question of what kind of consideration other living beings are entitled to is beyond the scope of this book. But research on the so-called "higher" mammals suggests that primates, elephants and cetaceans are more like us than most humans would probably like to think. That is, these beings may very well have enough intellectual and emotional sophistication to qualify as *nonhuman persons*. And this means that when we hold an ethical yardstick against human actions that lead to the death, injury and emotional suffering of at least these beings, it's a new game. As philosophers put it, these beings may be entitled to "moral standing." And their interests would have to be taken into account in a moral calculation. That means that our species is now confronted with a series of difficult questions that stem from the stark clash of human and dolphin interests:

- A certain way of fishing for tuna produces important benefits to humans, while harming dolphins. Some dolphins die; some are injured; others are simply harassed. Is any or all of this wrong? Does the good to humans outweigh the harm to dolphins? Are the dolphins entitled to better treatment? How do we determine which rights they have in this situation?
- Captive dolphins provide humans with entertainment. Research on dolphins lets us learn about and maybe help them. There are also therapeutic uses of captive dolphins. Is captivity wrong? If the dolphins are well cared for, are they actually being harmed? Does it matter whether they're being used for entertainment, research, therapy or military purposes? Again, are there dolphin rights that we're obligated to respect in these situations? And what about competing human rights?

This investigation also challenges our species to think in new ways. Marine scientist Diana Reiss has referred to dolphins as "an alien intelligence," and she has observed that, "The dolphin is a superb model for helping us formulate ways of describing and understanding intelligence in nonhuman species."[3] The idea that dolphins are probably the closest thing we have on the planet to an "alien being" is an intriguing and different way of looking at things. It's also a surprisingly accurate perspective.

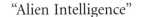

"Alien Intelligence"

The idea that dolphins are, in relation to humans, *alien* beings is a surprisingly effective conceptual model. Not only does this bolster the conceptual foundation for the idea that dolphins might be nonhuman persons, it also suggests that even such important concepts as "the self" and "intelligence" might manifest themselves in fundamentally different ways in humans and dolphins.

The possibility that dolphins are so different from us that they're *alien* also helps guard against the dangers of anthropocentrism in our investigation. *Anthropocentrism* means looking at the world through a strictly human perspective, which then leads to *speciesism* – inappropriately (even if unintentionally) applying standards that are grounded in one species to make judgments about other species. Many environmental ethicists argue that speciesism is as wrong as racism and sexism. They claim that using the traits of our species as the standard by which to judge all other species is as blatantly a matter of irrational prejudice as it is to claim that the traits of one race or sex determine the norm for the entire species.

Reiss's idea that dolphins represent an *alien* intelligence, then, helps us avoid anthropocentrism by suggesting a new and important set of questions. How do we make sure that our evaluation of the intellectual and emotional abilities of dolphins doesn't assume that "different" means "inferior"? Are traits like *intelligence* best defined in a way that is specific to different species? Is *person* the best concept to use in such an investigation? Is there another concept we can use in our investigation to ensure that our characterization of dolphins is free of unintentional species bias?

[3]   Diana Reiss, "The Dolphin: An Alien Intelligence," in Ben Bova and Byron Preiss (eds) *First Contact: The Search for Extraterrestrial Intelligence* (New York: NAL Books, 1990), p. 32.

In particular, what is the significance of the profound differences between humans and dolphins when it comes to evaluating the ethical character of current human/dolphin contact? Recall that philosophers typically understand the concept of personhood to imply a specific set of rights: life, health, freedom from harm, liberty, privacy, respect for the dignity of the individual person, and the like. However, if we think about dolphins as alien beings, we encounter the possibility that differences in the nature of human and nonhuman persons might be so fundamental that humans and dolphins might have different rights – or, at least that there are major differences in how we'd have to behave to respect a specific right in the life of a particular species. Take the right to be free from harm, or to have one's dignity respected. Is it possible that what counts as harm could differ between species? Is it possible that we have to behave differently to respect the dignity of persons of different species? Violating the privacy of a human person, for instance, is generally considered to be ethically questionable. But why should we assume that's also the case with a nonhuman like dolphins? Observing the public character of dolphin sexual behavior leaves one wondering whether dolphins have any need for privacy, that is, whether it served any purpose in their evolution. Is it possible that respecting the dignity of dolphins requires us to behave in a way that isn't necessary in our interactions with humans?

In other words, thinking about dolphins as an "alien intelligence" should help us be more alert to the differences between our species and more sensitive to their philosophical – and especially their ethical – significance.

--------------------------------- Two Questions ---------------------------------

This book ultimately boils down to just two questions: *What kind of beings are dolphins?* And, *What does our answer to the first question say about the ethical character of human/dolphin contact?* Chapters 2 through 6 tackle the first question; Chapter 7 handles the second.

We'll start with basic information about dolphins – their anatomy and physiology, including the dolphin brain (Chapter 2). Then we'll proceed to the type of consciousness and intelligence this brain makes possible (Chapters 3–5). Once we have a sense of what the scientific research suggests, we'll explore the philosophical questions that this picture raises: What kind of beings are dolphins? Are dolphins nonhuman persons? (Chapter 6) Given what we now know about dolphins, is the current state of human/dolphin contact ethically defensible (Chapter 7)?

This investigation will primarily be grounded in current scientific research, but it will occasionally include some nonscientific elements. We'll consider anecdotes I've been told as well as my own personal experiences that I've found philosophically suggestive. And we will see where the notion that dolphins are an alien being takes us.

All I ask is that you approach this with an open mind.

CHAPTER 2

The Anatomy and Physiology of Living in the Water

Reiss's idea that dolphins represent an *alien intelligence* may take some getting used to. But you'd probably agree that humans and dolphins are at least profoundly different. When you first look at dolphins, all they seem to have in common with humans is a head, eyes, a mouth and teeth. Of course, dolphins live in the water, so we should expect more differences than similarities. At the same time, however, much of the reason that humans find dolphins engaging is the feeling that our two species share important traits. How are any meaningful similarities possible when we look so different from each other? And in precisely what ways are dolphins so different from us that we should regard them as truly alien from us?

Let's start approaching the question of what kind of beings dolphins are, then, with some basic scientific facts and see what this reveals about our similarities and differences.

Basic Facts about Dolphins

Dolphins and humans start off with much in common because we are both animals. However, because dolphins belong to the biological order known as *cetacea* (whale), we ultimately end up on different branches of the family tree. The cetaceans are divided into two *suborders* – the mysticetes and the odontocetes. Dolphins belong to the latter, which makes them a toothed whale. Dolphins constitute a separate biological family (*delphinidae*), and there are more than 30 different species of dolphins, including spotted, spinner, dusky, common, and white-sided dolphins. Humans are most familiar with the bottlenose dolphin.[1]

Humans and cetaceans are also both mammals. That is, like humans, dolphins breathe air, are warm-blooded, bear their young alive, nurse their babies via mammary glands, and have hair.[2] The fact that we're both mammals points up the fact that scientists believe that the common ancestor of all modern whales and dolphins was a land animal – a hoofed mammal (ungulate) called the Mesonyx.[3] This animal may have looked like an aquatic version of a large dog or wolf, and it began its return to the water approximately 50 million years ago – probably to find food.

Ancient cetaceans went through a number of stages before they arrived at their current shape, size and design. The modern dolphin emerged about 10 to 15 million years ago. By comparison, the maximum amount of time that humans of one sort or another have been on the planet is about 5 million years, and modern *Homo sapiens* is only about 100,000 years old.

─────────── Adaptations to Living in the Water ───────────

Even though dolphins started like us as land mammals, they look the way they do because they had to adjust to surviving in the water. Water is denser than air. It transmits sound better than light. It mutes the effect of gravity. It draws heat away more quickly than air does. It allows for some technologies, but makes others impossible. The body of a dolphin is the result of a dynamic process – the interaction between an organism and the environment in which it's trying to survive – that ultimately produces a successful formula.

Precisely how did dolphins adapt?

[1]   The bottlenose (*Tursiops truncatus*) adapted well to captivity and is the type of dolphin seen most frequently in theme parks and aquaria and on television shows and in motion pictures. "Flipper" is a bottlenose dolphin. Most of the dolphin research that has been conducted in captivity has been done on bottlenose dolphins. However, it's not clear how much we can generalize from one species to another.

[2]   A baby dolphin is born with a few hair follicles on its snout or rostrum, although dolphins lose this hair fairly quickly.

[3]   Having an ungulate as an ancestor, dolphins are closer to such animals as deer, pigs, camels, cows and horses than to primates and humans. Dolphins' nearest land-based relative may be the hippopotamus.

Body design

Ancient cetaceans started off with hair, but because skin is more hydrodynamic, they lost their fur. Their body temperature is about the same as ours, however, so they had to find a way to stay warm. Their bodies responded by developing a layer of fat or blubber. Their circulatory system also grew more efficient at preserving body heat. They may even be able to preserve heat by consciously reducing the flow of blood to their pectoral fins and their flukes.

In developing a streamlined design, dolphins lost their rear limbs; their front limbs became pectoral flippers; and they developed tail flukes and a dorsal fin on their back. The dolphin head developed a more hydrodynamic, elongated rostrum with teeth positioned to grab food. External ears were replaced by pin-holes on either side of the head. Male and female dolphins look the same from a distance because sexual organs and mammary glands are tucked inside. Because an erection is a voluntary action for male dolphins, however, as long as the penis of a particular species is long enough, dolphins can use the organ as something of an appendage, towing an article along with it or even wrapping it around something.

Their head took on a fixed design to maximize movement through the water. Unlike humans and the other primates, dolphins have no "face." That is, there are no muscles that they can manipulate to communicate something about their inner state, as we do.

All references to the dolphin's famous "smile," then, are mistaken and misleading. This is not a sign of a good mood and a pleasant disposition, it is a design dictated by hydrodynamics. A spontaneous display of teeth is not a "toothy grin," but more likely aggressive or sexual behavior.

The perennial misreading of the dolphin "smile," however, is an instructive mistake worth reflecting on for a moment because it reveals something about the challenge of understanding a being so different from ourselves. As primates, we focus a good deal on one other's faces. We have an impressive level of control over the muscles in our face, and we use this control to communicate both positive and negative feelings via a large repertory of facial expressions. Our body language may reveal something about how we feel, but humans probably automatically focus on facial expression more than anything else.

Our inclination to attend to facial expression is understandable. No doubt, this is the product of our own evolutionary history. (Other primates, like chimps, also communicate via facial expression.) But this is an unfortunate disposition

FIGURE 2.1   The dolphin "smile" – hydrodynamics, not emotions

to have when studying dolphins, because a dolphin's "face" actually reveals very little. And this means that it's important for us to recognize that any visual signals that dolphins send may be different from the ones humans send. We may need to force ourselves to pay more attention to signals that come from other parts of a dolphin's body.

Consider, for a moment, what it would be like to play charades with someone wearing a mask with a big smile on it. Your partner is trying to communicate something having to do with sadness or anger. Think about how likely it is that, without even realizing it, you would be tempted to interpret his or her signals in a way that's consistent with the "smile." This is the same situation we're in when we observe dolphins. Humans are virtually hard-wired to focus on faces; a dolphin's "mask" has an obvious "smile"; so we've had an automatic tendency to interpret their behavior accordingly. At least in the general news media, we've even characterized their entire nature through this lens and created a stereotype. Think about the number of times you've read, heard or watched stories about dolphins that refer to them as "playful" or "happy." Think about the number of times you've seen pictures of dolphins that describe them as "playing" or "cavorting." More importantly, now think about the number of times you've wondered at those moments whether those labels or characterizations were really accurate. My guess is that this *rarely* crossed your mind.

Breathing

Cetaceans did a superb job of handling the challenges that being air-breathers presented.

- Dolphins now breathe through a blowhole on the top of their head. Over millions of years, their nostrils merged and migrated to the blowhole's current location. There's no connection between their mouths and lungs. The esophagus leads only to the stomach.
- Dolphins became particularly efficient breathers. Whereas humans exchange about 10 percent of the air in our lungs with each breath, dolphins exchange about 80 percent to 90 percent. They extract more oxygen from each breath. Dolphins can even exhale and inhale in a fraction of a second. The amount of time between breaths varies depending on conditions, but bottlenose dolphins have been known to remain submerged for as long as 8–10 minutes.
- Cetaceans have also become the world's best freedivers. Diving to 500 feet is probably relatively easy for them. The deepest dive on record for a trained dolphin is 1,795 feet. They can store more oxygen in their muscles than we can. They have a greater tolerance for CO_2. A variety of mechanisms give them resistance to nitrogen narcosis (the "bends") – a potentially fatal condition that affects human divers. And, as a way of coping with the pressure of the ocean, dolphins developed hinged ribs.
- One of the most striking adaptations that separate cetaceans from land mammals is that whales and dolphins became conscious breathers. Humans breathe automatically. But in a dolphin's life, each breath is a voluntary act – and this makes sleep especially problematic. As anyone who has spent any time on a small boat knows, the constant motion of the ocean makes sleeping on the water more difficult than sleeping on land. More importantly, the ocean is a much more active – and dangerous – place at night than during the day. If there were any early cetaceans who returned to the land each night or who somehow mastered the art of sleeping at sea, they didn't survive to pass on their genes to any descendants. Accordingly, dolphins don't sleep the way that we do. Dolphins may rest at or just below the surface in a partially alert state. Some evidence suggests that when

dolphins rest, they shut down half of their brain at a time, and that they can spend up to a third of the day this way. But there is some debate on this issue, as well as on the question of whether they dream.

• Being conscious breathers means that dolphins cannot afford to lose consciousness. If they do, they won't breathe, and they'll suffocate and die. Dolphins also are very much aware of the danger that other dolphins face if they lose consciousness, and they'll often try to help other dolphins who might pass out. They may jostle them to keep them awake and hold them against the surface so that they can breathe. In fact, this behavior is so strongly ingrained in them that it may be part of what underlies the many stories of dolphins coming to the aid of distressed human swimmers.

Echolocation

Unquestionably, dolphins' most interesting and impressive adaptation is the way that they dealt with the fact that vision is of only limited use in the water. Dolphins' eyesight is surprisingly good (although one species of river dolphin is, for all practical purposes, blind), but they probably don't see colors. Unlike humans, their eyes operate independently of one another – one eye can look forward while the other looks back. However, dolphins must also be able to negotiate the oceans throughout the night, when both food and predators are more abundant than during the day. In order to survive, cetaceans had to develop the ability to operate in the dark.

Vision may be too problematic to rely on in the ocean for gathering information about one's environment, but hearing is not. Sound travels better in water than it does on land, and sound moves as well in darkness as it does in light. Sound travels more than 4 times faster in the water than it does on land. It can travel almost a mile in just one second. And sound can travel much farther than light. Hearing, then, is a better sense to rely on in the water than vision is.

It's not surprising that dolphins' sense of hearing is substantially more developed than our own. First, dolphins can handle a wider range of sounds than we can. Bottlenose dolphins can hear sounds from 150 to 150,000 Hz, while our frequency range runs from about 20 Hz (a little lower than the first key on a piano) to 20,000 Hz (about two octaves higher than the last key on a piano). Dolphins make and hear sounds about 8 times higher than the upper limit of our hearing range.

Second, dolphin hearing evolved into a highly sophisticated sonar system. *Echolocation* is the aquatic version of the mechanism bats use to navigate.

It's a biological version of the technology used by submarines. It's a personal ultrasound device. But it's vastly superior to all of these.

Echolocation is the primary means that dolphins use to get information about their environment. There are a series of air sacs underneath their blowhole, and dolphins can use the air in these sacs to create clicks that last less than a thousandth of a second. These clicks are projected off the some-what parabolic, almost satellite-shaped surface of the front of the skull and pass through the melon – fatty tissue that dolphins may be able to manipulate like a lens. The clicks bounce off objects, return as echoes, are retrieved through the dolphin's lower jaw and pass to the inner ear. Clicks vary in intensity and frequency. Lower frequency clicks (which sound something like a creaking door) probably give a rough sense of the item and are used for objects at a greater distance. Higher frequency clicks (which sound more like a high-pitched buzz) give more detail. Depending on the circumstance, dolphins emit between 8 and 2000 clicks per second. After a certain point, the clicks are so fast that separate clicks are indiscernible to human ears and all we can hear is a buzz. Dolphins are able to separate them, however, because a dolphin doesn't send out a new click until the first one returns. Some researchers even claim that in the first six clicks, the dolphin is modifying its clicks to get the best information – "tuning the signal," as it were.[4]

Echolocation produces very precise information. In one experiment, two discs 1/16 inch thick were put behind something that would block a dolphin's sight, but not its sonar. The only difference between the discs was that one was aluminum and the other was copper. The dolphin could tell the differ-ence. In other experiments, dolphins could tell if a square was made of metal, wood or plastic from 100 feet away. They could tell differences in shapes (a circle from a triangle) and size (a smaller circle from a larger circle).[5]

In one especially impressive experiment, dolphins could even detect a dif-ference of a few tenths of a millimeter – about the thickness of a fingernail – in the thickness of two metal cylinders from about 30 feet away. How? A click bounces off the front of a cylinder, but some of the sound energy appar-ently also penetrates the cylinder and produces a separate echo from the back edge. The length of the delay between the first and second echo depends on how thick the cylinder is. The dolphin could discern the time difference and

[4]   Rory Howlett, "Flipper's Secret," *New Scientist*, 28 June 1997, p. 34.
[5]   There is an extensive literature on dolphin echolocation. See, for example, Witlow W. Au, *The Sonar of Dolphins* (New York: Springer-Verlag, 1993) and W. W. L. Au, P. W. B. Moore, and D. Pawloski, "Echolocating Transmitting Beam of the Atlantic Bottlenose Dolphin," *Journal of the Acoustical Society of America* 80 (1986): 688–691.

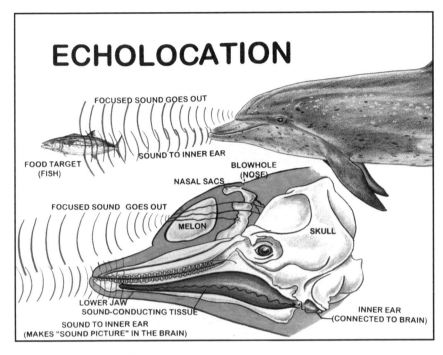

FIGURE 2.2   Dolphin echolocation
Source © 2002 Robin Lee Makowski

therefore could tell which cylinder was thicker. This seems reasonable until you realize that the time difference the dolphin was noticing was between .5 and .6 millionths of a second![6]

The explanation of how dolphins differentiated between these two cylinders suggests perhaps the most striking feature of this biotechnology. That is, echolocation gives dolphins *three-dimensional* information. Dolphins can tell the difference between objects with different geometric shapes, for example, cylinders, cubes and spheres. In addition, since sound travels through living tissue, echolocation allows dolphins literally to see through objects. Dolphins can see into each other's bodies, which could let them know something of each other's physical condition. Some dolphins have been known to take special interest in pregnant women and people with surgical steel in their bodies.

---

[6]   Howlett, "Flipper's Secret."

I've been told that there was even at least one instance at the Dolphin Research Center when a dolphin suggested that a woman was pregnant before the woman herself knew it. One day, when a visibly pregnant trainer was working with a dolphin who was pregnant herself, the dolphin sonared the woman's abdomen and flipped over so that the woman could touch the dolphin's belly in what almost seemed to be a moment of: "You're pregnant. I'm pregnant. Isn't that nice?" Shortly afterwards, the same dolphin did the same thing with a woman during a swim. She was told that the only time this dolphin had acted this way was with the pregnant trainer. So the inevitable question was: "Are you pregnant?" To which the woman's husband replied: "I hope not." In reality, however, it turned out that the woman was pregnant – even if barely pregnant on the day of the swim.[7]

The ability of dolphins to observe the inner workings of one another's bodies raises the interesting question of whether their echolocation lets them know about each other's emotional states. Our own emotions are usually accompanied by certain physical responses. When we get nervous, our palms sweat, our hearts beat faster, and we breathe more often and more shallowly. Presumably, fear or anxiety causes changes in a dolphin's body, and dolphins might readily observe such changes. Most intriguing is the question of whether this ability might limit dolphins' capacity to deceive each other. After all, polygraphs measure our bodies' reactions as we attempt to lie. If dolphins had an analogous reaction to deception or to some other behavior that provoked an internal reaction, would it be apparent to their neighbors?

We know little about how dolphins use their sonar in their dealings with each other, but scientists have made two interesting suggestions. Despite the traditional assumption that dolphins use whistles to communicate and clicks to echolocate, it's possible that clicks may be used in communication.[8] It's also

[7] Recognizing a pregnancy at such an early stage is not only testimony to the sophistication of a dolphin's sonar but to this particular dolphin's knowledge of human anatomy and physiology. That is, she apparently recognized the fetus for what it was, not simply some unusual tissue.

[8] Peter Tyack, for example, notes that "there are several dolphin species that appear to use 'echolocation' clicks for social communication." Peter L. Tyack, "Functional Aspects of Cetacean Communication," in J. Mann, R. C. Connor, P. L. Tyack and H. Whitehead (eds) *Cetacean Societies: Field Studies of Dolphins and Whales* (Chicago: University of Chicago Press, 2000), p. 303.

been suggested that dolphins can "eavesdrop" on one another's echolocation echoes.[9]

We do know that echolocation is an important tool in finding food. Dolphins use it to spot schools of fish that are swimming at a distance. But dolphins can also use it to locate fish beneath the sand. On research trips with marine scientist Denise Herzing, we've observed spotted dolphins in the Bahamas sonaring the bottom and then plucking out a fish from just below the sand. A more dramatic example of such behavior, however, is called "crater feeding." Herzing has observed that bottlenose dolphins in the Bahamas will swim along the bottom and scan down into the sand.[10] When they detect a particular kind of fish, they'll go vertical to the bottom and burrow after their prey. Sometimes they'll drill themselves into the bottom all the way to their pectoral fins. They scan the whole time and sound something like a dentist's drill. The process leaves a small crater on the bottom – hence the name "crater feeding."

Perhaps the most intriguing way that dolphins might be using sound in getting food, however, is the suggestion that dolphins can use sound as a weapon. Dolphins are capable of producing remarkably intense sounds. In addition to echolocation clicks, they make what are called "burst pulse" sounds. One bottlenose, for example, has been recorded as having emitted a sound of 228 decibels. To appreciate just how loud this is, note that the sound level of an ordinary conversation is about 70 decibels, the sound of a jet engine is about 120 decibels, and that of an air-raid siren is about 150 decibels. Humans typically find sounds above 140 decibels painful. The level that dolphins can reach is so high that it's virtually at the physical limit of sound. That is, adding more energy would produce not more sound, but heat.[11]

Dubbed the "big bang" theory, the idea that dolphins use sound to stun fish was first suggested by the late dolphin researcher Kenneth Norris of the University of California at Santa Cruz. Norris pointed out that at certain intensities, sound takes on a tactile quality. When a dolphin scans you, for

[9] H. E. Harley, M. J. Xitco Jr., and H. L. Roitblat, "Echolocation, Cognition, and the Dolphin's World," in R. A. Kastelein, J. A. Thomas, and P. E. Nachtigall (eds) *Sensory Systems of Aquatic Mammals* (Woerden, The Netherlands: De Spil Publishers, 1995), pp. 529–542.

[10] D. L. Herzing and C. M. Johnson, "Interspecific Interaction between Atlantic Spotted Dolphins (*Stenella frontalis*) and Bottlenose Dolphins (*Tursiops truncatus*) in the Bahamas, 1985–1995," *Aquatic Mammals*, 23(2) (1997): 85–99.

[11] Au, *The Sonar of Dolphins*, p. 129; K. S. Norris, *Dolphin Days* (New York: W. W. Norton, 1991), pp. 283–285.

FIGURE 2.3   Bottlenose dolphin "crater feeding"

example, you may feel a slight tingling. Dolphins also "buzz" one another's genital regions from a distance, and there's little question that this produces a pleasurable sensation. If the intensity of their clicks is dramatically increased, however, Norris believed that the sound generated could be strong enough to disorient, if not kill, a fish.[12] Dolphins are also able to produce a very loud burst of sound that differs from ordinary echolocation clicks and sounds something like a rifle shot. While no one has yet directly observed dolphins using sounds this way in the wild, scientists have confirmed the plausibility of Norris's thesis with recordings of bottlenose dolphins and orcas making such sounds while they're feeding.[13]

---

[12]   K. S. Norris and B. Mohl, "Can Odontocetes Debilitate Prey with Sound?" *American Naturalist*, 122(1) (1983): 85–104; Norris, *Dolphin Days*, pp. 283–285.
[13]   Tim Beardsley, "Sonic Punch," *Scientific American*, 287(4) (October 1987): 34–36.

The place of sound

We'll continue this discussion of dolphin anatomy and physiology by look-ing at the dolphin brain. But it's important to pause at this point and reflect on the fact that the place of sound in a dolphin's experience is one of the most important differences between humans and cetaceans. As important as sound is to us, humans are, on balance, primarily visual creatures. So the subjective experience of being a dolphin may be very different from the subjective experience of being a human.

Imagine that you yourself have abilities equivalent to a dolphin's echoloca-tion. Think what it would be like to have three-dimensional information about the objects and people around you whenever you want – and to live in a world where everyone else has this ability as well. When you focus on an object, you instantly get a comprehensive and integrated sense of its outward appearance, internal structure, the density and condition of its component parts – top to bottom, front to back, inside and out. When you focus on an object, you even get some information about what the parts facing away from you are like. Matter would for the most part be either transparent or translucent to you. Relatively little would be opaque. If you put something "inside" a box, for example, it wouldn't mean that the object was "hidden from view," but that it "couldn't be touched." However, it may not even mean that – because while you couldn't touch it with your hands, you could use your sonic sense to "touch" it that way. And your "sonic touch" would even reveal differences in the density of the materials that objects are made of. Nothing would be private, not even the inner workings of our bodies.

If you sit with this idea for a minute, you'll realize that there's nothing analogous to this experience in our lives as humans. Focusing on an object with our echolocation – let's say an old-fashioned watch with a mainspring – would give us more information in an instant than we could get if we spent a considerable amount of time examining it from every angle, studying its workings, taking it apart and putting it back together. Or imagine focusing on someone else's hand. You could quickly get a sense of how that appendage works that would be far more detailed and comprehensive than even our most sophisticated medical technology can currently arrive at.

Now imagine that you come across someone who lacks these enhanced abilities and can see only the surface of objects with their eyes. They have to take things apart and carve them up to get to the inner workings. What's your reaction? Surprise? Amusement? Do you feel sorry for them? Superior to them? What's your sense of what they're like? (In your everyday life now, if you're fortunate enough to have all of your senses in good working order, how do you refer to people who have problems with their sight or hearing, for example? Do you see them as "disabled"? How do you label the difference between you and them?)

Dolphins surely recognize that we lack their echolocation abilities in the same way that they recognize that we can't swim as well as they can. We obviously don't know if they have any conscious reaction to our lack on this score, but it's an interesting question to consider. What do you suppose their reaction is? Surprise? Amusement? Do they feel sorry for us? Superior to us? What's their sense of what we're like?

The Dolphin Brain

The dolphin brain is one of the most important topics we'll consider in this book because of how much "intelligence" means to humans. Our big brain virtually defines us. We call ourselves *Homo sapiens* – "*thinking* humans." We see ourselves as having developed the most advanced brain on the planet. We believe that this brain gives us powers that no other species on the planet has and that this puts us at the top of a biological hierarchy on the planet. Many humans believe that because humans are intelligent and nonhumans aren't, we have the right to use all other living beings largely as we see fit. In fact, many humans regard nonhuman animals more like *things* than *beings*. They're "just animals" – a "what," not a "who." Such an outlook defends killing or injuring unintelligent, nonhuman animals as long as it benefits us and as long as the nonhumans involved die "humanely."

The dolphin brain is a critical topic in our investigation because it is a large, complex brain that has led to some controversial claims about cetacean intelligence. The most famous were made by John Lilly, a physician who specialized in the brain and did extensive research on dolphins from the 1950s to the 1970s. Lilly made a variety of startling assertions. For example, he wrote, "The brains of Cetaceans are superior to ours in unique and effective areas."[14] He also believed that dolphins have language and ethics.[15]

---

[14]   John C. Lilly, *Communication between Man and Dolphin: The Possibilities of Talking with Other Species* (New York: Julian Press, 1978), p. 137.

[15]   In addition to *Communication between Man and Dolphin*, see *Lilly on Dolphins: Humans of the Sea* (New York: Anchor Press, 1975).

If these assertions are only partly true, humanity's claim to the pinnacle of creation – and the ethical defensibility of most human/dolphin interaction – are highly questionable.

Lilly was never able to prove his boldest claims. However, the dolphin brain is a focal point in our inquiry because there are undeniable similarities and unexplained differences between dolphin and human brains that continue to fuel speculation about dolphin intelligence:

- Simply in size and outward appearance, the human and dolphin brains set themselves apart from the brains of other animals.
- The brain of the bottlenose dolphin is 40 percent larger than the human brain, and much of the increased size is in the part of the brain that governs most of our higher functions. The surface of the dolphin brain is more convoluted than the human brain, and this larger number of foldings means that the dolphin brain has a bigger cerebral cortex than the human brain. And since it's our "gray matter" that determines the fact that humans have so much intellectual capacity, this is no small matter.
- Dolphins, however, have a different, and older, evolutionary history, and this has produced a brain with a different structure from ours. It lacks some features that our brain has, but it also has some traits that ours doesn't.

What have scientists uncovered about the dolphin brain? Is it a sophisticated enough piece of biological machinery to allow for the possibility of intelligence? Or, if we look under the hood, do we find out that it ultimately lacks the necessary horsepower?

(As important a topic as this is, if you're more interested at this point in what the dolphin brain can do, feel free to move on to Chapter 4 and return to read about its structure later.)

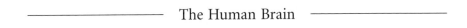

The Human Brain

The best way to start a discussion of the dolphin brain is with a quick review of the human brain. Human and dolphin brains are both large and complex, and we're both mammals. Scientists know a good deal about how the human brain supports advanced intellectual abilities, so perhaps we can infer some things about the dolphin brain from the similarities and differences with our own brains.

The human brain is made up of four major parts: (1) the *brain stem*; (2) the *cerebellum*; (3) the *limbic system*; and (4) the *cerebrum*. Actually, the brains of all vertebrates have these same major parts. The difference is in their relative size. In fish, the cerebrum is the *smallest* part. In primates and cetaceans, it's the *largest* part. In humans, the cerebrum accounts for about 85 percent of the brain's weight.

The brain stem sits at the top of the spinal cord, and is the earliest and most primitive part of the brain. It first developed in animals about 500 million years ago. It controls the body's most basic functions – like breathing, heart rate, blood pressure, a variety of reflex reactions, sleep patterns and the brain's level of alertness.

The cerebellum is an interesting structure attached to the back of the brain stem. It not only governs balance and helps to fine-tune our voluntary movements, it is also involved in sensory processing, memory, cognition and language.

The limbic system developed in mammals, and sits in the center of the brain, connecting the brain stem and cerebellum to the cerebrum. It consists of a variety of structures plus a small layer of cortex. The limbic system plays a central role in the human brain.

First, all sensory messages that are generated elsewhere in the body pass through the limbic system on their way to the "higher" parts of the brain that decide how to respond to sensory information. So do the returning instructions that produce bodily movements and regulate the autonomic function of internal body organs. The limbic system also plays a role in a variety of basic appetites – eating, drinking, sleep and sexual activity.

With the limbic system, we also start getting more complicated abilities. For example, one part of the limbic system (the hippocampus) plays a role in preparing perceptions to be stored elsewhere in the brain as long-term memories. Another part (the amygdala) appears to be the storehouse of memories of events that are highly charged emotionally.

The limbic system also generates all of our emotions – although not the conscious awareness of them. In response to an event, the limbic system sends signals to a higher part of the brain, where we consciously experience emotions. At the same time, it sends directions to the body to produce the physical states that accompany our emotions (increased heart rate and respirations, higher blood pressure, etc.). The conscious brain interprets the situation and sometimes moderates both the feelings and the physical response. This complex process thus produces the emotional charge that events have for us and the overall emotional coloring that's such an important part of our everyday experience of life.

The cerebrum is the largest part of the human brain, and – with its characteristic convoluted surface – is probably what most people think of when they hear the word "brain." The majority of this part of the brain is devoted to processing sensory information. However, this is also the location of all high level brain functions.

The outer layer of the cerebrum is called the *cerebral cortex*. The cortex is characterized by folds and valleys (gyri, sulci and fissures) and is also referred to as "gray matter" because of its color. The folding makes it possible to have more surface area within the limited space allowed by a skull.

Humans emphasize the size and complexity of our cerebral cortex because it's the primary anatomical fact that supports most humans' belief in the huge gulf between "people" and "animals." The cerebral cortex of virtually every other mammal is much smoother than the human brain because there's less cerebral cortex in the skulls of those animals. Differences in cerebral cortex produce important differences in abilities. Humans have more of it than virtually any other mammal, and that's what gives us our edge.

The most recent addition to the human brain is the front part of the cerebral cortex. In fact, the current shape of the human head is the result of the expansion of the skull to accommodate the development of this part of the brain.

Humans also have more of a type of cortex that apparently is responsible for "thinking." The cerebral cortex can be divided into *projection cortex* and *association cortex*. The former essentially runs the body. Association areas, on the other hand, are devoted to working with, analyzing and integrating the information provided by the projection areas. In organisms with simpler brains, the brain is all projection cortex. In more complex brains, we find association cortex. We find a good deal of it in the gorilla, orangutan and chimpanzee, but we find more in the human brain. The primary difference between our brains and those of our primate relatives is that we have even more association cortex.

Parts of the cerebral cortex

A deep fissure down the middle of the cerebral cortex separates it into two "hemispheres." For the most part, each hemisphere controls the opposite side of the body (right hemisphere/left side of the body, left hemisphere/right side). But each hemisphere also governs different functions, which has led to the references you've heard between "left-brained" versus "right-brained" activities and "left-brained" and "right-brained" people. The two sides of the brain communicate with each other by means of a thick bundle of nerves underneath the cerebral cortex called the "corpus callosum."

The major sulci and fissures of the cerebrum further divide the cerebral cortex into four areas or "lobes." Each handles different functions in the body:

- The "occipital" lobe governs largely visual functions.
- The "parietal" lobe is concerned mainly with functions connected with movement, orientation, calculation and certain types of recognition.
- The "temporal" lobe deals with some aspects of memory, sound and, in the left temporal lobe, speech comprehension.
- The "frontal" lobe is concerned with abstract functions such as thinking and planning.

Temporal and frontal lobes

The majority of the brain is devoted to running the body – that is, to processing sensory information and controlling our movements. However, the *temporal* and *frontal* lobes are the location of the abilities that we consider most distinctively human – memory, language and abstract thinking.

The temporal lobes make some of our most impressive abilities possible. They are the primary storehouse for our long-term memories. The temporal lobes are thought to have a role in generating insight. In addition, in most of us, the left temporal and frontal lobes make it possible for us to understand language (Wernicke's area) and to speak (Broca's area). The left temporal lobe also appears to play an important role in our emotional stability. In keeping with the differences between the left and right hemispheres, the right temporal lobe lets us read facial expressions, understand the meaning of verbal tones, sense rhythm and appreciate music.

The frontal lobe is the most recent evolutionary addition to the human brain. It is the largest lobe and accounts for about 28 percent of the entire cortex, and it is responsible for the abilities that we humans take most pride in.

The most evolved part of our brain, however, is the front part of the frontal lobe – the *prefrontal cortex*. It is also called the "silent associational area" because it is the only part of the brain that does not have a direct link to sensory or motor functions. The prefrontal cortex makes possible an impressive array of sophisticated abilities and lets us: have a sense of "self"; work with concepts; experience and express emotions; determine whether our actions are appropriate or inappropriate; set goals; make plans; make choices; delay

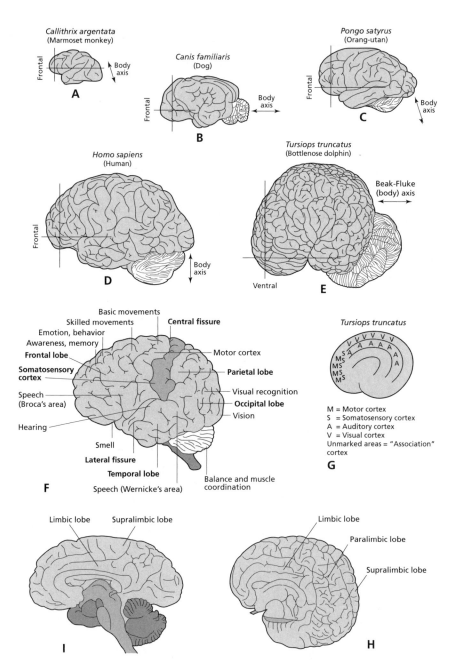

FIGURE 2.4 A comparison of the external appearances of the brains of a variety of animals (images A–E) shows that the dolphin and human brains are significantly more convoluted. Images F–I illustrate major differences between the human and dolphin brains. a) In the human brain, the sensory and motor functions are spread out over different parts of the brain, while in the dolphin brain, sensory and motor functions are adjacent to each other (images F, G). b) The dolphin brain contains a "paralimbic" lobe not found in the human brain (images H, I).

gratification; change our behavior or set a new strategy when we encounter obstacles; learn from our mistakes.

The Human Brain: Summary

The human brain, then, is a remarkable piece of biological hardware. It has older parts that it shares with virtually every other animal on the planet, and this lets us control a complicated body. It also has newer parts that give us a self-conscious "inner" world and the unusual ability to think and to feel.

Our most impressive abilities appear to result from:

- a large, complex cerebral cortex;
- well-developed temporal and frontal lobes;
- the impressive amount of associational cortex that constitutes the prefrontal cortex.

The Dolphin Brain Compared to the Human Brain

The dolphin brain is one of the most interesting – and one of the most difficult – parts of cetacean anatomy to discuss. It is interesting because, like the human brain, it is large and complex. It is difficult to discuss because, in comparison to what we know about the human brain, we know much less about it.

We also face major challenges because dolphins come from a different part of the animal kingdom than we do, they have a longer evolutionary history than we do, and they evolved in a different medium than we did.

Basic appearance

When we look at the dolphin brain, we immediately see similarities with the human brain. Both brains are large, and they have surfaces that are more convoluted than the brains of other mammals. This means that, like the human brain, the dolphin brain has a large *cerebral cortex* (and, hence, a good deal of "gray matter"). In fact, at first, the dolphin brain seems to have an edge

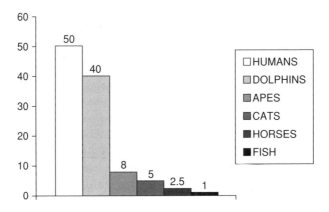

FIGURE 2.5   Ratio of brain weight to spinal cord weight

over the human brain. The brains of bottlenose dolphins are usually larger than ours: human brains weigh about three pounds, bottlenose dolphins' brains about three and a half. And the dolphin brain also has more sulci and gyri – which means that it looks like they've been able to fit more cerebral cortex into their skulls than we have in ours.

Comparative measures

The combination of size and complexity has sparked much speculation about "dolphin intelligence." Fortunately, scientists have a couple of measures that give us at least a general estimate of a brain's cognitive potential. One figure is the *ratio of brain weight to spinal cord weight*. In humans, the ratio is 50 to 1; in bottlenose dolphins, 40 to 1; in apes, 8 to 1; in cats, 5 to 1; in horses, 2.5 to 1; and in fishes, the brain weighs less than the cord.[16] According to this measure, the dolphin brain is impressive.

A more sophisticated index is based on the relationship between the weight of the body and the weight of the brain. The idea is to use a formula that lets us subtract out the part of the brain needed to run the body. What's left connotes purely cognitive ability. This *encephalization quotient* (EQ)

[16]   Sam H. Ridgway, "The Central Nervous System of the Bottlenose Dolphin," in Stephen Leatherwood and Randall R. Reeves (eds) *The Bottlenose Dolphin* (San Diego: Academic Press, 1990), p. 87.

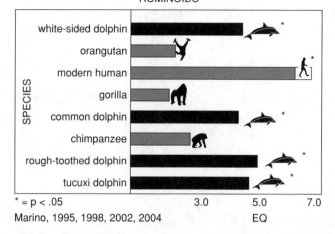

MEAN EQ FOR SOME MODERN DELPHINIDS AND HOMINOIDS

FIGURE 2.6   Mean EQ for some modern delphinids and hominoids
Source: Lori Marino, "Convergence of Complex Cognitive Abilities in Cetaceans and Primates," *Brain, Behavior and Evolution* 59 (2002): p. 26. © 2002 S. Karger AG, Basel

presumably correlates with the degree of behavioral complexity and cognitive capacity (what some might call "intelligence"). It's a convenient way to make comparisons across species.

Once again, the dolphin brain does well. In general, EQ calculations show that dolphins have an impressive brain – at least the second most impressive one on the planet. While dolphins fall below humans, they rank higher than all other mammals. *Homo sapiens* comes in at 7.0. Depending on the species, dolphins range from 4.1 to 4.95 – considerably higher than all of our primate relatives (chimpanzee, 2.3; orangutan, 1.8; and gorilla, 1.6). This places dolphins second on the planet only to *Homo sapiens* with an EQ equivalent to that estimated for one of our ancestors, *Homo habilis*.[17]

Moreover, two scientists suggest that the EQ figures for dolphins are *underestimated* because they don't take into account the difference between living

[17]   Lori Ann Marino, "Brain-Behavior Relationships in Cetaceans and Primates: Implications for the Evolution of Complex Intelligence," PhD dissertation, State University of New York at Albany, 1995, p. 173; Lori Marino, "Convergence of Complex Cognitive Abilities in Cetaceans and Primates," *Brain, Behavior and Evolution*, 59 (2002): 21–32; Patrick R. Hof, Rebecca Chanis and Lori Marino, "Cortical Complexity in Cetacean Brains," *The Anatomical Record*, Part A 287A (2005): 1142–1152. The EQ values are based on the equation by H. J. Jerison (1973).

on land versus living in the water.[18] And if we include these factors, the difference between humans and dolphins decreases.

For openers, then, the most basic empirical measures suggest that the dolphin brain should have considerable cognitive ability.

Brain structure: important differences

While the overall size and the appearance of the brain's outer layer suggest important similarities with the human brain, as soon as we start looking beneath the surface, we find significant differences.

Of course, the dolphin brain has the same basic parts as the brains of all mammals. It has a *brain stem, cerebellum, limbic system* and *cerebrum*. However, noteworthy differences surface immediately:

- The cerebellum is significantly larger than in the human brain, relative to brain size. It accounts for about 15 percent of total weight versus about 10 percent in humans. After taking into account differences in the overall size of the brain, the average dolphin cerebellum is more than 50 percent larger than the average human cerebellum.[19]
- Similarly, as in humans, the cerebrum is the largest part of the dolphin brain. However, dolphin cortex is only about half as thick as human cortex, the neurons are less densely packed, the dolphin cortex usually doesn't have as many layers as the human brain does, and so its total volume is probably only 80 percent of the human cortex.
- The dolphin brain is also like ours in being divided into two hemispheres that are connected by a corpus callosum. But the dolphin corpus callosum is considerably smaller, which suggests that each hemisphere operates more independently than in our brain.

[18]   Lori Marino points out that because the buoyancy of water reduces the pull of gravity, cetaceans may be able to get bigger bodies without increasing the size of their brains. Also, in order to stay warm, cetaceans have a higher percentage of body fat that humans do – and body fat requires no additional brain power. Lori Marino, "A Comparison of Encephalization between Odontocete Cetaceans and Anthropoid Primates," *Brain, Behavior, and Evolution*, 51 (1998): 236. Sam Ridgway observes that dolphins "have smaller body surface areas than terrestrial mammals of similar body weight . . . Thus if we related brain size directly to body surface area, odontocetes would rank still higher." S. H. Ridgway, "Dolphin Brain Size," in M. M. Bryden and R. J. Harrison (eds) *Research on Dolphins* (Oxford: Oxford University Press, 1986), p. 63.

[19]   Lori Marino, James K. Rilling, Shinko K. Lin, and Sam H. Ridgway, "Relative Volume of the Cerebellum in Dolphins and Comparison with Anthropoid Primates," *Brain, Behavior and Evolution*, 56 (2000): 204–211.

- Predictably, cells and structures devoted to hearing are dramatically larger in the dolphin brain than in the human brain. Odontocetes have the largest diameter acoustic nerve fibers.
- The dolphin brain is also shaped differently from ours. Whereas the human brain grew by developing neocortex in the front part of the brain (producing the all-important prefrontal cortex), the dolphin brain grew by getting wider – developing in what we call the temporal and parietal regions of the human brain. As a result, it's more spherical or globular than the human brain.

Major difference #1: lobes

This different growth pattern of the dolphin brain leads to fundamental differences in how the cerebral cortex is divided. As in the human brain, the large cerebral cortex is characterized by many grooves and foldings (gyri and sulci), and the major fissures divide the dolphin brain into three different lobes. Dolphin researchers label them the *limbic* lobe, the *paralimbic* lobe and the *supralimbic* lobe.

This middle, *paralimbic lobe*, however, is missing in the human brain. In addition, while the supralimbic lobe of the human brain is then divided into the four lobes mentioned above (occipital, parietal, temporal and frontal), we don't see those same divisions in the supralimbic lobe of dolphin brain.

There are, then, fundamental, structural differences in the human and dolphin brains. We may be tempted to think that since the dolphin brain lacks a prefrontal cortex of the sort that we have, it can't have the advanced capacities that ours has. But that's not the case.[20] In addition, the human brain lacks a paralimbic lobe, and this structure may give the dolphin brain advantages that we lack.

Supralimbic lobe and association cortex

The majority of the dolphin supralimbic lobe, however, is made up of "association" cortex – the same type of cortex that makes up our prefrontal cortex. And it's possible that dolphin association cortex could be capable of higher

[20]   Self-awareness in humans is made possible by our prefrontal cortex. Despite the fact that the dolphin brain lacks a prefrontal cortex, there is evidence for self-awareness in dolphins (as we'll see in the next chapter). See Lori Marino, "Convergence of Complex Cognitive Abilities in Cetaceans and Primates," p. 24.

order functions. According to at least one theory about how evolution works, a time of rapid evolutionary growth can produce profound, complex, qualitative changes – great leaps forward – that do not happen in slow, steady progression. Within two million years, for example, the relative size of the human brain tripled. And this explosive growth is one explanation for the emergence of human language. By the same token, in the space of five to ten million years, the relative size of the dolphin brain increased by a multiple of four.[21] And Lori Marino, the most recent commentator on the dolphin brain, argues that some species of dolphins "may have developed an analogously sophisticated cognitive mechanism during their rapid evolution."[22]

Major difference #2: sensory/motor areas

In addition to the structural difference between the human and dolphin brains, another basic difference can be seen in the location of sensory and motor functions. In our brain, the sensory and motor functions are spread out across different parts of the brain and are separated by cortex. (We have a "motor strip" and a "touch strip"; vision is located in the back; hearing, on the side.) In the dolphin brain, however, most of the sensory-motor functions appear to be located in the paralimbic lobe. In addition, sensory and motor functions actually "bump up" against each other, and they also directly abut the limbic system.

"Cortical adjacency"

This difference in the location of sensory/motor functions, however, has led to a fascinating line of speculation by Lori Marino, who argues that the fact that the sensory/motor regions interlock with each other allows for the possibility that information is processed differently than in the human brain. She contends this "cortical adjacency" may let dolphins process information in a more "integrated" fashion than we do.[23]

---

[21] Dolphin EQ increased significantly near the Eocene-Oligocene boundary from an average EQ of .5 for Eocene archoaecetes (extinct first suborder) to 2.0 for the earliest neoceti (new dolphins). Lori Marino, Daniel W. McShea and Mark D. Uhen, "Origin and Evolution of Large Brains in Toothed Whales," *The Anatomical Record*, Part A, 281A (2004): 1247–1255.

[22] Marino "Brain-Behavior Relationships in Cetaceans and Primates," p. 386.

[23] "The cortical adjacency found in cetacean brains suggests that cetaceans may process, at least auditory and somato-sensory, information in a more integrated manner than primates." Marino, "Brain-Behavior Relationships in Cetaceans and Primates," p. 387. A similar point is made by Sterling Bunnell:

To see what "cortical adjacency" means in practice, consider the following research into dolphins' ability to "see through sound." In a study directed by Louis Herman at the Kewalo Basin Marine Laboratory in Hawaii, a dolphin was first shown an abstract, complexly shaped object in the air or on a television screen. Since echolocation doesn't work in air, this means that the dolphin had to use her eyes. Then two objects – one identical to the one just shown, and another that was different – were placed in an underwater box constructed of materials that the dolphin could sonar through but not see through. The dolphin was tested to see if she could make the match to the first object. Then the process was reversed. One object was first placed in the box, two were shown in the air, and the dolphin was tested. In each case, the dolphin had a very high success rate, and typically took no more than a couple of seconds to make up her mind. The researchers concluded that "the dolphin appears capable of 'visualizing' an object's shape through sound alone."[24] And the fact that her decision was virtually immediate suggests that she got a sense of the entire object all at once, not just isolated features of it. The fact that dolphins performed equally well no matter which order the tests were conducted (seeing the object, then matching it with echolocation; using sonar first, then matching the object with vision) led these researchers to make an interesting observation. Research on "cross-modal matching ability" in humans that used vision and touch suggests that we don't do as well as dolphins going in both directions. We do better looking at something and then using our hands to find a match than we do starting with our hands and trying to match the object by viewing different possibilities.[25] Why the difference in the performance of the two species? Visual and auditory cortex abut in the dolphin brain, while there is considerably greater distance between vision and touch centers in the human brain.

> For us to make an integrated perception from sight, sound and touch, the impulses must travel by long fiber tracts with a great loss of time and information. The Cetaceans' paralimbic lobe makes possible the very rapid formation of integrated perceptions with a richness of information unimaginable to us. Motor expression of perceived patterns thorough vocalization could be especially subtle.
> (Sterling Bunnell "The Evolution of Cetacean Intelligence," in
> Joan McIntyre (ed.) *Mind in the Waters* (New York:
> Charles Scribner's Sons, 1974), pp. 56–57)

[24]   Louis M. Herman, Adam A. Pack, and Matthias Hoffmann-Kuhnt, "Seeing Through Sound: Dolphins (*Tursiops truncatus*) Perceive the Spatial Structure of Objects Through Echolocation," *Journal of Comparative Psychology*, 112(3) (1998): 293.
[25]   Eugene Abravanel, "Retention of Shape Information under Haptic or Visual Acquisition," *Perceptual and Motor Skills*, 36(3, Part 1) (1973): 683–690.

Or consider this example of "integrated" information processing from human experience. One of the legendary differences between men and women has to do with what we pay attention to when we talk to each other. The stereotype is that men tend to focus primarily on the words someone speaks, while women pay attention to much more – words, facial expression, "body language," the speaker's emotions, and even the listener's own emotional reactions to what someone says (or avoids saying) and how they say it. Many men are perfectly comfortable looking away from the person talking to them or even walking around while still listening – something that many women take to mean that the man isn't really listening to them or at least doesn't take what she's saying seriously. In reality, women simply process more information than men do in situations like this. That is, women get a more "integrated" or multi-dimensional sense of what's going on because they're simultaneously processing auditory, visual and emotional information while men are processing mainly auditory information. This difference in communication style may be the result of the fact that women typically use more of their brains than men do in a variety of tasks connected with language – a difference that may also explain why girls typically speak earlier than boys, learn to read more easily, have fewer learning disabilities, and decode non-verbal communication better than men do.[26] Of course, the flip side of this is that women probably send out a more "integrated" package of information than men do when they communicate. So understanding the complete message is more complicated than simply understanding the words spoken.

It's possible that the "cortical adjacency" of the dolphin brain produces something similar to, but even more pronounced than this multi-dimensional data processing that we see in human females. That is, it's possible that when dolphins perceive reality (receive data) they take in a wider range of sensory information than humans do. And if they do, it's logical that when they communicate (transmit data), they also send out a wider range of data. The late Kenneth Norris, one of the world's greatest dolphin researchers, observed that dolphins always make body movements when they generate sounds. He hypothesized that these movements are "packets of information" which are part of dolphin communication.[27] And this would fit with the idea that the dolphin brain processes information in an integrated or multi-dimensional fashion.

---

[26] See, for example, Robert Lee Hotz, "Women Use More of Brain When Listening, Study Says," *Los Angeles Times*, November 29, 2000, A-1.
[27] Private communication.

Limbic or emotional information

Another difference with the human brain is that the dolphin brain has an older architecture on the microscopic level. But, once again, "older" may not mean "inferior." An intriguing implication of an older architecture is the possibility that *emotional information* may play a bigger role in the dolphin brain than in the human brain.

To understand this point, we have to start with the fact that scientists can identify the cellular structures that came earlier from an evolutionary perspective versus the structures that came later. The human limbic system, for example, is considered to be composed of cortex that appeared much earlier than the cortex in the human prefrontal cortex. The assumption is that more recent cortex is capable of more sophisticated or advanced cognitive operations. And this is all part of the general line of thought that would argue that our *emotional* responses to situations (which originate in the limbic system) are more "primitive" than our more "advanced" *rational* responses in the prefrontal cortex.

Some evidence suggests, however, that there is not the same sharp division between older and newer cortex in the dolphin brain. This has led some scientists to conclude that, on a microscopic level, the entire dolphin cortex is organized according to an older architecture.[28] And this raises the possibility that the limbic system in the dolphin brain has more of an impact on the processing of information than is the case in the human brain. As Denise Herzing explains it, the dolphin limbic system may be stretched out over more of the brain, and limbic (that is, emotional) information may be more integrated into a variety of brain functions than is the case with the human brain. The dolphin brain may have less cortex of a recent architecture than

---

[28]   As Morgane et al. explain:

> Layer II is also strongly accentuated over the entire cortical formation of the dolphin brain . . . This effectively means that the cortex in the dolphin is entirely covered with a paleo-archicortical [ancient-old cortex] type of organization which represents a primitive architectonic feature.
>
> (P. J. Morgane, M. S. Jacobs, and Albert Galaburda, "Evolutionary Morphology of the Dolphin Brain," in Ronald J. Schusterman, Jeanette A. Thomas and Forrest G. Wood (eds) *Dolphin Cognition and Behavior: A Comparative Approach* (Hillsdale, NJ: Lawrence Erlbaum Associates, 1986), p. 16)

Jerison makes a similar observation when he observes, "Neocortical structures in dolphins seem to be organized as if they were paleocortical [ancient cortex]. Harry J. Jerison, "The Perceptual World of Dolphins," in Schusterman et al., *Dolphin Cognition and Behavior*, p. 162.

the human brain does, but it may have more of a "global connection" to limbic information.[29]

What does this mean in ordinary language? In theory, between the fact that the sensory/motor areas of the dolphin brain abut the limbic lobe and the fact that there may be more of a connection between the limbic lobe and the rest of the cortex, it's possible that emotional data play more of a role in the information processing of the dolphin brain than in the human brain.

But what does this mean in practice? A few possibilities suggest themselves:

- First, Harry Jerison has suggested that this brain architecture could lead dolphins to have deeper emotional attachments than humans experience.[30]
- More extensive access to the emotional content of the brain could make it virtually impossible to be "in denial" or "out of touch" with one's feelings – common psychological phenomena among humans. This could also move emotional issues and relationships more to the center of life.
- The owner of a brain with these properties could experience less of a distinction between "rational" and "emotional" – or at least more of a balance between the two – than comes about with our brains.[31]

---

[29]   Denise Herzing, private communication. Jerison suggests something akin to this possibility when he remarks:

> [R]ecognizing structural similarities between "neocortex" in dolphins and paleocortical structures in other mammals, it may be that there are functional similarities as well. Further, recognizing that paleocortical systems in rats, cats and monkeys are important in autonomic, emotional and motivational activities, it may be that higher brain functions in dolphins are more strongly represented on those dimensions (or in those domains) than are comparable human functions.
>
> (Jerison, "The Perceptual World of Dolphins," p. 162)

[30]   Developing one of the implications of dolphin brain architecture, Jerison notes, "Social bonding might involve deeper and, in a sense, more primitive attachments in dolphins than we usually see in humans." Jerison, "Perceptual World," p. 162.

[31]   Herzing notes:

> [cortical adjacency] places the higher functions in direct connection with the major sensory areas and it may explain the emotional/subtle nature of dolphin's communication. A society based on emotions and relationships might run everything through those channels first, and might also allow equal time to the association areas for sensory information. If so, the rational wouldn't necessarily override the emotional, and might provide more of a balance between these two elements.
>
> (Denise L. Herzing and Thomas I. White, "Dolphins and the Question of Personhood," *Etica & Animali*, 9 (1998): 74)

Limbic system and emotional health

Finally, there's one more difference between the dolphin and human brains related to the limbic system that raises yet another interesting point.

As explained in our discussion of the human brain, even though the cerebral cortex performs the brain's higher functions, the emotional signals from the limbic system plays an important role in its operation. One medical researcher notes that evidence from brain damaged humans suggests that a high ratio of association neurons in the neocortex to neurons in the limbic system and brain stem is necessary in humans for a variety of higher functions, including abstract thought, creativity and emotional self-control.[32] Dolphins, however, have a *higher* ratio in this regard than humans. We don't know if this ratio means the same thing in the dolphin brain, but it raises some intriguing questions.

- Is it possible that dolphins have greater emotional self-control than humans?
- Could this explain why dolphins don't act more aggressively to humans in circumstances that would probably provoke a violent response in humans?
- Is it possible that the average dolphin is emotionally healthier than the average human?

---

[32] Sterling Bunnell writes:

The neocortex forms perceptions, memories, and thoughts, but its motivation comes from the emotional activity of the so-called limbic system, or primitive core brain. Evidence from cases of brain damage in humans indicates that a high ratio of neocortical association neurons to limbic system-brain stem neurons is necessary for such qualities as reality orientation, objectivity, human, emotional self-control, and the capacity for logically consistent abstract thought, as well as the higher forms of creativity, while a decreased neocortical–limbic ratio is associated with impulsiveness, emotional instability, and irritability, impaired memory, loss of objectivity and humor, marked egocentricity, stereotyped behavior, and sometimes obsessions, mania, delusions, or hallucinations. Dolphins have a higher neocortical-limbic ratio than even healthy, intelligent humans, and captive dolphins and orcas have often shown humor, empathy, and self-control that few of us could match under comparable circumstances.

(Bunnell, "The Evolution of Cetacean Intelligence," pp. 56–57)

————————— The Dolphin Brain: Summary —————————

The dolphin brain is such a complex organ that we could go into ever increasing detail in exploring it. However, what we've seen suggests that the dolphin brain may be capable of impressive higher order functions.

- It has a large cerebral cortex and a substantial amount of associational neocortex. Most anatomical ratios that assess cognitive capacity (brain weight/spinal cord, encephalization quotient) place it second only to the human brain.
- From this perspective, the dolphin brain appears to be, at the very least, the second most complicated and powerful brain on the planet.
- The dolphin brain has a "paralimbic" lobe lacking in the human brain. Its pattern of "cortical adjacency" may produce more integrated information processing. And limbic or emotional information may play a larger role in the dolphin brain than in the human brain. The human and dolphin brains appear to have different specializations. The human brain may emphasize detail, while the dolphin brain may emphasize speed.
- The dolphin brain may compensate with its size what it lacks structurally, it may have adapted in unexpected ways, or operate according to somewhat different rules.[33] Remember that dolphins have had this brain design for 15 million years – during which time the brain has had more opportunity to develop the nuances of its potential than the human brain has.

[33] Morgane et al. write, "The cortical expanse in whales is enormous and perhaps the rules governing its organization, still unknown, are altogether different in their Order. In some way quantity may compensate for quality, or perhaps quality takes on a different form which still remains to be specified." Morgane et al., "Evolutionary Aspects," p. 95. Elsewhere Morgane et al. make an important observation in this regard. They write:

> It should be emphasized that expansion and differentiation of neocortex has proceeded independently in the major mammalian lines of descent. The whales, having left terrestrial life many million of years ago . . . seem to reflect in their present neocortical structure the conservative features of those early mammalian stages that were perhaps preserved because of the decisive lack of further somatic sensory experience of land life for both groups of animals. Lacking this possible stimulus for higher neocortical differentiation, the neocortical evolution in the whales may, therefore, have taken a different path leading, among other things, to the enormous surface spread of the neocortex, compensating or even hypercompensating in this manner for the reduced level of cortical differentiation.
>
> (P. J. Morgane, M. S. Jacobs and Albert Galaburda, "Evolutionary Morphology of the Dolphin Brain," pp. 22–23)

The dolphin and human brains are, therefore, so different in both known and unknown ways that it would be a mistake to think that the dolphin brain is incapable of advanced cognitive processes simply because it's structurally different from the human brain. In fact, research that we'll review in succeeding chapters reveals that the dolphin brain is capable of a variety of advanced cognitive abilities: self-recognition, problem solving, artificial "language" comprehension and sophisticated social behavior. This, then, is evidence for a mechanism that scientists call "convergence." "Convergence" is a process by which species that aren't related to one another are nonetheless able to develop similar abilities by adapting to similar environmental pressures. Birds, insects and bats, for example, all developed the ability to fly – but they aren't related to each other and they use different mechanisms. Humans and dolphins have developed similar complex cognitive abilities with signifcantly different brains. As Lori Marino puts it, "the brains of humans and great apes, on the one hand, and cetaceans, on the other, have managed to get to the same 'cognitive place' by different neuroanatomical routes."[34]

In a way, then, this reinforces Diana Reiss's idea that dolphins are so different from us that we should think of them as a kind of "alien" intelligence. The dolphin brain is sufficiently different from ours in important ways that we have to be prepared to consider the possibility that the experience of living life in the water with a brain of that sort is fundamentally different from living life on the land with a brain of the sort that we have.

We can't settle the issue of what cognitive abilities dolphins are capable of, then, simply by studying the details of the dolphin brain. So our next step will be to look at the research into dolphin intelligence that's based on dolphin behavior. Are dolphins self-aware? Do they have an inner life of thoughts and feelings? Can dolphins solve complex problems? Is there any evidence of their using abstract concepts and language? That's what we'll look at in the following chapters.

---

[34]   Lori Marino, "Convergence in Complex Cognitive Abilities in Cetaceans and Primates" and private communication.

CHAPTER 3

Do Dolphins Think and Feel?

The potential of the dolphin brain to support higher order functions is critical to our investigation because, for most humans, "intelligence" is the great divider between "humans" and "animals." Many humans think that we're the only intelligent beings on the planet, that we therefore deserve special treatment at the hands of one another, and that we also have the right to treat other living things virtually any way we want to.

Of course, not everyone thinks that a being must be intelligent to deserve decent treatment. The modern "animal rights" movement is based on the idea that the ability to feel pain is more important than advanced cognitive abilities – and this capacity is something that we share with all nonhuman animals. Indeed, the eighteenth-century philosopher Jeremy Bentham argued that "The question is not, Can [nonhumans] reason? nor Can they talk? but, Can they suffer?"[1] In the opinion of contemporary philosophers like Peter Singer, it's even wrong for us to kill nonhumans for food or clothing. Other thinkers simply call for better treatment of nonhumans until they're killed (calling for "free-ranging" chickens, for example).

Whatever philosophical merit these positions may have, however, most humans disagree with Bentham, Singer and animal rights proponents. For most humans, the issue is indeed whether nonhumans can think. But this shouldn't be read as a form of blind prejudice that we might call "sentient-ism" – a bias that contends that only sentient beings have rights because we're innately superior. Rather, we believe that our complex brains give us specific, advanced capacities that provide logical, objective, and scientific grounds for

---

[1] Jeremy Bentham, *Principles of Morals and Legislation* (New York: Hafner, 1948), p. 311.

our claim that we have a right to be treated in certain ways. By the same token, we believe that nonhumans lack these same cognitive abilities, and therefore lack the right to be treated like us. In essence, we presume that the capacities of a species' brain determine what constitutes "harm" to members of that species and, therefore, how we can treat other species.

So if dolphins (or any other nonhumans, for that matter) have the same advanced cognitive abilities that we do, most people would agree that we would need to rethink how we treat them.

Do dolphins' brains actually give them the abilities that matter? As we're about to see – yes. Do humans, as a result, need to change how they treat dolphins? Yes.

------------------------- Human Consciousness -------------------------

Before we can appreciate the ethical significance of what the dolphin brain can do, however, it's crucial to understand why humans think that such advanced abilities merit us special treatment, or, as some thinkers put it, give us "moral standing."[2]

The key here is that the human brain gives us a sophisticated *consciousness*. This consciousness makes it possible for us to be the unusual beings that we are: *special, self-conscious, unique individuals (with distinctive personalities, life-long memories and personal histories) who are vulnerable to pain and harm in unusual ways, and who have the power to reflect upon and choose our actions.*

- Having "self-consciousness" means that we are aware of our experiences. We're also aware of ourselves existing through time. We live in the present, but we also have a sense of the past and future.
- Our brains give us the capacity for a wide range of thoughts and emotions, as well as physical sensations. This makes us vulnerable to pain connected with our minds and hearts, as well as our bodies.

---

[2] To say that a being has "moral standing" means simply that, at least to some degree, its interests are entitled to be respected. Historically, humans have argued that nonhumans have little or no moral standing because they lack the advanced cognitive and affective abilities that humans possess.

● Our sense of self, our thoughts and our feelings are strong enough to control our actions. Two important points flow from this: (1) this *freedom* to behave as we choose is so much at the center of who we are that we have a fundamental need to control our actions, and (2) the fact that the people around us can control *their* actions means that pain at the hands of other humans is not inevitable.

The brain and the self, self-awareness and personal identity

The most distinctive feature of the type of consciousness in question is the fact that *we are aware of our own existence*. We have *self-awareness* or *self-consciousness*. We can look inside ourselves and say, "I."

Self-consciousness is made possible by advanced intellectual abilities, and it is one of the most fundamental traits that define our species. Each of us experiences ourselves as a unique individual with a continuous identity through time. This "self" persists throughout our lives and is the crucial, common thread that weaves together everything that we experience into some unified whole. It gives us the sense of personal identity that we carry with us through space and time. We may move from one location to another. We may associate with different groups of people. Our bodies change. We may even change our name. But throughout everything, there's something constant – an identity – that holds together and contains all of those changes and different experiences.

Our uniqueness makes us think that each one of us is special and irreplaceable. That is, we see each individual as having what philosophers refer to as "intrinsic worth." Apart from whatever tangible good or harm we may do in our lives, we believe that we have an *intangible* value that comes from the simple fact that we exist as unique individuals. Indeed, most of us think that the life of a human being is so valuable that we cannot put a price tag on it. No matter who we are or what we do, we believe that each individual life is valuable – and deserves to be respected as such. We believe that any time a human being dies, something precious and irreplaceable is lost. Accordingly, since each individual has, for all practical purpose an infinite value, we believe that this entitles us to special treatment at the hands of one other.

The great German philosopher Immanuel Kant captured this idea when he wrote that "everything has either a *price* or a *dignity*. Whatever has a price can be replaced by something else as its equivalent; on the other hand, whatever is above all price, and therefore admits of no equivalent, has a dignity."[3] For Kant, human beings have a dignity. We're worthy of respect just by virtue of our nature as self-aware, unique beings.

Self-awareness, an "inner life" and experiencing pain

Our sense of individuality and uniqueness, however, comes from more than the ability to look inside and say, "I." Our brains also give us powerful memories, impressive analytical abilities and the ability to experience a wide range of emotions. And when we combine these capacities with self-awareness, we get an entirely new, complex dimension to our lives – a rich "inner life" comprised of thoughts and emotions that stretch across our entire lives and are different for each one of us. Our "self," then, becomes something like a receptacle that contains the unique combination of ideas, feelings, memories, hopes, dreams, fears, disappointments, traits, talents, strengths, weaknesses, and the like that we experience from birth to death.

Human consciousness, however, is a two-edged sword. Self-awareness and the ability to reflect on our experiences may add an extraordinarily rich dimension to human life. But our consciousness also exposes us to a wide range of harm and pain. We are as vulnerable to emotional pain as we are to physical pain. We remember hurts from the past. We worry about pain and loss that we may experience in the future. At any moment, we're vulnerable to an enormous range of negative feelings: fear, terror, grief, guilt, shame, regret, anger, hatred, betrayal and the like. And the more intense these feelings are, the more fixed they become in our memory, and the more they may affect our sense of life, our sense of who we are and our behavior in the future. Emotional trauma, for example, can have a life-long impact on someone.

The self and control

Our brains, however, give us more than the capacity to be aware of what happens to us and to react with thoughts and feelings. Self-consciousness also gives us the power to think about and to *control* our actions.

We don't go through life like riders on a roller coaster – observers who experience and react to every dip and turn, but are powerless over what happens next. Our actions aren't mindless responses to physical stimuli or the product of the irresistible pull of instinct or emotion. Our brains give us

---

[3] Immanuel Kant, *Grounding for the Metaphysics of Morals*, trans. J. E. Ellington (Indianapolis, IN: Hackett Publishing Company, 1993), Ak 4: 434.

the power to resist our first impulse and to think before we act. We can assess situations and consider a variety of factors – our own wants and needs, those of others, the consequences of our actions, the norms of our society, ideas of right and wrong, and so on. We can then identify our options and choose the behavior we deem most appropriate for the circumstance. In fact, our *freedom* to choose our actions is so much at the core of who we are that we believe that we have an absolutely vital need to control our actions. Any significant interference with that freedom counts as *harm*.

This freedom to choose our actions is another reason that philosophers like Kant set beings like us apart from everything else. The ability to fashion our own destiny means that free beings are qualitatively different from tables and chairs and should be treated appropriately. If other people try to use us as means to their ends, or if they try to impose their will on ours, they're treating free and autonomous beings like inanimate objects. This deprives us of something central to our nature. In Kant's opinion, manipulating or forcing free beings to do something that they don't choose to do is wrong because it fails to treat free and autonomous individuals with appropriate respect for their special nature.

Moreover, since all of us control our actions, we feel justified in expecting other people to treat us appropriately. Other people have the ability to consider the consequences of their actions before they act. Accordingly, we think it's reasonable for them to stop themselves from doing anything that could hurt someone – or to accept the responsibility if they do.

Consciousness and harm

A sophisticated consciousness characterized by self-awareness, an inner life of thoughts and feelings, and control over our actions, then, is the basis of our claim that humans deserve to be treated in certain ways. Our sense that we have the right to be treated in certain ways by other people essentially proceeds from the nature of our consciousness. Indeed, the restrictions that we place on one another's actions – through laws, codes of ethics, and even norms like courtesy and respect – ultimately proceed from the nature of human consciousness. That is, "human harm" and "appropriate treatment" are ultimately determined by the type of consciousness that the human brain makes possible.

- *Harm is individual.* Self-awareness means that every individual member of our species is conscious of the harm that befalls us. So humans claim that *each one of us* is entitled not to experience harm.

- *Harm is emotional as well as physical.* Our brains let us experience life in such a way that harm doesn't mean just physical pain, injury or death. It extends to emotional pain as well.

- *Harm includes limiting our freedom.* The fact that our consciousness enables us to choose our actions means that harm also encompasses anything that compromises our freedom. We can even be hurt by deception or manipulation that produces neither physical nor emotional pain. In fact, in the case of deception that we never discover, we believe that we are harmed without ever knowing it.

- *We are responsible for our actions.* The power to control our actions also means that harm at the hands of humans isn't something like the weather or other natural events – something that simply happens. We cause what we do, so we are responsible for the consequences of our actions.

- *We can avoid hurting others.* Because we can understand how our actions affect others, we think that it's reasonable to expect one another to avoid hurting other people. Accordingly, we say that we have a duty to treat other humans appropriately – and we formalize these obligations in a variety of ways. We establish laws that carry punishments if we fail to obey them. We propound lists of rights that we expect to be honored. And we offer norms of morality and traditions of courtesy and respect as further guidance.

- *Limits in consciousness limit duties, rights and harm.* The fact that the nature of our consciousness determines what we consider appropriate ways to treat one another is also apparent in the exceptions we make to the rule that everyone should be held responsible for their actions and to the idea that people are entitled to make their own choices. For example, we don't hold small children responsible for their deeds because they haven't developed the ability to restrain themselves yet, they don't understand the consequences of their actions, and they can't understand the world well enough to be safe making their own choices. We might say that small children have an "undeveloped consciousness." We also recognize that some adults are not responsible for their actions because they have what we might call an "impaired consciousness." This includes, for example, people who have serious emotional problems (lack impulse control) or are mentally ill (suffer from temporary or permanent insanity). We don't see people with an undeveloped or impaired consciousness as having truly chosen their actions, so we don't see them as the authors of what they do. Therefore, we have a different sense of what's reasonable to expect from them, what's appropriate in how we treat them and what counts as harm in their cases. We don't expect to be able to reason with, communicate with and negotiate with a small child or someone who's psychotic. We think there's nothing harmful about restricting the freedom of children or people who are so ill mentally that they would hurt themselves or others if left to their own devices.

— Nonhumans, Consciousness and Appropriate Treatment —

Of course, when humans specify what we think is appropriate treatment of nonhumans, we also rely on the nature of a being's consciousness. The only difference is that many humans have traditionally put all nonhuman animals into the same category with children and the dangerously insane. Nonhumans are "just animals" – "pets" or "beasts." We assume that if nonhumans have any kind of consciousness, it lacks all of the advanced abilities that ours has. Accordingly, we neither feel any duty to treat them with the same consideration that we give humans, nor hold them responsible for their actions in the same way we do each other. We think that since "animals" have an unsophisticated consciousness, there's a large difference between how we should treat humans and how we can treat them:

- *No individual harm.* The absence of self-consciousness means that nonhumans do not experience themselves as unique and self-conscious individuals. Having a less sophisticated awareness of their experiences than we do, they lack intrinsic value. Accordingly, the deaths of *individual* nonhuman animals aren't seen as a matter of great consequence, unless we have an emotional attachment to a particular nonhuman. The extinction of an *entire species* of nonhumans may matter to us. But as long as this isn't at risk, the death of individual nonhumans is ethically acceptable.
- *Less counts as harm.* We assume that since nonhumans have a less sophisticated consciousness, they don't experience pain the way we do. Most humans believe that even though other animals feel physical pain (and possibly some kind of emotional pain), their lack of self-awareness means that pain isn't as bad for them as it is for us. We assume they have a simpler subjective experience of life than we do. We presume that nonhumans have a less complicated awareness of the world around them that consists of reacting to the physical stimuli immediately present in their environment, or responding to stimuli according to hard-wired instinct.

We believe that nonhumans can't reflect on their present experiences, file them away as memories that they recall at another time, or project forward and think about life in the future. So we think that relatively little counts as significant *harm*.

- *No dread or grief in livestock.* One of the reasons that we believe there's nothing wrong with raising nonhumans for food is that most of us think that these beings can't grasp the grave nature of their situation. We believe that they're unable to feel such emotions as dread about their future fate, grief over the disappearance of any of their number who are now gone, a sense of betrayal at the hands of ostensibly loving caretakers, trauma from being separated from members of their family, long-term emotional suffering that comes from the memory of a lifetime of harsh physical conditions, and the like. As far as most of us are concerned, as long as chicken, cattle and pigs don't experience unnecessary pain while they're being raised, and as long as they don't suffer needlessly when they're killed, we don't have any moral reservations about what's going on.

- *No power to choose.* We assume that nonhumans lack the type of consciousness that gives them the power to think about and *choose* their actions. We assume that their actions result from instinct or the automatic response to particular physical stimuli – not from *free choice*. Nonhumans are either "wild animals" who are driven so strongly by the forces of nature that they're fundamentally dangerous creatures, or they're "pets" or "domesticated animals," who have been "broken" or "bred" into a condition that renders them safe for us to be around. Limiting the freedom of nonhumans by keeping them captive or physically forcing them to do things, then, strikes us as perfectly acceptable ways to treat them.

In sum, a simpler type of consciousness means that there's a major difference between what counts as harm to nonhumans and what counts as harm to us. Because we claim that the brains of nonhumans lack our advanced cognitive and affective capacities, we argue that situations or events that seriously harm humans (death, captivity, emotional trauma, the absence of freedom and the like) are largely inconsequential when done to nonhumans.

The possibility of a sophisticated consciousness in nonhumans

The way that humans think about nonhumans, however, is based on a crucial assumption – that they lack the type of consciousness that we have. *If all* nonhumans have the simple consciousness we've always believed they did, then most of us are comfortable that there's nothing wrong with how we treat them. But that's a big "if."

What if we're wrong, however?[4] If any nonhumans have a sophisticated consciousness, we humans would be forced to re-evaluate our relationship with those beings.

- If any nonhumans can experience self-awareness and a sense of individuality, then, presumably, they should be regarded as having a similar kind of "intrinsic worth" and "moral standing" that human beings do. And this would mean that the injury, suffering or death of an *individual* nonhuman – not merely the death of all members of a species – would be an event of considerable ethical consequence.
- By the same token, if any nonhuman animals have complex intellectual and emotional abilities and a sense of personal identity, they would probably experience pain in a way that's closer to the human experience of pain than most of us imagine.
- And if the consciousness of any nonhumans is powerful enough to give them control over their actions, then restricting their freedom through physical coercion or captivity might also count as a kind of harm.

This, then, is why the issue of "dolphin intelligence" is so important. If the dolphin brain supports significant cognitive and affective abilities, then the way that humans currently treat dolphins raises important ethical issues. If dolphins are self-conscious, if they can file experiences away as memories and later recall them, if they can think about the future, if they can choose their actions, and if they're aware of their own mortality and that of others, then they probably feel pain as badly as we do and they are unique individuals with "intrinsic worth."

---

[4]   There is, in fact, good reason to think that we are wrong. This book examines only the issue of what type of consciousness dolphins may have. However, for discussion of the possibility of awareness in a variety of nonhumans, see, in particular, the work of Donald Griffin (*The Question of Animal Awareness: Evolutionary Continuity of Mental Experience* [New York: The Rockefeller University Press, 1976]; *Animal Thinking* [Cambridge, MA: Harvard University Press, 1984]; and *Animal Minds* [Chicago: The University of Chicago Press, 1992]). For a popular treatment of the question of whether nonhumans can think and feel, see Jeffrey Moussaief Masson and Susan McCarthy's *When Elephants Weep: The Emotional Lives of Animals* (New York: Delacourt Press, 1995).

If dolphins have these abilities, then, it would be hard to imagine how anyone could defend, for example, practices in parts of the fishing industry that harass dolphin communities and lead to the death and injury of individual dolphins. The use of captive dolphins for research and entertainment as well as the entertainment industry's programs of captive breeding of dolphins would be morally problematic. In addition, a variety of human practices that make the oceans less livable for cetaceans would also become ethically questionable: dumping toxic waste into the oceans, performing sonic experiments that could harm the echolocation abilities of whales and dolphins, setting off explosions in the ocean, and the like.

For thousands of years, humans have been telling stories about dolphins that suggest that these cetaceans have at least some kind of intelligence. We've already seen that dolphins have large, complex brains. Even though the dolphin brain is different from the human brain, there doesn't appear to be anything about the dolphin brain that precludes the possibility of some kind of higher order awareness. Indeed, on the contrary, there's reason to believe that the dolphin brain does support higher order cognitive functions.

——————————————— Dolphin consciousness ———————————————

The question we're faced with, then, is whether any scientific research tells us what type of consciousness the dolphin brain makes possible. Not surprisingly, given just how important *intelligence* is to humans, there's such a substantial body of research into various facets of *dolphin intelligence* that it will take us more than one chapter to look at it.

For the remainder of this chapter, we'll focus on the four most basic questions for determining the main lines of their consciousness:

- Are dolphins self-aware?
- Do dolphins recognize the existence of other self-aware beings?
- Do dolphins think and feel?
- Do dolphins control their actions?

If dolphins possess these traits, then these cetaceans are clearly a "who," rather than a "what." That is, their brains give them a consciousness that, at least to some degree, has the same fundamental characteristics as ours – attributes that humans offer as reasons why we have "moral standing."

Self-awareness and signature whistles

We start our investigation of dolphin consciousness with *self-awareness*. Do dolphins share with us the ability to look inside and say, "I"?

Of course, the easiest way to determine whether dolphins are self-aware would be for us simply to go up to a dolphin and say something like: "Hi, my name is Tom. What's yours?" But since humans and dolphins don't engage in two-way communication with a common language, the image of introducing ourselves and asking a dolphin for his or her name must seem silly.

Or is it?

This picture actually isn't as foolish as it first seems. Just because a dolphin won't tell us its name when we ask doesn't mean that it doesn't have one. In fact, it may. Two scientists claimed to discover in 1965 that each dolphin has a unique whistle that may be the equivalent of a "name." It's called a "signature whistle." Scientists who believe that each dolphin has a signature whistles claim that it remains the same throughout a dolphin's life, that dolphins use it a great deal, and that its main function seems to be to broadcast the dolphin's identity (and perhaps information about itself) to other dolphins in the vicinity.[5] Signature whistles are reportedly often used as contact calls between individuals, e.g. mother and calves, separated by some distance.[6] Moreover, dolphins have also been recorded making the signature

---

[5] M. C. Caldwell and D. K. Caldwell, "Individualized Whistle Contours in Bottlenosed Dolphins (Tursiops Truncatus), *Nature (London)*, 207 (1965): 434–435. Also see, Melba C. Caldwell, David K. Caldwell and Peter L. Tyack, "Review of the Signature-Whistle Hypothesis for the Atlantic Bottlenose Dolphin," in S. Leatherwood and R. Reeves (eds) *The Bottlenose Dolphin* (San Diego: Academic Press, 1990), pp. 199–234. In a more recent study of signature whistles, researchers discovered that "bottlenose dolphins extract identity information from signature whistles even after all voice features have been removed from the signal. Thus, dolphins are the only animals other than humans that have been shown to transmit identity information independent of the caller's voice or location." V. M. Janik, L. S. Sayigh, and R. S. Wells, "Signature Whistle Shape Conveys Identity Information to Bottlenose Dolphins," *Proceedings of the National Academy of Sciences*, 103(21) (May 23, 2006): 8293–8297.

[6] D. L. Herzing, "Vocalizations and Associated Underwater Behavior of Free-Ranging Atlantic Spotted Dolphins, *Stenella Frontalis*, and Bottlenose Dolphins, *Tursiops Truncatus*," *Aquatic Mammals*, 22 (1996): 61–79. Also see L. S. Sayigh, P. L. Tyack, R. S. Wells, and M. D. Scott, "Signature Whistles of Free-ranging Bottlenose Dolphins *Tursiops Truncatus*: Stability and Mother–Offspring Comparisons," *Behavioral and Ecological Sociobiology*, 26 (1990): 247–260, and R. A. Smolker, J. Mann, and B. B. Smuts, "Use of Signature Whistles during Separations and Reunions by Wild Bottlenose Dolphin Mothers and Infants," *Behavioral and Ecological Sociobiology*, 33 (1993): 393–402. Peter L. Tyack and Laela S. Sayigh, "Those Dolphins Aren't Just Whistling in the Dark," *Oceanus*, 32(1) (Spring 1989): 80–83.

whistle of another dolphin – perhaps in the same way that we say the name of a friend to get his or her attention.[7] Human names, of course, refer to unique, self-aware individuals. So it's possible that "dolphin names" could refer to the same thing. That is, signature whistles offer at least some preliminary evidence to suggest self-awareness – that is, that dolphins, like humans, are conscious of themselves and other dolphins as individuals.[8]

As suggestive as signature whistles might be, however, researchers have uncovered even stronger grounds for thinking that these cetaceans have a sense of self.

Self-awareness and mirror tests

One of the most important findings that suggests that dolphins possess self-consciousness is that dolphins are able to pass a standard test of self-awareness that we use with humans. It involves how we behave when we see our reflection in a mirror.

This test comes from the world of developmental psychology and uses a mirror to determine whether a human baby has developed to the point where he or she has a sense of self. Until the age of about 18 to 24 months, when babies see their reflection in a mirror, they think that they're looking at another child. After their brain has developed more, however, they recognize the image as their own. Psychologists test for this by putting something like a piece of colored paper on a child's clothes when he or she isn't looking and then observing the reaction when the child looks at a mirror. Children who have achieved self-awareness will look at their reflection and then look down at and touch the piece of paper. They recognize that what is true of the image in the mirror is true of themselves. The idea behind the test is that you

---

[7] Ibid.;. Peter L. Tyack, "Functional Aspects of Cetacean Communication," in J. Mann, R. C. Connor, P. L. Tyack and H. Whitehead (eds) *Cetacean Societies: Field Studies of Dolphins and Whales* (Chicago: University of Chicago Press, 2000), p. 303.

[8] Not all scientists believe that dolphins have signature whistles. See, for example, Brenda McCowan and Diana Reiss, "The Fallacy of 'Signature Whistles' in Bottlenose Dolphins: A Comparative Perspective of 'Signature Information' in Animal Vocalizations," *Animal Behaviour* 62 (2001): 1151–1162. This study claims that the dolphins studied used "a predominant and shared whistle type rather than individually distinctive signature whistles." However, the authors also report that "subtle variations within this one whistle type could be partially attributed to individual identity." That is, the variations could contain "signature information." Even if dolphins lack "signature whistles," when we take into account the general picture we get from research into dolphin cognitive abilities, such "signature information" might just as readily suggest self-awareness as "signature whistles" do.

couldn't recognize yourself in the mirror unless you were already aware of yourself as an independent, autonomous, self-conscious being.

The mirror test has been used in primate research since 1970. Researchers place a conspicuous mark on their subject's forehead while he or she is anesthetized. What's significant is how the subjects respond to the reflection after they wake up. Trying to remove the mark suggests self-awareness; acting as though the reflection is another animal suggests a lack of self-awareness. Given the test's effectiveness with other species (chimpanzees, orangutans and at least one gorilla have so far demonstrated self-recognition), scientists wondered how dolphins would do on it.

Determining whether dolphins can recognize their reflections actually involves research on two different matters, because passing the mirror test requires two different cognitive abilities.

1   It requires that someone grasp the concept of *an image that represents reality*. To take a crude example, when we see a photograph of an apple, we understand that this two-dimensional image on a piece of paper represents a real-life, three-dimensional piece of fruit. In the same way, when we stare into a mirror, we understand that the visual image that we look at – the reflection – is separate from but represents an actual object – a human body. And we're then able to place the images into the appropriate cognitive context and respond appropriately.

2   The mirror test then requires that we recognize that this image represents *us* – not someone else. We know that we're looking at *our* face, *our* hands, and so on.

Dolphins and the representations of reality

The question of whether dolphins recognize representations of reality has been explored by two scientists: Ken Marten, the former chief scientist for Earthtrust's Project Delphis in Hawaii, and Louis Herman, director of the Kewalo Basin Marine Mammal Laboratory at the University of Hawaii in Honolulu. Both men have turned up interesting results.

Ken Marten is a cetacean biologist who was on the research faculty at the University of California at Santa Cruz. However, Marten also served at one time as a government observer aboard tuna boats, with the depressing job of counting the number of dolphins who were killed or injured in the purse seine nets. The experience was a driving force behind Marten's research into self-awareness in dolphins.

Marten approached the question by showing captive dolphins a tele-vised image of a human throwing fish into the pool. Obviously, a small, two-dimensional televised image is very different from three-dimensional reality, so if the dolphins reacted appropriately, it would suggest that they understood what the image was representing. Here is Marten's account of the experiment:

> To test if dolphins treat images on their TV as a representation of reality, we played the dolphins Keola, Hot Rod, Okoa, Tinkerbell, and Maui a videotape of their trainer feeding them. The "feeding tape" had been filmed from the oppos-ite side of the tank, zoomed in on the trainer, so it showed fish being thrown down to the dolphins, almost from the dolphins' viewpoint. We hypothesized that if the dolphins viewed TV as a representation of reality they would swim away from the TV monitor in the big tank and go to their feeding station in the small tank. We were surprised by the actual result: Keola, Hot Rod, and to a lesser extent Tinkerbell, appeared to try to "catch" the TV fish by opening their mouths each time a fish was thrown. After doing this for about a minute they finally left the monitor and went to the small tank (where they were accus-tomed to being fed); the fact that TV may represent reality for dolphins was thus confirmed. This result occurred with Keola and Hot Rod the first time they saw the feeding tape, before any conditioning could occur. In one instance when Hot Rod was watching the feeding tape, the video came to an end with the trainer packing up her fish buckets and leaving, which resulted in Hot Rod rushing to the small tank. Because in our research subtle motions on the TV screen occasionally elicit mouth openings such as the dolphins' "catching" response, more research is needed to fully understand the dolphins' perception of TV, and to know whether the dolphin was trying to catch the fish, or just reacting to the motion on the TV screen. Our results bode well for the continued use of TV as a dolphin cognition research tool.[9]

Lou Herman is a psychologist who has done groundbreaking research on dolphins' ability to understand an artificial "language" – research that we'll examine in Chapter 5. He used a television screen in his language research, but he also used it to investigate whether dolphins recognize the images they see as representations of actions.

The two dolphins that Herman worked with, Phoenix and Akeakamai, had already been trained to mimic the behavior of either another dolphin or a human in the pool with them. The "model" would perform an action (e.g.,

[9]   Ken Marten and Suchi Psarakos, "Do Dolphins Perceive Television as a Representation of Reality?" *Earthtrust Chronicles* (Fall, 1992): 8.

tossing a ball in the air, twirling a Frisbee, pulling a rope, swimming over a surfboard, and the like), the dolphin would be given an "imitate" command, and the dolphin would attempt to perform the same behavior. Herman then asked the dolphins to perform the same task by watching a televised picture of the task being performed. As in the case of Marten's research, Herman's dolphins appeared to understand what they were seeing. Commenting on their performance, Herman notes:

> It is worth remembering that the TV images are greatly decreased in image size, contrast, and resolution from that of the live situation. The important point to remember is not the perceptual feat alone which recognition of a TV image implies, but the conceptual accomplishment which is predicated on it. That is, the dolphin appears to interpret a scene on a TV display as an analog of the real world event. Yet, the dolphin distinguishes between the TV world and the real world in that the behavior is demonstrated away from station such as tossing a ball through a hoop. The dolphin does not attempt to retrieve the ball shown on the TV screen, but instead retrieves the ball in its own tank and swims to the real world net for its "layup."[10]

So, it appears that dolphins can take the first step to self-awareness and recognize images for what they are.

Mirror/video tests

What happens, then, when dolphins confront images of themselves? Do they behave in a way that implies self-awareness? Research on more than one group of dolphins suggests that this is the case.

The pioneer on this front is Project Delphis's Ken Marten. Marten chose the mirror test because its successful use with primates makes it a respected scientific procedure. In this experiment, researchers worked with five captive dolphins at Sea Life Park in Hawaii. They rubbed some zinc oxide onto a spot that the dolphins could see only by using the mirror. While there were some individual differences in how the dolphins responded to the mirror, all of them behaved in ways that suggested that they were using the mirror to examine the mark. In the following sequence of photographs, for example,

---

[10] L. M. Herman, P. Morrel-Samuels, and L. A. Brown, "Recognition and Imitation of Television Scenes by Bottlenosed Dolphins," paper presented at Eighth Biennial Conference on the Biology of Marine Mammals, Pacific Grove, California, December 7–11, 1989.

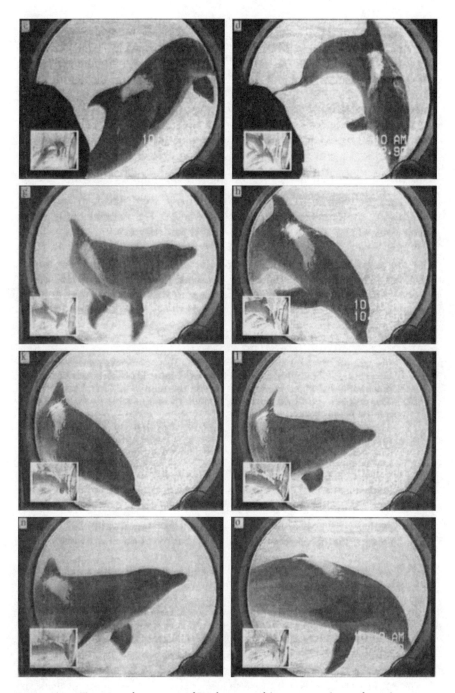

Figure 3.1   Ten-second sequence of Keola engaged in maneuvering and turning postures in front of a 1.2 meter diameter one-way mirror
Source: Kenneth Martin and Suchi Psarakos, "Evidence of Self-Awareness in the Bottlenose Dolphin (*Tursiops truncatus*)," *Self-Awareness in Animals and Humans: Developmental Perspectives*, ed. Sue Taylor Parker, Robert W. Mitchell, and Maria L. Boccia, chapter 24, pp. 361–79. New York: Cambridge University Press, 1995

you can see the dolphin Keola twisting and maneuvering himself in ways suggesting that he's looking at the mark on his back. Because this is very different behavior from what researchers observed when dolphins interacted with a new dolphin in person, they conclude that the mirror behavior suggests self-awareness.[11]

In addition to the mirror test, however, Ken Marten also exposed dolphins to other circumstances designed to determine whether they recognized an image of themselves for what it was – or thought it was another dolphin.[12] In the first test, researchers alternated between showing three dolphins (Keola and Kamalii, two adult males and Hot Rod, a juvenile male) live video images of themselves on a television screen for about 10 minutes ("mirror mode") and then the playback of these same images ("playback mode"). In Marten's opinion, "each dolphin distinguished playback from mirror mode in his own way, suggesting self-examination over social behavior."

Hot Rod and, especially, Keola paid more attention to the television screen when it was in "mirror mode" than "playback mode." In "playback mode," the dolphins tended to be less active in front of the screen. But in "mirror mode," Keola would watch himself while he moved his head and opened his mouth.

Even more conclusive than Marten's findings, however, is the work of Diana Reiss and Lori Marino. In one test done at California's Marine World Africa USA, the researchers observed how Pan and Delphi, two young male dolphins responded, first, to having a mirror in their pool for ten days and, then, to being marked with zinc oxide on day eleven.[13] During the first ten days, the dolphins appeared to watch their reflection as they performed a number of head movements and body postures in front of the mirror. They also seemed to use the mirror to examine the insides of their mouths. (The mirror may even have led to increased sexual behavior between the two. Dolphins ordinarily are highly sexual beings (a dimension of their nature that

---

[11]   Kenneth Martin and Suchi Psarakos, "Evidence of Self-Awareness in the Bottlenose Dolphin (*Tursiops truncatus*)," in Sue Taylor Parker, Robert W. Mitchell, and Maria L. Boccia (eds) *Self-Awareness in Animals and Humans: Developmental Perspectives* (New York: Cambridge University Press, 1995), pp. 361–379.

[12]   Ken Marten and Suchi Psarakos, "Using Self-View Television to Distinguish between Self-Examination and Social Behavior in the Bottlenose Dolphin (*Tursiops truncatus*)," *Consciousness and Cognition*, 4(2) (1995): 205–224.

[13]   Lori Marino, Diana Reiss and Gordon Gallup, "Mirror Self-recognition in Bottlenose Dolphins: Implications for Comparative Study of Highly Dissimilar Species," in Sue Taylor Parker, Robert W. Mitchell, and Maria L. Boccia (eds) *Self-Awareness in Animals and Humans*, pp. 380–391.

we will discuss later in this book), but when the mirror was available, they engaged in sexual behavior much more often than when it was covered – and *only* in front of the mirror. For example, during one 30-minute period, Pan tried to have sex with Delphi 24 times and Delphi tried to have sex with Pan 19 times. Moreover, if they drifted out of view of the mirror, they'd stop the sex, go back in front of the mirror, and then continue.) The most compelling evidence, however, occurred after they were marked with zinc oxide. When the researchers called the dolphins and started removing the marks, the dolphins would swim back to the mirror to check the progress of the removal. In other words, they were using the mirror to examine themselves.

However, Reiss and Marino did the conclusive research on this matter with two different dolphins at the New York Aquarium under scientific controls so strict that there can be no question that the dolphins were capable of recognizing themselves in a mirror.[14] When the dolphins were marked, they used a mirror or another reflective surface in the pool to examine themselves. When they were "sham marked," they used the reflection to see if they'd been marked or not. They spent more time at the mirror when marked than under any other conditions. And the study even brought out some unique behavior. As the scientists report: "[One] dolphin, upon being marked for the first and only time on the tongue, immediately swam to the Plexiglas mirror and engaged in a mouth opening and closing sequence never before observed by him during the study." That is, the dolphins clearly appeared to understand that they were looking at a reflection of their own bodies.

Equally significant about all of these mirror and video studies is that at no time did any of the dolphins behave towards the reflection as though it were another dolphin. The head-to-head position that these dolphins often had to take in order to view either their reflection or the tape playback is typically an aggressive stance for dolphins.

And when you see dolphins go head-to-head in the wild, there's no question that it's an aggressive exchange. They typically make squawking sounds at each other, and they may also take a run at each other in what almost looks like a game of "chicken." Yet there was none of this sort of behavior when the dolphins studied by Marten, Reiss and Marino interacted with their images. Especially when you study tapes of dolphins watching their images, there's no reason to think that they are mistaking their image for another dolphin.

[14] Diana Reiss and Lori Marino, "Mirror Self-Recognition in the Bottlenose Dolphin: A Case of Cognitive Convergence," *Proceedings of the National Academy of Science*, 98(10) (May 8, 2001): 5937–5942.

FIGURE 3.2   Dolphin examining its image in a mirror
Source: Diana Reiss, PhD The Wildlife Conservation Society

FIGURE 3.3   Aggressive behavior

FIGURE 3.4   Aggressive behavior

Dolphin self-awareness? Probably

So, in the first step of our inquiry into the type of consciousness that the dolphin brain supports, we find some impressive facts.

- Dolphins may have "signature whistles" that appear to be used in a way that's equivalent to a "name." This is highly suggestive of self-awareness.
- Dolphins can recognize their reflections in a mirror – something that requires not only self-awareness, but the sophisticated intellectual ability to grasp the distinction between real-life *objects* and the *representations* of objects.

It's impossible to overestimate the importance of the presence of self-awareness in dolphins because self-awareness is the crucial foundation of the kind of intelligence that humans have claimed is unique to our species. If dolphins are self-aware, this opens the door to accepting the idea that dolphins are similar to us in ways that we've always said were unique to humans – self-conscious individuals with a rich inner life of thoughts and emotions, vulnerability to emotional pain, and the ability to control our actions.

Self-consciousness and a mental "workbench"

It's critical to understand precisely why self-consciousness is so important for the question of whether dolphins use their large brains in the same way that humans do – that is, that they self-consciously feel and think in a way that's similar to the way that we do. After all, the point is not simply that they're like us. It's what self-consciousness allows. And the crucial point is that self-consciousness makes it possible for a being *to reflect on the contents of its consciousness.*[15]

All animals can feel fear and physical pain, for example. But only self-conscious animals, in addition to experiencing the pain, can take a mental step back and *reflect* on what's happening to them. Only self-conscious animals, in addition to feeling fear, can reflect on the fact that they are experiencing such an emotion. Self-consciousness creates a kind of "mental space" in which we can analyze our experiences – as they happen, or after they've taken place. We can even mull something over that we anticipate will happen in the future.

For want of a better analogy, we might say that self-consciousness gives us a kind of "mental workbench" onto which we can place our experience of emotions, concepts, memories of events, representations of physical objects and the like. And then we use this "workbench" to work with them in any number of ways:

- We can take our experiences apart, and understand them better.
- We can look at our emotional reaction to events from a different angle, in order to determine whether our responses were appropriate.
- We can examine a variety of possible ways of acting and evaluate which we would choose to do.
- We can study our memories of the actions of other people, and understand them better.
- We can concentrate on a difficult idea until we grasp it.
- We can scrutinize a problem in a way that lets us solve it more efficiently than trial and error. The result of our reflections can lead to our learning new actions or patterns in a way that's far more efficient than positive and negative reinforcement.
- We can use this "mental workbench" to create something new – something artistic, mechanical, humorous, etc.

The list of what we are able to do by reflecting on the contents of our consciousness is as limitless as it is impressive. And all of this would be impossible without self-consciousness.

---

[15]   Mirror self-recognition studies aren't the only evidence that dolphins can reflect on the contents of their consciousness. This is also suggested by the capacity to register "uncertainty." See, for example, J. David Smith et al., "The Uncertain Response in the Bottlenosed Dolphin (*Tursiops truncatus*)," *Journal of Experimental Psychology: General*, 124(4) (1995): 391–408.

────────── Do Dolphins Recognize Other Minds? ──────────

As important as self-awareness may be, however, it's still a fairly elementary ability in comparison to what the average human is capable of. Can dolphins take the next step and recognize self-awareness in others? That is, do they recognize other minds?

The ability to recognize the existence of other minds is critical for a variety of reasons:

- Like the mirror test, it is one of the benchmarks of human cognitive development. Between the ages of 15 months and 4 years, human children develop a variety of abilities connected with understanding the minds of others. If dolphins have a sophisticated consciousness, this is a trait we'd expect them to have.
- Recognizing other minds is surely a necessary trait of a sophisticated consciousness. The brain of a self-aware being that fails to recognize other similar beings would be a poor instrument for understanding reality. After all, we know that billions of self-aware beings exist – us. A consciousness that supports self-awareness but fails to recognize this same trait in others provides such an inaccurate picture of the world as to be horribly defective.
- One reason it's so important to humans that we have an accurate picture of reality on this score is that our ability to recognize other self-aware beings undergirds the expectations we place on each other about how we act. Recognizing the existence of other self-aware beings lets us understand the difference between using a baseball bat to hit a baseball and using it to hit our neighbor. Our brains give us a consciousness that distinguishes between a *what* (the ball) and a *who* (Herbert), recognize the difference between *sport* and *assault*, and act appropriately. Surely, most of us would insist that if dolphins are to be recognized as having a "moral standing" equivalent to humans, they must have the ability to distinguish between "humans" and "lunch" – and act appropriately.
- If dolphins are aware of other minds in a way that they understand that the actions of others result from mental "intentions," this implies that they themselves *choose* their actions in the same way. And this suggests that they then have the power to fashion their actions based on a respect for the difference between a *who* and a *what*.
- Our own recognition of other minds is also one of the factors that makes us vulnerable to a certain type of pain – cruelty or unfairness at the hands

of another. If you slipped on a patch of ice and broke your wrist, in addition to physical pain, you'd also feel disappointment at your bad luck. However, if you ended up with a broken wrist because a robber, after taking your money at gunpoint, decided to beat you for his amusement, you'd feel more than wrist pain and disappointment. You'd feel a host of powerful, painful emotions that flow from the fact that someone with no respect for other people had deliberately victimized you. If dolphins are also capable of recognizing that harm at the hands of other "self-aware" beings can result from negligence (at best) or malice (at worst), then they, too, are probably vulnerable to a significant type of emotional pain. Thus, harm that may result from their contact with humans could be intensified by the awareness that we are beings with the power to act differently, but choose not to.

So, how do dolphins fare on this score? Is there reason to think that they can distinguish between a *what* and a *who*? Yes.

Other minds, pointing and intentions

The research that is most suggestive of dolphins' abilities to recognize other minds relates to something surprisingly simple – *pointing*. Pointing may seem an unlikely way to explore a dolphin's grasp of "other minds," but consider this. You're walking along with a friend and she silently raises her arm to the front and points her finger at something in the distance. What do you do? You look to see what she's pointing at. But *why* do you think the reason for her gesture is to direct your attention to something ahead? Better yet, why *don't* you think that she simply wants you to look at her finger? Or that she's just stretching her arm and not trying to communicate anything at all to you? You read the action correctly because silent gestures are an important part of how humans communicate with each other, and you've learned to recognize the signals that we use when we gesture in a meaningful way. In this case, you know that holding the arm still (not waving it around), extending one finger (not a closed fist, open hand or a number of fingers) and pointing in a purposeful way into the distance is a nonverbal way of saying, "Look at that!"

The most significant part of this process, however, is that you understand the meaning of your friend's gesture because you correctly infer the *intention* behind her action. That is, you infer something about your friend's *thoughts* from her action – specifically, that she wants you to look at something in the direction her finger is pointing. Humans understand gestures like pointing because we make the link between *the body movement* and *the content of someone's mind*. Therefore, if dolphins can figure out the thought or intention behind a human action like pointing, it suggests that they can recognize other minds.

Moreover, like self-awareness, the ability to understand someone's intention behind pointing follows a developmental progression in the human brain. At 9 months, a baby can understand pointing as long as the objects aren't more than 20 inches away. At 12 months the range extends to objects about 8 feet away. And not until 15 months will the baby be able to disregard nearer objects and grasp the idea that the pointer is referring to a more distant object.[16] This progression is taken to be a sign that the child is developing what psychologists call a "theory of mind" that captures how both its own mind and other minds operate. As with self-awareness, we'd probably expect to see this ability developed in dolphins if they, too, have a "theory of mind."

Understanding pointing is seen as an important sign of the sophistication of the human brain. Therefore, if dolphins can understand pointing, then this would be more evidence that dolphins may have the kind of sophisticated consciousness that recognizes the existence of other minds.

The main scientist who has looked into this is again the University of Hawaii's Lou Herman.[17] In one representative study, Herman's team worked with the two dolphins we met earlier in this chapter (Akeakamai and Phoenix) who had already been taught to understand and carry out a series of commands – for example, "fetch the pipe."[18] (Akeakamai understood hand and arm signals; Phoenix, computer-generated whistles; the "grammar" that governed these different types of signals also differed.) The question was whether – without any additional training – the dolphins could understand what the researchers meant when, instead of using one of the usual signals to refer to an object in the pool, they *pointed* to it. For example, instead of receiving the signal for "pipe" and then the signal for "fetch," the dolphin first saw the human point to an object and then got the command for "fetch." Each time, there were three objects in the pool – one to the dolphin's left, one to her right and the other behind her:

[16] Louis M. Herman, Adam A. Pack et al., "Dolphins (*Tursiops truncatus*) Comprehend the Referential Character of the Human Pointing Gesture," *Journal of Comparative Psychology*, 113(4) (1999): 347.
[17] Ibid., pp. 347–364. Louis M. Herman and Robert K. Uyeyama, "The Dolphin's Grammatical Competency: Comments on Kako (1999)," *Animal Learning and Behavior*, 27(1) (1999): 18–23.
[18] Herman's research on these dolphins' "linguistic" abilities will be described in detail in Chapter 4.

- In the first experiment, the objects were fairly far away (about 30 feet left or right and 45 feet to the back). The experimenter pointed straight at the object with his outstretched arm and index finger for about a second and then gave the command that told the dolphin what to do with the object. Both dolphins performed well with the objects to the side, but had trouble understanding the experimenter when he pointed to the object behind them.
- In the second experiment (with just Akeakamai), the objects were moved closer (about 10 feet left, right and behind) to see if this would help. Ake didn't do better with the object behind her until the experimenter added something extra to the pointing – a body lean in the direction of the object. However, after some experience with this "exaggerated pointing," she no longer needed the extra information and performed well with simple arm/hand pointing.
- In the third experiment, researchers used a more complicated set of instructions involving two objects and a command about what to do with them – for example, "pipe + basket + fetch" ("get the pipe and take it to the basket"). Sometimes the experimenter pointed at each of the different objects involved, sometimes he pointed at one and used a hand gesture to indicate the other, and sometime he used a gesture for the first and then pointed. In all of the combinations, the dolphin's performance was significantly better than chance. In general, she was correct about 75 percent of the time.

In all three experiments, the dolphins' performance was impressive. They apparently understood the *intention* behind the pointing – to refer to an object at some distance from the experimenter's hand. This is a sophisticated mental operation and a crucial bit of evidence that suggests the ability to understand other minds.

Pointing and a new twist – gazing

The more often that experiments can be successfully repeated, the more confirmation there is that the conclusions are legitimate. So it's significant that Herman's findings about the ability of dolphins to understand pointing were replicated by a group of researchers studying six different dolphins at a Sea World facility in Durban, South Africa.[19] However, these scientists added

[19] Alain Tschudin, Josep Call, R. I. M. Dunbar, Gabrielle Harriss and Charmaine van der Elst, "Comprehension of Signs by Dolphins (*Tursiops truncatus*)," *Journal of Comparative Psychology*, 115(1) (2001): 100–105.

an interesting twist to their experiments. They also investigated whether the dolphins could understand a command based on a more ambiguous way to refer to an object than pointing at it – simply *gazing in its direction*.

The Durban group followed Herman in basing the experiment on asking the dolphins to fetch an object. Two objects were placed about 4 feet from the dolphin, one to the left and the other to the right. A researcher gave the hand signal for "fetch" and then indicated the intended object by pointing or gazing. Four of the six dolphins did better than chance on the pointing experiment, and all of them did better than chance on the gazing experiment. The official conclusion of the study was, "In this case, we have been able to demonstrate that at least some dolphins are able to interpret human pointing and gaze direction signals without prior training."[20] Accordingly, this seems to strengthen the claim that dolphins have the type of consciousness that includes an awareness of other self-aware beings whose actions are the result of their thoughts.

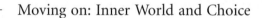

Moving on: Inner World and Choice

The research we've looked at so far in this chapter is impressive. The mirror studies of Marten, Reiss and Marino, Herman's pointing studies and the Durban pointing and gazing experiments suggest that dolphins' brains give them a sophisticated consciousness. That is, dolphins appear to have self-awareness and the ability to recognize other minds.

What about the other traits that dolphins need to have in order to qualify for moral standing and special treatment?

- Do they have an "inner world"? That is, do they have a consciousness characterized by *emotions* and *thoughts*?
- More importantly, if dolphins have feelings and thoughts, are they strong enough to be factors in dolphin behavior? That is, do dolphins *control* and *freely choose* their actions? Do they experience *freedom*?

Contents of consciousness: thoughts and feelings

Until relatively recently in the history of western science, it would be considered foolish – even heretical – to ask whether nonhumans think and feel.

[20] Ibid., p. 102.

The prevailing assumption was that nonhumans were essentially mindless, bio-logical automata and, therefore, had no emotional and intellectual capacities to speak of. Thanks to the work of pioneers like Donald Griffin, however, many scientists are now willing to concede that many nonhumans have at least some sort of a consciousness with affective and cognitive properties. The differences between humans and nonhumans on this score, then, are more a matter of degree than of kind.

Exploring the inner world of beings with whom we can't easily commun-icate, however, is an extraordinarily difficult task. So, for the purposes of this chapter, our investigation into the consciousness of dolphins will stay at a very basic level. Accordingly, when we ask, "Do dolphins have emotions and thoughts?," we aren't asking whether they can suffer from suicidal depression or whether they can handle advanced mathematics. For now, we just want to know whether their brains (1) let them have some experience of emotions; and (2) allow them to form and reflect on basic concepts. If so, the next question will be whether these thoughts and feelings are strong enough to control a dolphin's actions.

Do Dolphins Have Emotions?

In approaching the issue of whether dolphins have emotions, we should start with the fact that virtually all mammals probably have emotions.

First of all, the brains of all mammals have limbic systems – the part of the brain that generates emotions, although not the conscious awareness of them. In fact, since all mammals have a limbic system in their brains, the debate about whether nonhumans have emotions is more properly about whether they experience *conscious* emotional states that are in some way analogous to the ones we have when we say, "I feel afraid," "I feel happy," and the like.

Second, emotions are part of a highly efficient system for processing in-formation in a way that increases the likelihood that an animal will survive. This is especially true in any nonhumans who can't think, and it's even the case with humans. Imagine that you're walking along a mountain path and you see a huge boulder ahead break loose and start rolling in your direction. As you see the rock pick up speed, you'll feel fear, your body will release adrenaline, and you'll run to get out of the way. That is, your brain quickly processes the information and triggers an emotional reaction that saves your life. In fact, this is faster and more efficient than if you stopped to think about what was happening and made a calculated decision about what to do. (Indeed, the odds are that the rock would already have run over you by the time you assessed the data and decided on the best course of action.) Obviously, for any nonhuman species that lacks our abilities to think, appropriate emotional states are critical for survival.

It would be surprising, then, if dolphins did not have emotions. Like humans, dolphins have a limbic system. (Indeed, recall that the dolphin limbic system may be spread out over more of their brain and have more of an impact on how they process information than is the case in the human brain.) Adding the fact that dolphins are self-aware greatly increases the likelihood that they consciously experience emotional states. After all, self-consciousness means being able to reflect on the contents of your consciousness and have the awareness that all of these sensations are somehow *yours*.

Dolphin researchers generally have no problem attributing at least some emotions to dolphins. It may be difficult to say conclusively that dolphins feel "happy," "playful" or "curious," but researchers don't hesitate to label certain behaviors as "aggressive": tail slaps and open mouth behaviors, for example. And these likely result from such feelings as frustration, annoyance or aggression.

Ronald Schusterman describes a particularly interesting episode of dolphin aggression because it involves throwing something at someone – behavior that has not been reported as taking place in the wild among dolphins. He writes:

> One of my most vivid memories of hurling behavior as an aggressive act was one that took place at Kewalo Basin in Hawaii during research on teaching dolphins an artificial language. The female dolphin Ake had just been given a series of gestural signals by a young intern. The cues were produced at the side of the pool, and when Ake didn't respond correctly, she was given negative feedback. A moment later, the dolphin grabbed a large plastic pipe floating on the water's surface and flung it unerringly at the poor, unsuspecting intern. The pipe missed the young lady's head by inches, and all of the students, volunteers, and researchers around the pool gasped.[21]

However, dolphins also appear capable of other emotions, as suggested in Denise Herzing's touching account of grief among female Atlantic spotted dolphins in the wild.

---

[21] Ronald J. Schusterman, "Pitching a Fit," in Marc Bekoff (ed.) *The Smile of a Dolphin: Remarkable Accounts of Animal Emotions* (New York: Discovery Books, 2000), p. 106.

I arrived in the Bahamas in 1985 to study Atlantic spotted dolphins. Among the first I met were Rosemole, Little Gash, and Mugsy, three juvenile females in the middle of their childhood years . . . As the years passed, all three females became engaged in courtship and mating with the ever-persistent maturing male spotted dolphins. By 1990, both Rosemole and Mugsy were pregnant for the first time . . . As I left in the fall, I thought how exciting it would be to come back the next year and see both these females that I'd grown up with during the last five years with their first babies.

The following May we returned to our field site and met up with a mother/calf group that included both Rosemole and Mugsy. Rosemole had a healthy young female baby, Rosebud, and they were surrounded by other mothers who proudly swam along with their calves. But on the periphery was Mugsy, in formation but without a calf. She might have had a miscarriage or lost her calf, either to a predator or from natural causes. Swimming slowly and despondently on the edge of the group, she stayed in line but left a space beneath her, as though she had a phantom calf in tow. She showed no interest in her friends or in mating again. Month after month Mugsy left her train of grief, as clear as a luminescent streak in the dark water.

The grieving process isn't unique to mothers and their first offspring; it's also strong in mothers who have multiple young. The previous year I had observed a lone dolphin swimming on a shipwreck we often used for anchorage. On approaching her, I saw that she had a large shark bite above her left pectoral fin. She was emaciated, and a remora was clinging to her. Her swimming appeared despondent and disoriented. It's very unusual to see a dolphin swimming alone, except when one is sick or wounded. Days later, I reviewed my video-tape and realized that this individual was one I knew well but hadn't recognized at the time. It was Gemini, mother of a three-year-old, Gemer.

Gemer had been a spunky little dolphin, and we'd often recognized her partly by the presence of a telltale remora, a clingy fish, that was always with her. But now there was no Gemer with Gemini, nor was the baby ever seen again. Defending her offspring, Gemini had likely done battle with a predator. Perhaps she's lost Gemer in the fray, and the remora once attached to the baby had switched to the wounded mother.

It's amazing Gemini survived at all, mourning and wounded as she was, and emaciated from the inability or unwillingness to eat. Her wounds eventually healed, however, and she regained her weight and went on to have two more healthy calves. Grief had been experienced and processed, and life had returned to the business of renewal, a new chance at life.[22]

---

[22] Denise L. Herzing, "A Trail of Grief," *The Smile of a Dolphin*, pp. 138–139.

————————— Do Dolphins Think? —————————

Dolphins, then, seem capable of at least some basic emotions. But can they think? We saw in the last chapter that the dolphin brain may allow for the possibility of sophisticated cognitive abilities. It has a large cerebral cortex and a substantial amount of associational neocortex. And most anatomical ratios that assess cognitive capacity (brain weight/spinal cord, encephalization quotient) place it second only to the human brain. The hardware may be there, but what do dolphins do with it?

Some of the ground that we covered earlier in this chapter actually gives us a number of examples of dolphins working with concepts. Recall that in order to recognize its reflection in a mirror, a dolphin must first be able to understand an image as a representation of reality. We saw that both Ken Marten and Lou Herman found that their dolphins treated televised images as representations. And they would have been unable to do this without engaging in *abstract, conceptual* thinking.

For example, in order for any of us to understand that the televised image of an apple *represents* a real-life apple, we must be able to think abstractly. We must be able to create, recall and use what we might call a "mental apple." An oversimplified description of the process would go as follows:

1   We see a real-life apple with our eyes.
2   We identify the defining traits of this object, create a "mental apple," and store it in our memory.
3   We see an image of the apple on the screen.
4   We then recognize that the image refers to the original apple we encountered by retrieving our "mental apple" and comparing it to the image on the screen.

If we couldn't perform this mental operation, we would simply have two different and unrelated sensory experiences – seeing the actual apple and seeing the televised image of the apple. We grasp that the image of the apple stands for the actual apple because of what goes on in our brains.

Creating such "mental objects" – what philosophers call "concepts" – and storing, retrieving and working with them are the most fundamental features of abstract, conceptual thought. When we think, we create and manipulate "ideas." Some of them may be fairly simple (representations of physical objects like tables, chairs and apples); but others are quite complicated (abstract notions like the self, fairness, justice, and the meaning of life).

The dolphins in Marten's and Herman's television screen experiments must have employed concepts of the physical objects involved. In addition, the dolphins in the mirror experiments would have engaged in abstract thought of a more sophisticated sort. Any self-aware being must be able to form and understand the concept of "I." So, the dolphin brain appears to allow for at least some abstract, conceptual thought.

Choice and freedom

The research that we've looked at so far in this chapter suggests that dolphins seem to have a consciousness that lets them self-consciously experience at least basic feelings and thoughts. However, can they, like us, use their thoughts or feelings to shape their actions? That is, can dolphins *choose* their actions?

The question of whether dolphins choose their actions is particularly important because this would mean that dolphins experience one of the most distinctive traits of *our* lives – freedom. The traditional picture of nonhumans is that their actions result from instinct or a kind of genetic programming that compels them to respond to certain stimuli in particular ways. Even learned behaviors – everything from rats running mazes in laboratories to dolphins leaping on command in theme parks – are usually interpreted as the product of carefully designed positive reinforcement. So the prospect that a nonhuman can be the author of its own actions would be a striking challenge to the belief among humans that we alone have this power.

We can approach this issue in two ways. On the one hand, we can look at events so unusual that the best explanation is that they result from deliberation and choice. But the unusual event is a two-edged sword. What it gives us in dramatic value, it takes away in dependability. Because such events are in fact so out of the ordinary and can't be replicated on demand, it's impossible to determine exactly what's going on. From a scientific perspective, then, the unusual event is problematic precisely because it is exceptional. The other approach is more dependable, but less exciting. We look for more mundane behavior that is easier to find, observe and explain as a function of choice. We'll take both approaches, and we'll see what the combination suggests.

The unusual event: the lost tool box

Rachel Smolker, cofounder of the Monkey Mia Dolphin Project at Shark Bay on the west coast of Australia, describes a fascinating event involving a bottlenose dolphin that she named Holly. In May, 1988, a terrible storm rolled over the study site. Smolker was fortunate. The only thing of value that she lost was a tool kit that had been in her small boat. The dinghy had been tossed about and sunk by powerful winds, and the tool kit had been thrown out. An interesting incident took place about a week later. The scientist writes:

> A week or so after things have settled back down again, I wake up early and go down to see the dolphins. Holly is in at the beach and in a languid mood. I have the urge to jump into the water with her this morning, so I don my snorkel and mask. She stays just offshore, watching me get dressed, and I can tell by her patient, attentive waiting that she too is in the mood for a swimming partner. In my excitement, I fall over trying to get my flippers on. Holly is whistling as I slide into the water alongside her . . . Side by side we progress slowly out into deeper water . . . Then she gently moves out from under my arm and heads down toward the bottom. We are in about twenty feet of water, and I try to dive with her, but my awkward flailing seems inappropriate so I retreat to wait at the surface. Below me, she is poking at something on the bottom, but the water is too murky for me to see. A moment later she comes back up toward me, dragging something large, white, and apparently heavy, which she is holding in her jaws. She comes directly to me and delivers a plastic bag into my hands. I take it, and she moves away, diving again at some distance from me. She is done swimming with me for now, and it would be useless to try to catch up to her . . . I tread water for a moment and untie the plastic bag. It looks vaguely familiar somehow. Inside are a ratchet wrench set, pliers, screwdrivers, some spark plugs, and flares. It is the tool kit from my boat.[23]

It is difficult to imagine a more likely explanation for this unusual event than deliberation and choice on the part of Holly.

The mundane event: choice and fishing

What about more ordinary behavior that's easier to observe? Is there anything that dolphins regularly do that also suggests deliberation and choice? The best commonplace example is probably *fishing*. Dolphin fishing strategies can be

---

[23]   Rachel Smolker, *To Touch a Wild Dolphin* (New York: Doubleday, 2001), pp. 221–222.

so varied and complex that it's hard to explain them away as unthinking responses to appropriate stimuli. Here are three examples:

- *Mud rings*: A community of bottlenose dolphins in Florida Bay has developed a fascinating strategy perfectly adapted to the shallow waters in which they live. Upon finding a school of mullet, two or three dolphins position themselves in front of the school while another dolphin circles the fish and stirs up a curtain of mud. As soon as the dolphin completes the circle and joins its companions, the mullet simply jump out of the water into the waiting dolphins' open mouths. The dolphins just move along repeating the strategy, getting food with surprisingly little effort.
- *Hydroplaning*: A different, but risky shallow water hunting strategy has been seen used in Shark Bay, Australia. A small number of dolphins have learned how to hydroplane in just inches of water – a tactic that lets them catch fish trying to escape into the shallows.[24]
- *Herding*: Bernd Würsig has observed dusky dolphins in the deep water off of Patagonia employ a highly cooperative feeding strategy.[25] When small groups of dolphins discover a school of anchovies, they herd them together, signal nearby dolphins about the catch, and wait until the others join them before eating. Even while the feeding is going on, the dolphins take turns at different roles. Some eat while others keep the fish contained, and then they switch. As many as 300 dolphins may join in the process.

In each case, the dolphins have solved a fundamental problem (how to get food) with an effective strategy that is tailored to the peculiarities of the situation. The strategies are novel, efficient, complex and, to some degree, imaginative. Whether they somehow stumbled upon these tactics by accident or reasoned their way to them, the complexity of these fishing practices argues for the idea that choice is involved.

- *Mud rings*: The appropriate coalition of dolphins must first be formed, the mullet located and each dolphin must perform its appropriate role.
- *Hydroplaning*: The dolphin must consider a variety of factors (speed, depth and the likelihood of success) before deciding on whether on not to make

---

[24] P. Berggren and J. Skelton, "Beaching Foraging Strategy of Bottlenose Dolphins (Tursiops sp.) in Shark Bay, Western Australia," paper presented at Eleventh Biennial Conference on Marine Mammals, Orlando, FL, 1995.
[25] Bernd Würsig, "The Question of Dolphin Awareness Approached through Studies in Nature," *Cetus*, 5(1) (1985): 6.

a run at the fish being sought. The fact that the other dolphins in the community feed in more conventional ways suggests that, while they're aware of hydroplaning, they choose to avoid it for some reason.

- *Herding*: As Bernd Würsig explains:

> Herding and holding of prey are not a stereotyped series of actions. At times, the fish school may fragment into smaller balls. When that occurs, a few of the dolphins break off from the group and herd the fish back into the central fish school. It is a dynamic, ever-changing system, which may require organization by these large-brained and communicative social animals. Differential role-playing and premeditation (such as a decision that certain members do particular things in order to meet various contingencies) may be important in this kind of cooperation. The degree of behavioral flexibility to encompass novel situations appears well developed.[26]

In addition, in order to keep the anchovies from scattering and escaping, the dusky dolphins must restrain the desire to swim through the ball until it is tight enough, and they must also take turns managing the ball while their companions feed.

Since we know from the mirror self-awareness experiments that dolphins are probably aware of the contents of their consciousness, and since other dolphins survive in similar environments using more conventional feeding practices, the most likely explanation for these three complex strategies is that they're the product of deliberation and choice. We may be able to construct alternative explanations that could account for these strategies through such "natural" mechanisms as adaptation, instinct, genetic programming, stimulus/response and the like. But given the number of variables we'd have to account for, such explanations would probably end up being quite complicated. This would make the "natural" explanation less plausible than the one that most humans would initially find harder to believe – that a non-human being is making conscious choices.

Accordingly, between the unusual event of the Monkey Mia dolphin finding Rachel Smolker's toolbox and the everyday feeding practices of the Florida Bay, Shark Bay and Patagonia dolphins, a reasonable case can be made for the idea that dolphins are capable of choice. That is, the dolphin brain appears to produce a consciousness whose thoughts and feelings are strong enough to let dolphins control their actions.

[26] Ibid., p. 6.

Conclusion: Dolphin Consciousness and Moral Standing

What we've seen in this chapter about the type of consciousness that dolphins have is impressive. The dolphin brain appears to support a consciousness that lets these nonhumans:

- be aware of themselves and others;
- experience at least basic emotions;
- engage in some degree of abstract, conceptual thought;
- choose their actions.

Surely, then, a plausible case can be made for the idea that dolphins are a "who," not a "what" – that is, that they experience life in a way that approximates ours. In particular, the combination of self-awareness, thoughts and feelings means that they probably experience themselves as individual beings who feel pain as we do. That is, they know who they are, they suffer both physically and emotionally, and they may even experience pain associated with unhappy events remembered from the past or feared in the future.

As beings of this sort, dolphins would therefore seem to be entitled to "moral standing" for the same reasons that humans are:

- We claim that because each of us is a unique, self-aware individual, humans have "intrinsic worth."
- We also claim that the advanced intellectual and emotional capacities of our consciousness make us far more vulnerable to pain and harm than beings who lack these abilities, but also give us the power of choice.

As we've seen, dolphins appear to have self-awareness and some intellectual and emotional abilities strong enough to let them control their actions. Therefore, from an ethical perspective, they would seem to share with us the right to some kind of special status and protections.

Humans, however, have a bad habit of "raising the bar" when it comes to giving up privilege. So it's important that we explore as much as we can about what's been uncovered about what the dolphin brain can do. Accordingly, the next two chapters will discuss still more dimensions of dolphin intelligence.

CHAPTER 4

Can Dolphins Solve Problems and Understand Language?

The last two chapters have given us a solid beginning into our inquiry about what kind of beings dolphins are. We've seen that the dolphin brain appears to be able to support sophisticated cognitive abilities, that dolphins have not only consciousness, but, more importantly, self-consciousness, and that dolphin consciousness appears to be strong enough to give these cetaceans the ability to control, reflect on and choose their own actions.

In this chapter, we examine evidence that suggests that dolphins can do even more impressive things with their large brains. Dolphins appear to be able to solve complex problems by thinking about them, to think creatively and abstractly, and to understand an artificial language. In short, we will encounter more reasons to think of dolphins as unusually complex beings entitled to better treatment by humans than they currently receive.

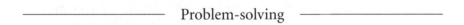

Problem-solving

Some of the most important research about the cognitive abilities of dolphins has been done by John Gory and Stan A. Kuczaj.[1] These two scientists studied the cognitive abilities of two bottlenose dolphins at the Living Seas

---

[1] Stan A. Kuczaj II and Rachel S. Thames, "How Do Dolphins Solve Problems?," in T. R. Zentall and E. Wasserman (eds) *Comparative Cognition: Experimental Explorations of Animal Intelligence* (Cambridge, MA: MIT Press, 2006); John D. Gory and Stan A. Kuczaj II, "Can Bottlenose Dolphins Plan their Behavior?" paper presented at the Biennial Conference on the Biology of Marine Mammals, Wailea, Maui, Hawaii, November–December, 1999.

portion of Disney World in Florida. Gory and Kuczaj worked with two, adult male bottlenose dolphins named Bob and Toby.

The researchers investigated whether these two dolphins could solve problems by *thinking* their way to a solution. The reason this is such an important question is that reasoning is something that has traditionally been considered to be an exclusively human ability. However, two experiments, in particular, suggest that Bob and Toby could indeed invent a strategy for solving a problem by thinking.

In one experiment, three clear plastic containers were placed in the pool fairly close to each other. When the dolphin dropped a weight into the top of any of the containers, the food compartment opened. In two of the containers, the weight would then fall to the tank floor – where it could be used again to open the food compartment of one of the other boxes. But in the third, the weight would fall into an obviously closed bottom – making it unavailable.

Gory and Kuczaj wanted to see if the dolphins could understand the implication of having both open-bottomed and closed-bottomed containers – that is, to get the maximum amount of fish, use the open-bottom container first. The scientists theorized that if the dolphins understood this, they would plan their behavior accordingly. Bob and Toby were run through six thirty-trial blocks. From the first block onward, both dolphins used the container with the closed bottom most often last – suggesting that they could solve a problem by *thinking* about the conditions of the test.

Gory and Kuczaj's other experiment involved a container that required the dolphin to use two tools in a particular order to get the food inside. First, the dolphin had to drop a weight into the container. This caused a sliding door on the side of the box to open. Then, the dolphin had to pick up a stick tool, swim to the side with the open door, and push the food out of the back of the container. The catch was that the door stayed open for only 15 seconds.

The dolphins learned how to open the container by observing humans use the weight and the stick in the correct order. At first, the two objects were placed close to the container, so the time limit wasn't a problem.

Once the dolphins were comfortable with opening the box, however, the researchers made the task more complicated. They moved the stick far enough away (about 75 feet) so that the sliding door would close before the dolphin returned. Gory and Kuczaj wanted to see if the dolphins would respond to the time limit by first picking up the stick and putting it near the site before putting the weight into the container.

First, both dolphins tried to beat the clock by swimming faster. While this was a good idea, it didn't work. But both dolphins did ultimately solve the problem. The scientists explain that Toby stumbled onto the solution "serendipitously." Bob tried an alternative strategy of carrying both tools at once, although he couldn't handle both. But Bob did recognize the correct solution after observing some humans show him the proper strategy a few times.

Even though the two dolphins didn't discover the solution themselves, their behavior does suggest significant cognitive ability. The fact that their first strategy was to swim faster showed that they understood the nature of the problem. (If the researchers hadn't designed the experiment so that no matter how fast the dolphins swam, they still wouldn't get to the container in time, the dolphins' first strategy would have worked.) Bob did try a second tactic (carrying both tools at once) – which also showed that he understood the nature of the problem. And when Bob and Toby finally came upon the correct strategy, they recognized it for what it was fairly quickly.

Bob also showed some interesting behavior after he had apparently learned that swimming faster wouldn't work, but before he'd solved the problem. In about a third of the test trials, he would start by picking up the weight and swimming toward the container – but then he'd stop, turn around, and go back and look at the stick. Gory and Kuczaj think that "It's possible that Bob knew that there was something wrong about the stick being far away, but didn't know what to do about it – or possibly, that the competing response of using the weight first, which was so well learned by this point, was too hard to suppress." It certainly seems possible that Bob was *thinking about* the problem, even if he hadn't solved it.

The significance of Gory and Kuczaj's research

Gory and Kuczaj's work with Bob and Toby is definitely significant for our examination of dolphin intelligence. In the open-bottom/closed-bottom test, the dolphins used their brains to solve the problem. And in the two-tool/time-limit test, they recognized the solution when they saw it (even if they didn't invent it).

Gory and Kuczaj believe that these three experiments strongly suggest that Bob and Toby were able to "create a novel and appropriate solution in advance of executing the solution."[2] The dolphins also demonstrated an impressive ability to learn things by simply observing the humans.

However, to appreciate the significance of the dolphins' accomplishments, it's important to recognize the cognitive abilities that were required for them to behave as they did.

[2] "Can Bottlenose Dolphins Plan their Behavior?" John D. Gory and Stan A. Kuczaj II.

Representing the causal structure of the environment

The reason the Bob and Toby's performance is so impressive in these experiments is that Gory and Kuczaj claim that creating novel solutions "can only be achieved if an animal has an ability *to represent the causal structure of its environment*."[3] To represent in one's mind the causal structure of one's environment is a very complex accomplishment.

1   First, it requires the ability to reflect on the contents of one's consciousness – something possible only with self-awareness. Bob and Toby needed, we might say, a "mental space" or "mental workbench" in which to hold and reflect on their experiences in the experimental trials.
2   It next requires an ability to create mental representations of physical objects. Bob and Toby had to construct mental containers, weights, sticks and fish, for example, that paralleled the actual physical objects with which they were working.
3   The dolphins also had to develop an understanding of the relationships that exist among the objects in their environment that are expressed in abstract concepts. In these experiments, specifically, they needed to formulate and work with such concepts as "causality" and "necessary conditions."

> *Causality.* Understanding cause and effect means grasping the abstract concept that one event (or sequence of events) will bring about another event (or sequence of events).
>
> *Causality, sense of time and memory.* Understanding causality also requires having at least a basic sense of time and enough of a memory to store and then recall the relevant experiences. Bob and Toby needed to be able to remember their successes and failures well enough to select and refine their strategy as they went through the experimental trials. Also, they couldn't grasp the causal relationships involved unless they had at least a rudimentary sense of past, present and future.
>
> *Causality, necessary and sufficient conditions.* Bob and Toby had to recognize that they had to perform certain actions in a particular order. This means that they needed to have a practical understanding of the necessary and sufficient conditions that have to be met before something else will happen.
>
> > "I will get 3 fish from the 3 boxes *if and only if* I use the one with the closed bottom last."

[3]   Ibid., italics added.

"The fish compartment will open *if and only if* I drop in the weight first and then use the stick tool."

4 Finally, in order "to represent the causal structure of [their] environment" to themselves, Bob and Toby needed to be able to *create something new* in their brains. They would have to take various features connected with their experience in the experiments (memories, abstract concepts, and observations about what worked and what didn't work) and then combine them to produce a new, overarching picture of their environment. They would have to generalize from their specific experiences and generate insights that go beyond the limits of their experiences in the experimental trials. To grasp the causal structure of one's environment means recognizing (at least intuitively or tacitly) what can be formulated as the general rules that govern specific actions and that can then be used to predict what will happen when certain actions are done. That is to say, to grasp the causal relationships of one's environment requires at least an intuitive sense of the basic physics that govern what's happening.

Operating in a foreign cognitive environment

Perhaps the most impressive part of Bob and Toby's performance, however, has to do with the fact that Gory and Kuczaj deliberately designed these experiments so that the dolphins were not being asked to perform behaviors that dolphins commonly do in the wild or that they'd previously learned in other experiments. As the two researchers explain, "We deliberately chose behaviors unlike natural or previously learned behaviors so that [the dolphins'] success could not be construed as simple generalizations of these kinds of behaviors. If the dolphins can stretch their minds, so to speak, to plan their behavior in these alien contexts, then it should only be easier for them to do so in more familiar domains." Gory and Kuczaj designed the experiments so that Bob and Toby faced problems of a sort they'd never seen before and that called for novel behaviors on their part. Accordingly, if, as happened, the dolphins accomplished such a difficult task, the most likely explanation would be native brainpower.

The ultimate significance of the novelty of both the problems and the required solutions is that Bob and Toby were thereby operating in what we can call a "foreign cognitive environment."[4] This would be like asking humans who had

---

[4] I owe this phrase to Denise Herzing.

never seen an automobile to figure out how to replace a flat tire. First, they would have to grasp the problem. Then, they would have to locate the spare tire, the jack and the wrench. And they would also need to learn how to use the tools, and devise an appropriate strategy. Only then could they change the tire.

The fact that Bob and Toby did so well in a cognitive arena different from what they normally experience says much about dolphin intelligence. It is particularly difficult to solve problems that fall outside one's ordinary experience and frame of reference. It's also very demanding to have to create behaviors that one usually doesn't use. And yet this is precisely what Bob and Toby did. It's hard to think of a being, other than a human, whose cognitive abilities are so significant and flexible.

Supporting evidence: problem-solving and innovative thinking

Gory and Kuczaj provide systematic evidence that dolphins apparently have the array of cognitive skills needed to solve new and complex problems. However, the serendipitous discoveries of another researcher – Karen Pryor – should also be noted, because they provide independent support for aspects of Gory and Kuczaj's findings on a couple of fronts.

Karen Pryor and innovation   Perhaps the most impressive supporting evidence for dolphins' ability to demonstrate novelty and creativity has been offered by Karen Pryor. Attempting to introduce some variety into the dolphin show at Hawaii's Sea Life Park in the 1960s, Pryor decided to show the audience how the dolphins learned the behaviors they performed in the shows. So she selected Malia, a female rough-toothed dolphin (*Steno bredanensis*). The idea was to start from scratch and use the process of reward and reinforcement to condition Malia to perform a new behavior. This meant teaching her a new behavior each show. And that meant that Malia had to learn that she was being rewarded not for performing a specific behavior (a tail slap, for example), but for something more abstract – performing a behavior that she had never done before. Within three days, Malia understood what she was being asked to do, and she then regularly invented novel behaviors when asked to do so in subsequent shows. The noted researcher Gregory Bateson, who was associated with Sea Life Park at the time, regarded Malia's accomplishment as an example of higher-order learning. He saw this as a case of Malia taking facts, combining them and learning a principle – no small cognitive leap.

Bateson encouraged Pryor to try the same thing with a different dolphin, only this time to set it up as a scientific experiment. Pryor chose a dolphin named Hou, another rough-toothed female, and succeeded with her as well. Hou learned that she was being asked to create original behaviors, she responded appropriately, and Pryor published the results in a scientific journal.[5]

Other researchers have subsequently trained other dolphins to create behaviors. But one of the most fascinating examples comes from Lou Herman, who found than when we asked *two* dolphins to create a new behavior and perform the same action *in tandem*, they did so.[6]

---

[5]   Karen Pryor, Richard Haag and Joseph O'Reilly, "The Creative Porpoise: Training for Novel Behavior," *Journal of the Experimental Analysis of Behavior*, 12 (1969): 653–661. In fairness to Pryor, we should note that she does not draw the same conclusions from the evidence that Bateson does. She notes, "The work did *not*, in my opinion, go to show how *smart* [dolphins] are. Given the training, many, many species of animals show the same kind of development" (Karen Pryor, *Lads Before the Wind: Diary of a Dolphin Trainer*, expanded edition, Waltham, MA: Sunshine Books, 2000, p. 248). Specifically, Pryor claims to have worked with pigeons and dogs who have learned that they would be rewarded only for innovative behavior (ibid., pp. 249, 322–323). Ken Norris concurs that other animals can do similar things, but he suggests a different conclusion: "it is clear that many, perhaps most, animals such as sea lions, monkeys, social carnivores such as dogs, and even some birds such as the African gray parrot can deal with abstractions like those developed between Karen and Malia" (Kenneth S. Norris, *Dolphin Days: The Life and Times of the Spinner Dolphin*, New York: W. W. Norton, 1991, p. 48). However, the fact that there is reason to think that dolphins are self-aware – while there is currently no evidence to think that pigeons and dogs are – suggests that there is a qualitative difference in what was going on in the brains of these different nonhumans.

[6]   Herman writes:

> Of particular interest was how a pair [of dolphins] might respond to the sequence *tandem create*. In effect, this sequence asks the pair to select or create together a behaviour of their own choosing, and carry it out synchronously. Typically, the pair will first swim about side-by-side, generally for a longer time than when given a specific behaviour to perform synchronously, then apparently select some behaviour in common and execute it in close synchrony. The selected behaviours may range from simple types, such as synchronous tail waves, a complex spinning leap while spitting water from their mouth. We have not been able to determine how the dolphins manage this task. Their apparent joint performance may be a case of near simultaneous mimicry, one following the other's action closely, but we have not been able to confirm this through detailed video analyses. Alternatively, underwater intention movements by one dolphin may guide the second dolphin to select that same behaviour.
>
> (Louis M. Herman, "Intelligence and Rational Behavior in the Bottlenosed Dolphins," in S. Hurley and M. Nudds (eds) *Rational Animals?* (Oxford: Oxford University Press, 2006), p. 454)

Creativity and personality   However, in addition to suggesting that these two dolphins could think creatively, Pryor's experiment produced some other very interesting findings. First, Pryor observed a significant difference in how the two dolphins responded to the experiment. As she describes it, "Malia's novel responses, judged in toto, are more spectacular and 'imaginative' than Hou's. We're used to this differentiation in people; we call it imagination. Or creativity. Or talent. It interested me that it could show up so clearly in animals."[7] Not only do these dolphins evidence a cognitive trait that we're more used to seeing in humans, they also show a similar sort of individual differences.

Even more significant, however, is that Pryor claims that once Hou understood that she was being asked to be creative, "[she] was a changed animal." Moreover, Pryor claims that the change was deep and permanent. She states, "The change in Hou's 'personality,' from a docile, inactive animal to an active, observant animal full of initiative was a permanent change."[8]

It's impossible to know what this change actually involved or precisely what caused it. So we're simply left with unprovable speculation. However, it's possible that the change in Hou was akin to a kind of intellectual awakening that we see in humans. Through more than three decades of teaching philosophy on the college level, I've often seen a change in students that's similar to what Pryor observed in Hou. However, instead of being stimulated by creativity, it's stirred by thinking critically. As these students are asked to question many of the heretofore unchallenged beliefs they arrived on campus with, many of them become intellectually engaged, curious and inquisitive. Like Hou, they go from being docile and passive to being active, observant and questioning. They no longer accept something as true just because an authority says it is. They need to know the reasons for thinking something. These students show a confidence, autonomy and independence of mind that wasn't there before. And, as in Hou's case, this change is permanent. Once they learn how to think for themselves, they stay that way.

Pryor, cognitive flexibility and problem solving

While Karen Pryor's work in teaching Hou and Malia to be creative is especially significant for our purposes, she also tells a fascinating story that suggests that her two dolphins show two other abilities that we saw with Bob and Toby – cognitive flexibility and problem-solving. Pryor describes in

---

[7]   Pryor, *Lads before the Wind*, p. 249.
[8]   Ibid., pp. 242, 247.

detail an intriguing episode that took place during one of the shows at Sea Life Park:

> In the show, each animal had her own repertoire of behaviors, and they performed separately, although they could watch each other through the gates. Malia did a training demonstration, showing off, on sound cues, several of the behaviors she herself had invented: the upside-down jump, the corkscrew, the "Look, Ma, no hands!" business of coasting with her tail in the air. She also jumped through a hoop 12 feet in the air. Hou wore blindfolds and evaded obstacles and retrieved three sinking rings on her rostrum, in a sonar demonstration. The training of the two animals did not overlap, except that Malia had been conditioned to accept blindfolds. She had never, however, been asked to do anything with them on. . . .
>
> One day, Ingrid was training and I was narrating, and we ran into trouble from the beginning of the show. When Malia's gate was opened, the animal came out and did everything she was asked to do – the back jump, the corkscrew, and the coasting with tail out – but in the wrong sequence, and with great agitation.
>
> Something was wrong. Was the cue machine not working? When we got to the high hoop jump, she leaped toward it, in a frantic and disorganized way, but fell far short of the desired 12 feet. Usually, this would have called for firm measures: time outs, and insistence from the trainer. Ingrid, whose sensitivity for the animals is quite remarkable, decided to make a concession and lower the hoop down to about 6 feet above the water, whereupon the animal leaped through it, without waiting for the signal.
>
> What was going on? The animal was so nervous that we were both glad when her part of the show was over and we could put her back and open Hou's gate.
>
> The second [dolphin] rushed out with an air of excitement. Ingrid had considerable difficulty getting her to accept the blindfolds. Twice they fell off, and the animal retrieved them from the tank floor. Finally the blindfolds were in place. She negotiated the maze of pipes we lowered in the tank by sonar and retrieved rings by sonar, but only one ring at a time, instead of the usual three. Again this animal seemed extremely nervous and excitable; one had the alarming sensation, as a trainer, that things were about to go completely to pieces. However, while everything was a little distorted, different from the usual pattern, we got through the show safely. I discussed the two animals' unusual nervousness with the audience over the mike, confessing myself at a loss to explain why they were upset and acting "funny," why Malia got her sound cues mixed up and Hou bucked the blindfolding. The show ended. Ingrid put the last animal back in the holding tank and then looked at me in utter astonishment. "Do you know what happened?"
>
> "No."

"We got the animals mixed up. Someone put Malia in Hou's holding tank and Hou in Malia's holding tank. They look so much alike now, I just never thought of that."

Hou had done Malia's part of the show, getting the cues confused but offering the behaviors so well that we didn't realize she didn't "know" them, and even managing the hoop jump, which normally takes weeks to train. Malia had done all Hou's blindfold stunts correctly, on the first try, nervously, but again well enough so that we thought it was Hou. I stopped the departing audience and told them what they had just seen; I'm not sure how many understood or believed it. I still hardly believe it myself.[9]

In terms of the question of what the dolphin brain can do, this episode is surely a remarkable example of sophisticated cognitive abilities.

Hou, Malia and sophisticated cognitive abilities

The first thing that suggests impressive cognitive abilities is what Hou and Malia did *not* do.

- They didn't just ignore the cues and do nothing. Presumably, if dolphins could *not* think in some fashion, and if their performances in the shows were simply the result of operant conditioning, a new cue would probably evoke no response.
- They didn't stubbornly insist on trying to do what they'd already been taught. Hou didn't sit and wait until she was blindfolded, and Malia didn't insist on doing the series of behaviors she typically performed. If the dolphins' actions were just the result of conditioning, and if they felt compelled to respond to the cues, they could have presented their usual behaviors.
- The dolphins also didn't respond to the new cues with a series of random behaviors that would amount to a mindless trial-and-error reaction. They didn't respond in a way that, in effect, meant: the dolphins recognized that some response was called for; they didn't know the correct response; so they offered all of the behaviors that they'd learned.
- In addition, Hou and Malia didn't present innovative behaviors. Since both dolphins had been trained to produce new, creative behaviors, they might have responded to an atypical cue in a show (even if not the "innovate" cue) as a request for something new. That is, since they'd been

[9]   Ibid., pp. 251–253.

conditioned to produce not only specific behaviors but also new behaviors, they could have responded with a series of novel responses until they got rewarded.

The fact that the two dolphins did none of these ("do nothing," "do a learned behavior" or "create a new behavior") and, instead, tried to do what they were being asked to do, suggests that their actions were the product of cognitive abilities that are stronger than their disciplined, formal conditioning.

Cognitive flexibility

First, the behavior of these dolphins suggests a good deal of *cognitive flexibility*. While Pryor used a formal process of conditioning to teach Hou and Malia the behaviors they would perform in the show, each dolphin apparently came to understand – on their own, spontaneously and informally – the behaviors and the cues that the other was learning. They surely would have observed each other's training sessions. But they had neither practiced the behaviors, nor tried to execute them in response to the appropriate cues. The dolphins simply picked up on their own an understanding of the behaviors and the cues involved. This episode, therefore, implies that these dolphins have the flexibility to learn things both formally and informally.

In one way, what Hou and Malia did is similar to what we saw above in Gory and Kuczaj's experiments when Bob learned the solution to the time-limit test by watching a human demonstrate the answer. However, Hou and Malia's performance is even more impressive because – unlike the case with Bob – there was no conscious attempt to teach them these behaviors.

Self-motivation to learn

This episode also suggests that Hou and Malia were somehow self-motivated to notice and remember what each was being taught. There were no apparent external rewards involved, so they must have been motivated internally. Dolphins are highly imitative, so perhaps there was an innate pull to notice and remember behaviors that were different from ones they'd mastered. Perhaps they were curious about what the other was learning and paid close enough attention for the behavior and the cues to register. Or maybe they were bored and just liked learning new things. But whatever the explanation, the two dolphins learned enough on their own to be able to perform the behaviors in question the first time they were asked to do them. The fact that they learned, remembered and recalled something that they had no reason to think they'd ever need to know says something significant about their internal, cognitive motivations and/or inclinations.

Problem-solving involving thought

Pryor's story also speaks to these dolphins' abilities to solve a problem by thinking about it. Hou and Malia were presented with a dilemma. They performed in shows frequently, but they were always given the same cues for behaviors they'd been taught. Now, however, they were being given cues for different behaviors. Surely, the situation would be confusing. As we saw above, if the dolphins' performances in the shows were simply the result of conditioning, they would have either done nothing, performed behaviors that they already knew or tried to create new behaviors. Instead, they performed the requested behaviors as best they could – even though they had never tried them before. The most likely explanation for this episode, then, is that there was some thought process going on that led to a conscious decision. Hou and Malia were presented with a problem and, relying on what they'd learned on their own, they thought their way to a decision and an appropriate solution.

Two anecdotes about problem-solving

As interesting and engaging as Pryor's account of this episode is, it admittedly takes us out of the world of controlled, scientific observation and into the less precise realm of anecdotes about unique events. In carefully designed experimental trials, scientists have the opportunity to watch dolphins repeat the behaviors in question. Researchers study the actions involved in enough detail to uncover what they reveal about a dolphin's abilities. But it's difficult to know what we can conclude from the unique, spontaneous event because so many different things could be going on. Such stories often lack objective, third-party observers, so we're left with only one or two individuals' personal and subjective opinion of what happened.

Many reputable observers, however, tell fascinating anecdotes about dolphins. And even if these stories lack the strength of scientific experiments, they're still highly suggestive and thought-provoking. Accordingly, I want to offer two more anecdotes that seem to be striking examples of problem-solving.

Human diver helps dolphin   Scuba diver Wayne Grover tells the story of an encounter he had with three bottlenose dolphins in which the dolphins solicited his help.[10] Grover was about 60 feet deep in the waters off of Palm Beach, Florida when he was approached by two adults and one baby bottlenose. The baby had a large fishing hook stuck into its tail about a foot ahead of its tail fluke. Also, monofilament fishing line attached to the hook was wrapped around the dolphin and was cutting into the tail fluke area. "Whether it was my imagination or a logical deduction," Grover writes, "I suddenly felt that I was being asked for help . . . The large [dolphins] closed in on the baby from either side until they were touching it with their pectoral flippers. They settled the baby to the sea floor right in front of me, still holding it from each side." After discovering that the hook was in too deep to be removed by simply unwinding the fishing line and pulling it out, Grover steadied the baby on the ocean floor and used his diving knife to remove the hook. The two adults observed the entire procedure. After the hook came out, Grover reports:

> The largest dolphin came to me, stopped at eye level, and looked into my eyes behind the mask. For a brief moment, we looked deeply into each other's eyes, and then the dolphin nudged me with its snout, pushing me slightly back.
>
> I had the distinct impression that we were communicating but, even as I thought it, my logical mind tried to dissuade me, saying it was imagined.
>
> Then the three dolphins were gone. Without a sound, they rapidly climbed upward toward the surface, leaving me alone again.

Grover's story is a remarkable tale of ingenious problem-solving on the part of the dolphins. But it's not unheard of for these marine mammals to seek out human help in this way. Rachel Smolker writes, for example,

> Wilf Mason had described an incident where a strange adult dolphin who was clearly in trouble came into the shallows at Monkey Mia and approached him. She had a large fishing hook lodged in her mouth. This dolphin, unaccustomed to human contact, had permitted Wilf to remove the hook with a pair of pliers. This is all the more remarkable because it must have hurt like hell to have the hook dislodged, yet she somehow understood that Wilf was helping her, that the pain was ultimately necessary, and that she would be better off in the long run if she tolerated it. I'd heard other similar and equally remarkable stories of dolphins seeking help from humans.[11]

---

[10]   Wayne Grover, "Dolphins: One Diver's Touching Experience," *Sea Frontiers* (January–February 1989): 28–30.
[11]   Rachel Smolker, *To Touch a Wild Dolphin* (New York: Doubleday, 2001), p. 250.

These dolphins involved in these incidents most likely had observed humans often enough to understand that a human could use hands and tools to help in this situation. Such a request could hardly be accidental or the result of conditioning. The most likely explanation, then, is that it was the product of thinking about the problem and a conscious decision to pursue this particular solution.

Dolphins help dolphin This next story was told me by Della Schuler, who worked in the late 1980s as a trainer at the Dolphin Research Center in the Florida Keys. It is no less touching than Grover's account, because it, too, involves a problem connected with a dolphin being in danger. Only this time, it's the dolphins who do the saving.

Not only does DRC host its own community of dolphins, but the facility is sometimes called on by various aquaria to care for dolphins who have become ill. In such situations, Schuler explained, it's very important to put the sick dolphin with long-term residents. This appears to reduce the stress at being in a new environment and helps their recovery. In one such case, the staff decided to place the new dolphin in with two veterans, Mr Gipper and Little Bit. In the history of DRC, Mr Gipper is well known as being an unusual dolphin. One way that he was unusual was that he especially liked to come and go from the facility. In fact, to make this easier, Gipper actually made a hole in the fence so that he wouldn't have to jump over it. (DRC is located on the Gulf side of Grassy Key. The dolphins live in a natural lagoon, not concrete tanks, and the fences that define the pools in which the dolphins live are more to keep other things out than to keep the dolphins in.) The staff made sure to patch the hole before putting the new dolphin into the pool, because if the new dolphin panicked and left the facility in such a weak state, her life would be at risk. Unknown to the staff, however, Gipper had re-opened the hole.

Unfortunately, after the new dolphin was put into the pool, she found the hole and headed out to sea. Before the staff could do anything, however, Gipper and Little Bit went after her, got on either side of her, turned her around and escorted her back. Now, however, the new dolphin didn't want to come back in. Dolphins appear to have an instinctive aversion to going through restrictive openings, and teaching them to do so ("gating") is a difficult process. So it's not surprising that now that the new dolphin had apparently calmed down, she'd balk at going through the fence. Again, the dolphins took the initiative. While Gipper stayed with the sick dolphin, Little Bit swam back and forth through the hole – showing that it wasn't dangerous. The new dolphin followed Little Bit's example and swam through the hole. And then Little Bit and Mr Gipper kept her away from the hole until the staff could fix it. Schuler observed that the sick dolphin "was in such a weakened state that if she'd gotten lost, she would have died for sure." The former trainer believed that Mr Gipper and Little Bit "kept her from dying that day; they knew this was the place she needed to stay."

This is another fascinating account that appears to be an example of problem-solving that involves thought. First, when the sick dolphin headed out to sea, Mr Gipper and Little Bit correctly recognized this as a serious matter. And they immediately took the appropriate action to bring her back. Then, when the sick dolphin refused to swim through the hole, they diagnosed the problem and again came up with a solution. These would be novel and unusual problems in the lives of these two dolphins, and there's no reason to think that Gipper and Little Bit's actions resulted from behavioral conditioning or stereotyped or instinctive behavior. Therefore, the most likely explanation again appears to be that the dolphins reasoned their way to a solution.

Summary: problem solving – Gory, Kuczaj, Pryor, Grover, DRC

When we look at the range of experimental studies and anecdotes that we've seen in this chapter, we get an impressive picture of the cognitive abilities of the dolphin brain. In everything we've seen – from John Gory and Stan Kuczaj's dolphins figuring out something as prosaic as how to open a container for a fish to DRC's veteran dolphins dramatically saving the life of a sick newcomer – sophisticated cognitive abilities are required. The dolphins involved needed to be able:

- to reflect on the contents of their consciousness;
- to handle abstract notions well enough to grasp the causal structure of their environment;
- to understand a problem and then to create something novel – either an original behavior or a new strategy – as a solution.

In addition, these dolphins had to have enough curiosity, interest or self-motivation to discover the solutions to the problems they were presented with. That is, the behaviors described above show that these dolphins had not only the appropriate cognitive capacities, but the inclination to use them when presented with novel problems. In brief, these experiments and stories imply that these dolphins not only *can* think, but *do* think on a regular basis.

──────────── Language Comprehension ────────────

Of all of the questions that humans ask about dolphins, perhaps the most intriguing is whether it will ever be possible for the two species to communicate with each other. Accordingly, some of the most fascinating research into the cognitive abilities of dolphins looks at their ability to handle language. By far the most extensive, thorough and important research in this area is the work of University of Hawaii psychologist Louis Herman.

The dolphins at the center of this research were Phoenix and Akeakamai. These two female bottlenose dolphins were captured in the Gulf of Mexico in 1978, when they were juveniles of 2–3 years old. After that, they lived at the Kewalo Basin Marine Mammal Laboratory on the island of Oahu and worked with Lou Herman and his staff until their deaths in 2003–4. As we saw in the last chapter, Herman has studied a wide range of dolphin cognitive abilities. However, his laboratory is best known for investigating questions about how well Phoenix and Akeakamai understood an artificial "language."[12]

Two dolphins, two languages

Herman's language research was based on observing how well Phoenix and Akeakamai could follow instructions given in an artificial language. The dolphins were never asked to *produce* any sentences in the languages they learned. So Herman's research is strictly about language comprehension, not interspecies communication.

In order to find out how extensive dolphin abilities are on this front, each dolphin was taught a different artificial language.[13] Phoenix was taught an acoustic language; Akeakamai was taught a gestural language. That is, Phoenix's

[12] Louis M. Herman, Douglas G. Richards, and James P. Wolz, "Comprehension of Sentences by Bottlenosed Dolphins," *Cognition*, 16 (1984), 129–219; Louis M. Herman, "Cognition and Language Competencies of Bottlenosed Dolphins," in Ronald J. Schusterman, Jeanette A. Thomas and Forrest G. Wood (eds) *Dolphin Cognition and Behavior: A Behavioral Approach* (Hillsdale, NJ: Lawrence Erlbaum Associates, 1984), pp. 221–252; Louis M. Herman, Adam A. Pack and Palmer Morrel-Samuels, "Representational and Conceptual Skills of Dolphins," in H. L. Roitblat, L. M. Herman, P. E. Nachtigall (eds) *Language and Communication: Comparative Perspectives* (Hillsdale, NJ: Lawrence Erlbaum Associates, 1993), pp. 403–442.
[13] Herman explains, "If both the acoustic and the visual mediums could be used successfully, it would greatly strengthen the case for a general capability of dolphins for understanding instructions specified by a sentence." Herman et al., "Sentence Comprehension," p. 135.

"vocabulary" consisted of computer-generated whistles that she'd hear from an underwater speaker, while Akeakamai was trained to respond to hand gestures given by someone at poolside.

The two languages also had different "grammars." That is, the same command would have a different structure for each dolphin. For example, when Phoenix was instructed to "get the hoop and take it to the pipe," she would hear, in a word order similar to English:

HOOP FETCH PIPE
(Direct object + Action + Indirect object).

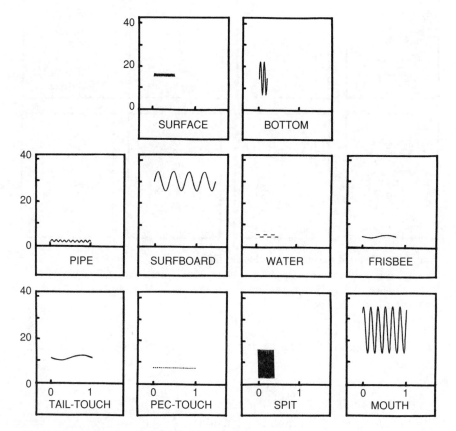

FIGURE 4.1   Selected sounds of the acoustic language
Source: Reprinted from *Cognition* 16: 1 (1984), p. 143, Louis Herman, Douglas Richards, James Wolz, "Comprehension of Sentences by Bottlenose Dolphins," © 1984, with permission from Elsevier

FIGURE 4.2   Selected signals used in the gestural language
Source: Reprinted from *Cognition* 16: 1 (1984), p. 143, Louis Herman, Douglas
Richards, James Wolz, "Comprehension of Sentences by Bottlenose Dolphins," © 1984,
with permission from Elsevier

The same command for Akeakamai, however, put the verb at the end of the
sentence:

PIPE HOOP FETCH
(Indirect object + Direct object + Action).

Akeakamai's grammar was thus closer to ancient Greek and Latin.
    Each dolphin learned a vocabulary of about 30 "words."

- One set referred to *objects* (e.g., GATE, SPEAKER, BALL, HOOP, FRISBEE, PERSON and the names of the two dolphins themselves).
- Another set designated *actions* (e.g., FETCH, GO OVER, GO UNDER, GO THROUGH, TOSS, IN [place one object in or on another], MIMIC [mimic the behavior of a model dolphin or human]).
- A third were *modifiers* that referred to direction. Phoenix was taught SURFACE and BOTTOM. Akeakamai learned LEFT and RIGHT.
- The dolphins learned a command (ERASE) that told them to cancel the instruction they'd just received.
- And they also learned how to operate YES and NO paddles in the pool (so that the dolphins could answer a question of the sort, "Is there a hoop in the tank?").

The first commands given to the dolphins consisted of two and three words (WINDOW TAIL-TOUCH, PIPE HOOP FETCH). However, the dolphins ultimately worked their way up to more complicated five-word sentences (Modifier + Direct object + Action + Modifier + Indirect object) – for example, SURFACE PIPE FETCH BOTTOM HOOP, that is, "take the pipe on the surface to the hoop on the bottom." In the course of the research, Phoenix's language came to consist of 368 unique sentences; Akeakamai's, 464.

The results and their significance

The two dolphins' performance throughout numerous experimental trials was very impressive. On the whole, Phoenix and Akeakamai correctly followed the instructions they received more than 80% of the time. Because this is far greater than what would result simply from chance, there's good reason to conclude that their performance came from understanding the sentences. Herman claims that this is "the first convincing evidence of the ability of animals to process both semantic and syntactic features of sentences."[14]

Semantics and syntax

The dolphins' performance was significant on a number of fronts. Overall, Phoenix and Akeakamai appear to have understood a variety of arbitrary symbols and the rules used to combine those symbols into sentences. Because

---

[14] "Sentence Comprehension," p. 130.

linguists see semantics and syntax as the core elements of human language, it is significant that these two dolphins demonstrated the ability to grasp them.

It's particularly important to note that the syntactic rules included the idea – common in human languages – that the place that a word occupies in a sentence conveys important information about the meaning of the sentence. For example, we all know that "dog bites man" means something very different than "man bites dog" because we understand that English is based on a Subject + Verb + Object structure. Despite the fact the two sentences contain the same three words, the different arrangements describe two different facts. Humans traditionally claimed that we were the only species with the cognitive sophistication to handle this. However, when Phoenix was given, for example, these two 5-word, "semantically reversible" sentences

SURFACE HOOP FETCH BOTTOM BASKET
("Go to the hoop at the surface and take it to the basket at the bottom")

and

BOTTOM BASKET FETCH SURFACE HOOP
("Go to the basket at the bottom and take it to the hoop at the surface"),

she followed instructions perfectly.

Words as symbols/generalization

Phoenix and Akeakamai also appear to have grasped the abstract, symbolic character of the words in their languages. This is seen primarily by the dolphins' ability to generalize. That is, the two cetaceans would first learn a new word in connection with a specific object. But then they immediately understood the word when it was applied to other, similar objects. For example, Herman explains,

> The word HOOP was taught with respect to a particular large, octagonal hoop constructed of plastic pipe. This design proved easy for the dolphins to demolish, so a large square hoop was substituted, without any decrement in performance. Similarly, small hoops, large hoops of much thicker pipe than had been used previously, hoops of dark colored pipe as well as white pipe, and hoops that sank to the bottom of the tank instead of floating, were introduced. In all

cases, these hoops were responded to immediately when a sentence containing the word HOOP was given.[15]

In other words, the dolphins understood that HOOP was a symbol for any object with the relevant central properties. This was true both for words that referred to objects and words that referred to actions.

A particularly interesting example of their apparently quick grasp of the broad meaning of a symbol is the way that Phoenix and Akeakamai generalized with PERSON. "Originally," Herman explains:

> PERSON was taught relative to one particular individual, a trainer named Cathy, who held her arm in the water. The dolphins responded to Cathy's arm when given an instruction containing PERSON, e.g., PERSON TAIL-TOUCH. Later, without any specific training, we demonstrated that a leg in the water, an elbow, or the whole person floating in the water would do as well as an arm for eliciting a response to PERSON. Still later, and again without specific training, both dolphins immediately responded correctly to a second person who was arbitrarily chosen, and then to any person at all.[16]

While it is tempting to regard the way that the dolphins' understood PERSON as no different from their learning that HOOP refers to big and small hoops alike, think about how much more difficult the process of teaching the concept to the dolphins could have been. That is, if Phoenix and Akeakamai had more modest cognitive abilities, they wouldn't have grasped the full reach of the concept so quickly. First, they would have understood PERSON just as "Cathy's arm." Then, it would have taken concentrated training to get them to expand the concept to "any part of Cathy." It probably also would have taken more work for the dolphins to understand that PERSON could refer to Cathy whether she was standing on the side of the pool or floating in the tank. Finally, it would have taken even more training to get Phoenix and Akeakamai to grasp the idea that PERSON could mean "any part of any human no matter where he or she is." The fact that the dolphins could make this progression without any specific training suggests an impressive level of cognitive ability.

It's also significant that the dolphins could understand how the same word could take on different roles – that is, that the dolphins could generalize a

---

[15]   Ibid., p. 178.
[16]   Ibid.

word over a variety of functions. For example, the dolphins had no trouble understanding PERSON when it was used in a variety of ways – "carrying out an action directly to a person, transporting an object to a person, transporting a person to an object, reporting whether a person is present in the dolphins tank, requiring an imitation of a person's behavior, or doing nothing at all with respect to a person."[17] That is, not only did they grasp the core, general meaning of the word. They also immediately understood the relationship between this object (or action) and the others in the sentence – a relationship indicated by the grammatical function of PERSON in the command (direct object, indirect object, etc.).

The idea that a symbol retains its core meaning while standing in different relationships to other objects or actions is, of course, one of the most fundamental conceptual building blocks of language. Again, we see these dolphins capable of a sophisticated cognitive operation.

Understanding new sentences

Another critical indicator of just how impressive Phoenix and Akeakamai's cognitive abilities are was their ability to handle new sentences the first time they were exposed to them. These new commands either included a new word, or they presented the dolphins with a new structure. If the dolphins followed the new instructions the first time they encountered them, it's a strong sign that they understood the linguistic issues involved.

The first group of new sentences contained words that the dolphins had learned the meaning of but had not heard or seen before in a command. The first time Phoenix and Akeakamai were given these sentences, they responded correctly more than 65% of the time. (Herman claims that there was only a 4% or less likelihood they'd be right by chance.)

In the new sentences with a novel structure, the dolphins were presented with a more complex type of sentence than they'd experienced before. For example, Akeakamai had been working with 3-word sentences of the sort

Modifier + Object + Action
(BOTTOM HOOP THRU – "go through the hoop on the bottom of the pool")

---

[17]   Louis M. Herman, Stan A. Kuczaj II, and Mark D. Holder, "Responses to Anomalous Gestural Sequences by a Language-trained Dolphin: Evidence for Processing of Semantic Relations and Syntactic Information," *Journal of Experimental Psychology: General*, 122(2) (1993): 186.

and

Indirect Object + Direct Object + Action
(HOOP PIPE FETCH – "take the pipe to the hoop").

Then she was given

Modifier + Indirect Object + Direct Object + Action
(e.g., RIGHT BASKET PIPE FETCH – "take the pipe to the basket on the right")

and

Indirect Object + Modifier + Direct Object + Action
(e.g., SPEAKER LEFT HOOP FETCH – "take the hoop on the left to the speaker").

Again, Phoenix and Akeakamai's performance was impressive. The first time the dolphins were given the more complicated sentence forms, they correctly carried out the tasks.

The dolphins' ability to understand new sentences is extremely significant. Indeed, Herman considers it "one of the most important findings on language understanding" because "the understanding and use of novel sentences was considered a hallmark of human language ability."[18]

—————————— Commands: FETCH, IN, MIMIC ——————————

From a conceptual standpoint, most of the actions in Phoenix and Akeakamai's vocabulary were relatively simple: TAIL-TOUCH (touch with flukes), PECTORAL TOUCH (touch with pectoral fin), MOUTH (grasp with mouth), OVER (swim over), UNDER (swim under), THROUGH (swim through), TOSS (throw object using rostrum), SPIT (squirt water from mouth at object). The commands based on these words simply asked the dolphins to perform an action to a named object, e.g., FRISBEE TOSS. In terms

[18] Herman, "Cognition and Language Competencies," p. 247; Herman, "Sentence Comprehension," p. 190.

of English grammar, the commands are based on verbs that take only direct objects. However, Phoenix and Akeakamai also learned three other commands that were significantly more complex.

The first two (FETCH and IN) are what Herman calls "relational words." They are verbs that refer to both direct and indirect objects at the same time. FETCH means "take object A to object B." IN means "place object A in or on object B." Both commands describe a more complex relationship than something like TOSS – and, hence, are cognitively more demanding.

The other complex command (MIMIC), however, required even more of Phoenix and Akeakamai – the ability to understand an abstract concept. Unlike all of the other action words in the dolphins' vocabulary, MIMIC doesn't refer to a specific, clearly identifiable action. When we read through the list of verbs used in the commands (TAIL-TOUCH, PECTORAL TOUCH, MOUTH, OVER, UNDER, THROUGH, TOSS, SPIT, FETCH and IN), we can easily get a mental picture of what action is involved. However, MIMIC has essentially no intrinsic, material content. Unless we know what behavior is supposed to be mimicked, we can't even imagine what's being asked. That's because the concept lacks any tangible component; it's purely abstract.

It's important to note, then, just how well Phoenix and Akeakamai handled such an abstract instruction.[19] In all of the following experiments, the dolphins performed far above what could be explained by chance:

- Akeakamai was asked to imitate a variety of new, arbitrary sounds that were different from the sounds that dolphins normally make. She was taught a MIMIC command and exposed to a wide-ranging variety of sounds. She was able to imitate them accurately.

- Akeakamai was taught to mimic sounds that were used to designate 5 specific objects (ball, pipe, hoop, person and Frisbee). Then she was asked to reproduce the "name" just by being shown the object. Again, she performed very well.

- Phoenix and Akeakamai were asked to imitate one another's actions. One dolphin would be told to do a specific behavior by means of a set of hand gestures that the other couldn't see; then the other would be given a MIMIC command.

[19]   Douglas G. Richards, James P. Wolz and Louis M. Herman, "Vocal Mimicry of Computer-Generated Sounds and Vocal Labeling of Objects by a Bottlenosed Dolphin, *Tursiops truncatus*," *Journal of Comparative Psychology*, 98(1) (1984): 10–28; Herman et al., "Representational and Conceptual Skills," pp. 414–421.

- In another experiment, a human was added to the mix. While Akeakamai looked on, Phoenix and the human were simultaneously told to perform different behaviors. Then Akeakamai was instructed either PERSON MIMIC or PHOENIX MIMIC. The vast majority of the time, Akeakamai chose the correct model and imitated the action.
- Phoenix and Akeakamai successfully mimicked both dolphin and human models even when the behavior in question and the MIMIC command were given to them over a television screen.

It's also important to note that the mimicking dolphin would sometimes have to wait almost a minute and a half before getting the MIMIC command. Moreover, sometimes she would be told to do something like swim on her back while she was waiting. The idea was that if the dolphins imitated the model correctly despite a delay or having to perform some distracting behavior, then they most likely were relying on a mental representation of the action involved.

Yet another piece of evidence for the idea that the dolphins were applying the abstract concept of mimicry and not simply engaging in mindless copying is an interesting response from Akeakamai when she was first imitating sounds. Akeakamai apparently had a preferred range in which she liked to whistle (5–10 kHz), and some of the sounds she was given to imitate were out of that range. Until Akeakamai got comfortable producing the sounds exactly, she'd transpose the sound either up or down an octave. This is similar to what most of us do when we're trying to sing a tune out of our range. We keep to the melody, but we take it up or down an octave.[20] If Akeakamai didn't understand the concept, it's difficult to believe she'd have responded this way.

The dolphins' performance throughout these varied experiments strongly implies that they understood and applied the abstract concept of mimicry. We see examples of successful imitation in relation to dolphin actions, human actions, sounds, behavior observed first hand and televised behavior. In fact, Herman claims that such varied evidence has never been seen in any other nonhumans and that this suggests "considerable representational abilities." Throughout the mimicking experiments, then, the performance of these dolphins yet again implies that their brains support sophisticated cognitive operations.

---

[20] Richards et al., "Vocal Mimicry," p. 17.

Answering questions: YES, NO and mental representations

Another part of Herman's research that suggests that the dolphins could think abstractly was Akekamai's ability to answer a question by using a pair of paddles she'd been trained on meaning YES and NO. The dolphin was taught a QUESTION symbol which, when paired with the symbol for an object, amounted to asking whether that object was in the pool. For example, BALL QUESTION would mean, "Is there a ball in the pool?" The dolphin would answer by pressing either a YES paddle or a NO paddle. When Akeakamai was tested on this, she responded correctly more than 75 percent of the time.[21]

This is an especially significant accomplishment because even though the question involved might seem simple, it requires sophisticated cognitive abilities. Consider for a moment what you need to do in your own brain if someone asks you, for example, "Is there a screwdriver under the chair in which you're currently sitting?" Of course, you need to know the meaning of "screwdriver," and you need to understand that "screwdriver" is an abstract symbol that refers to any number of objects with similar properties. More than that, however, you need to be able to call up from your memory an understanding of the concept of a screwdriver – a mental representation that you can access whether or not you're in the presence of screwdrivers. Then you can go ahead and compare what's in your mind against what is or isn't under your chair, and answer "yes" or "no." Akeakamai's ability to report on the absence of specific objects presumably demonstrates a similar ability to form, store, recall and work with concepts.

However, Akeakamai went on to use these paddles spontaneously in an interesting way that further suggests a significant level of cognitive ability. For example, she was given a standard sentence of the sort FRISBEE HOOP IN ("put the hoop on top of the Frisbee") – only sometimes one or the other of the two objects in the sentence was missing from the pool. If the first, destination object (Frisbee) wasn't there, Akeakamai would usually take the object that needed to be transported (the hoop) and put it on top of the NO pedal. However, if the object to be moved (the hoop) wasn't there, but the destination object (the Frisbee) was, she'd simply press the NO pedal with

---

[21]   "Representational and Conceptual Skills of Dolphins," p. 407. Louis M. Herman and Paul W. Forestell, "Reporting Presence or Absence of Named Objects by a Language-Trained Dolphin," *Neuroscience & Behavioral Reviews*, 5 (1985): 667–691.

her rostrum.[22] In essence, she developed a method – apparently of her own design – to communicate something roughly equivalent to the following: "You want me to do something with this hoop, but the object you want me to put it on isn't here, so this is as much as I can do," and "You want me to put a hoop onto the Frisbee that's here, but the hoop isn't here, so I can't even get started."

Interpreting instructions

Some parts of Herman's research even suggest that the dolphins actively process, interpret and evaluate their instructions – that is, that they think about them while they get them. For example, Akeakamai was given a series of "anomalous sentences," that is, commands that, according to the rules of her language, didn't make sense. She was given three word sentences of the form Object + Object + Action. However, the action word could take only a direct object – for example, BASKET SURFBOARD OVER or WATER HOOP TAIL-TOUCH. Such commands are grammatically meaningless. It would be like someone telling us to "sit on the car horse" or "paint the chair ceiling." If we couldn't ask this person what he or she meant, the best we could do would be to interpret the sentence and guess at what it was supposed to mean within the rules of how our language operates.

The first time that Akeakamai was given a series of such nonsense instructions, in 11 out of 12 cases, she ignored the first word and carried out the command as though it were a grammatically correct two-word sentence (SURFBOARD OVER and HOOP TAIL-TOUCH).[23] She didn't get so confused that she froze. She didn't try to apply the action to both objects (swimming over both the basket and the surfboard, for example). It's not unreasonable to speculate that in this case Akeakamai simply did her best to interpret and reconstruct the command according to the rules of the artificial language she'd been taught.

In fact, the dolphins' response to a supposedly anomalous sentence produced one of the most surprising moments in Herman's experimental trials. The scientist explains:

We considered the sentence [WATER TOSS] to be semantically anomalous, since the stream of water flowing from the suspended hose was nontransportable and

---

[22] "Representational and Conceptual Skills," p. 407.
[23] "Sentence Comprehension," p. 189.

hence, we believed, not tossable. Akeakamai, however, went to the water stream and, jerking her head rapidly through it, sent out a large spray of water. . . . Phoenix was later tested with the same sentence and performed exactly as did Akeakamai.[24]

The fact that the two dolphins saw a way to make sense of what a team of researchers thought was nonsense contains a lesson about the importance of being aware of how limited our thinking can sometimes be. It also testifies to the fact that, when it comes to the question of "animal intelligence," non-humans can probably surprise us more often than we think.

Other, more complicated research into how Akeakamai would respond to anomalous sentences reveals even more evidence about how intellectually active she apparently was in resolving the dilemmas that these new challenges created.[25] In these experiments, Akeakamai was given distinctly different types of anomalous sentences. Her responses were noteworthy:

- One set of sentences included a new, nonsense word in a grammatically correct command. With most of these, Akeakamai refused to respond, or she started to respond and then stopped. This is particularly significant because Akeakamai *never* refused to respond to a sentence – even a new sentence – as long as it was made up of meaningful words and was grammatically correct.
- Another set of sentences asked her to take an object that couldn't be moved (e.g., a speaker) from one place to another. Again, she usually refused to respond.
- Akeakamai was also given a variety of multi-word commands with a mismatch between the objects and the verbs. For example, some sentences had three objects and a verb that, in Akeakamai's grammar, could take only two (one direct and one indirect). Some had two objects and a verb that could take only one. Sometimes, it was the mix of a particular verb and movable and unmovable objects that didn't make sense. In the vast majority of cases, Akeakamai surveyed the elements available, followed the logic of the grammar of her language, constructed a meaningful sentence and performed it.

---

[24]   Ibid., p. 181.
[25]   Herman et al., "Responses to Anomalous Gestural Sequences," pp. 184–194. See also Edward Kato, "Elements of Syntax in the Systems of Three Language-Trained Animals," *Animal Learning & Behavior*, 27(1) (1999): 1–14, and Louis M. Herman and Robert K. Uyeyama, "The Dolphin's Grammatical Competency: Comments on Kako (1999)," *Animal Learning & Behavior*, 27(1) (1999): 18–23.

Two other cases where the two dolphins took an especially active role in following their instructions involved situations where, on the face of it, the commands couldn't be followed. After Phoenix had learned HOOP THROUGH ("swim through the hoop") and GATE THROUGH ("swim through the open gate"), she was again given the command GATE THROUGH – only this time the gate was closed. Phoenix swam to the gate and hesitated. But then she pushed the gate open and swam through it. Similarly, the first time Phoenix was given the command BOTTOM HOOP THROUGH ("swim through the hoop on the bottom of the pool"), there were two hoops in the pool – a weighted hoop lying on the bottom and a buoyant hoop suspended vertically in the pool. Phoenix swam to the bottom, lifted the hoop up until it was vertical and then swam through it.

Such a variety of examples of apparently active engagement surely suggests that Phoenix and Akeakamai were *thinking* their way through these experiments.

Language comprehension: overall significance

It is difficult to underestimate the significance of Lou Herman's research into the abilities of Phoenix and Akeakamai to understand the artificial languages that the scientist designed.

First, Herman's work strongly suggests that these two dolphins could understand and work with the basic elements of an artificial language:

- a vocabulary, that is, a variety of symbols that refer to both actions and objects and even to the presence and absence of objects (YES/NO),
- a vocabulary that incorporates the concept of generalization, that is, its symbols (words) refer to any object that has the relevant properties,
- grammatical rules and grammatical categories that assemble symbols into meaningful sentences,
- sentences as complex as five-word commands that include modifiers and both direct and indirect objects,
- questions as well as commands.

Second, the extent to which Phoenix and Akeakamai understood *new* sentences the first time they encountered them implies that their performance was truly the result of understanding the artificial languages involved.

Third, the dolphins' ability to follow a MIMIC command suggests the capacity to grasp an abstract concept. This is also implied by their use of mental representations in answering questions about whether or not particular objects are in the pool.

Fourth, the active role that the dolphins took in handling certain commands – especially in interpreting anomalous commands – implies a particularly sophisticated level of cognitive ability.

Humans have traditionally claimed that only members of our species have such intellectual capacities. It certainly appears that dolphins possess abilities far more sophisticated than had originally been thought.

The most important implication: operating in a foreign cognitive environment

The implications of Herman's research on language comprehension are unquestionably impressive and thought-provoking. However, the most significant dimension of this research never appears in the scientific reports of all of the experiments we've been reviewing. That is, as in Gory and Kuczaj's experiments on problem-solving described above, what is most impressive about Phoenix and Akeakamai is that they were able to perform so well *while operating in a foreign cognitive environment.*[26]

Phoenix and Akekamai learned and responded to artificial languages. Of course, it's tempting to think that they were able to do so because dolphins have their own language – that is, their own symbolic system and grammatical rules. This would mean, then, that the two dolphins' performance on Herman's experiments was simply the equivalent of learning a foreign language. However, there is no evidence that dolphins have a language equivalent to ours. Dolphins do communicate with one another as they engage in cooperative behavior, manage relationships in large schools, raise their young, and so on. But no scientist has uncovered even the main lines, never mind the details, of a formal language that dolphins use with each other. We know a few things about how they communicate. Tail-slaps are signs of displeasure. Certain postures signal aggression. Dolphins use signature whistles to identify themselves and to get one another's attention (as when mothers and calves use them as contact calls in the wild). So far, however, there is no evidence that they have the equivalent of a human language – "Dolphinese" – in which they converse.

However, if Phoenix and Akeakamai had nothing of their own to use as a convenient frame of reference for decoding the artificial languages they were presented with, then they were operating in a cognitive domain that was

---

[26]   I owe this point to Denise Herzing.

completely new to them. That is, if there is no dolphin parallel to a human language, what Phoenix and Akeakamai did was even more difficult, complicated and impressive than it first appears. Such an accomplishment has two important implications.

Efficacy of education   The first implication of the two dolphins' ability to operate in a foreign cognitive environment is that their brains must be able to respond to structured education of the sort that Herman exposed them to. Most humans acquire advanced cognitive skills only through an extended process of education. It would be extremely interesting if it turned out that both the dolphin and human brains are not only responsive to concentrated training, but actually require it in order to reach maximum cognitive development.

Cognitive flexibility   However, the more important implication of being able to operate so well in a foreign cognitive environment is that Phoenix and Akeakamai's brains must have been able to adapt to situations, demands and problems that were remarkably unlike anything a wild dolphin typically faces. These dolphins, then, demonstrated an extraordinary cognitive flexibility of the sort that has so far been documented only in humans.

It is difficult to find a simple example of what it would be like for us as humans to adapt to a similarly "foreign cognitive environment." The equivalent of the challenge that Phoenix and Akeakamai faced would be a situation where: we need to perform specific actions, for which the instructions are given in a series of symbols that we've never seen before, and they're presented to us through mechanisms that we've never been exposed to before, and we have to decode not only the meaning of the individual symbols but what it means when the symbols stand to each other in one sort of relationship or another. However, each of the following examples captures some dimension of the challenge.

- In one way, what Phoenix and Akeakamai did was analogous to Helen Keller's remarkable accomplishment. Despite being deaf and blind, Keller learned how to read, write and speak. That is, she was able to decode a symbolic system that was grounded in the two senses that she lacked. Most humans learn language first through sound and then through sight. Humans who are deaf learn sign language through sight. Lacking the standard way of assigning meaning to symbols, Helen Keller had to find a different way to grasp the meaning of symbols.
- Or, imagine that you're an explorer looking for a lost civilization. You come upon a huge door at the base of a mountain. Behind you is a swift,

white-water stream. What you haven't realized yet is that the stream is actually an artifact – made by the civilization for which you're searching. And the instructions for opening the door are contained in the recurring patterns and shapes that the water takes as it flows past you. The eddies, swirls and splashes are actually symbols that appear in the shape and order that they do because of the unique design of the stream. You must learn to break the code contained in the motion of the water if you're going to open the door. However, in order to do so, you must think very differently about what you're seeing when you look at the stream. You must demonstrate enormous cognitive flexibility.

When we look at what Phoenix and Akeakamai did against the backdrop of what it would be for humans to do something equivalent, it should be apparent that the dolphins demonstrated impressive cognitive abilities.

Broader implications

Phoenix and Akeakamai's performance throughout these experiments, then, is very impressive. But what does Lou Herman's research imply about the cognitive abilities of other dolphins? Can we draw any general conclusions?

The evidence actually suggests five possibilities. Let's see which is most likely.

1. Things aren't what they seem   The first possibility is that while it appears that Phoenix and Akeakamai's performance implies the ability to understand language, the reality is quite different. Maybe these dolphins were just very talented at learning the appropriate responses to behavioral stimuli. Wouldn't that be a simpler and more believable explanation than that these dolphins have significant cognitive abilities? Perhaps – but not if we consider the performance of Phoenix and Akeakamai against the backdrop of all of the other research that we've surveyed in the preceding chapters. No one experiment or story that we've considered may prove beyond the shadow of a doubt that dolphins have significant cognitive capabilities. But taken as a whole, the body of research suggests that these dolphins' brains have sophisticated abilities. Set in that context, it seems far more likely that what Herman is indeed showing us "the first convincing evidence of the ability of animals to process both semantic and syntactic features of sentences."[27]

---

[27]   "Sentence Comprehension," p. 130.

2. *Phoenix and Akeakamai's performance is so surprising that it probably means they're exceptional dolphins. Accordingly, we can't infer anything about other dolphins.*   The second possibility concedes Herman's claims, but limits what we can infer from his research. The issue here is whether or not Phoenix and Akeakamai are representative of other dolphins. If they aren't, then they're the equivalent of "brilliant" dolphins whom Herman simply had the good fortune to catch. Statistically, it's highly unlikely that a random capture would find unusual specimens. So the odds are good that Phoenix and Akeakamai's abilities are representative of other bottlenose dolphins.

3. *All dolphins have remarkable cognitive flexibility*   If we assume that Phoenix and Akeakamai are characteristic of the average bottlenose dolphin, and if we assume that dolphins have nothing analogous to human language, then the brain of virtually every member of this species has extraordinary cognitive abilities. Indeed, this suggests a greater degree (or, at least, a different sort) of cognitive flexibility than we find in most humans. Think again about the challenges that would be analogous for humans. How many of us could overcome the obstacles that Helen Keller faced? How many of us can solve problems that require us to think about the world in a completely different way from what our experience has prepared us for? How many of us can get our brains to cope with situations beyond what most humans encounter? Not many. As intelligent as we are, most of us don't demonstrate that level of ability. If virtually all dolphins can handle challenges equivalent to Helen Keller's, these cetaceans are definitely a cut above humans in terms of cognitive flexibility.

The problem with this possibility, however, is that it's difficult to find evidence for such cognitive flexibility in virtually every dolphin. To cite just one example, if the schools of dolphins in the eastern tropical Pacific ocean who are harmed by human tuna fishing had these kinds of abilities, it's difficult to believe that they wouldn't have found a way to avoid being killed or injured.[28]

4. *All dolphins would respond well to education*   The next possibility is that Phoenix and Akeakamai have no more cognitive ability than the average dolphin, but that ordinary dolphins respond extremely well to human education aimed at teaching them artificial language comprehension. At first, this seems more likely than either of the first three possibilities we've considered. After all, humans apparently require structured training for our brain to develop its most sophisticated abilities. And we don't grasp the details of human

---

[28]   For the details on this issue, see Chapter 7.

language without instruction. It's reasonable to think that the dolphin brain – which is complex in its own way – might operate the same way.

There are some problems with this idea, however. In the human brain, there is a specific area used for language. If the dolphin brain has a similar region that Herman's educational program stimulated, this would mean that this area was going unused for millions of years. However, it's not very likely that dolphins have been carrying around a fair amount of excess brainpower that didn't get tapped until they encountered human researchers. In terms of energy use, the brain is the most expensive organ in the body. Dolphins wouldn't have developed cognitive capacities in the first place unless they needed them and were using them in some way. And, particularly over millions of years, organs and abilities that go unused usually disappear. So it's highly unlikely that the modern dolphin brain has extensive untapped resources.

However, if Phoenix and Akeakamai aren't accessing spare resources, then their responsiveness to human education again implies that the dolphin brain is remarkably flexible. It would have to be able to shift gears so that cognitive abilities that are typically used for one purpose in the wild (understanding the natural environment and communicating with other dolphins, for example) can be used for something very different (understanding artificial languages) in captivity. But this also seems unlikely. Again, it's difficult to believe that such plasticity could exist unless we saw more evidence of this in the wild. If this capacity weren't used regularly, how could it persist in the dolphin brain for millions of years?

5. All dolphins have significant conceptual abilities and/or there's some dolphin analog to human language   Accordingly, perhaps the most likely implication of Herman's research is that Phoenix and Akeakamai arrived, we might say, hard-wired for the kinds of tasks they were asked to do. That is, maybe they weren't operating in as foreign a cognitive environment as it first seems.

In this possibility, either the two dolphins had developed at least a basic level of the cognitive skills required in the research before they were captured (e.g., generalization, abstract thinking, and understanding the elements of a symbolic system that represents the physical world around them), or they arrived at Herman's facility with brains whose development would naturally go in that direction as long as they received appropriate stimuli. In either case, Phoenix and Akeakamai would then have been applying typical dolphin cognitive skills to new situations or challenges. This, then, would be somewhat equivalent to what we as humans do when we take cognitive skills that we've learned in one domain and apply them in another. For example, imagine that you're traveling in a country where you don't speak the language. You encounter the following situations: you want to find a restaurant; you need to order a meal; because you're coming down with a cold, you need to find a pharmacy and then explain to the pharmacist what kind of medicine you need. You'd probably make your way through these challenges by a combination of gestures and sounds that would get your point across. You wouldn't be using language, but you'd be taking your language skills and applying them in an inventive way in order to communicate.

This possibility would suggest, then, that, as a matter of course, dolphins in the wild regularly use abstract thought and symbolic representational systems. This even raises the possibility that there could be some kind of dolphin equivalent to the artificial languages Herman was using – even though there is, so far, no evidence for such an analog. However, the idea that dolphins have advanced cognitive skills and something analogous to human language may turn out to be the simplest and most likely explanation for Phoenix and Akeakamai's performance in Lou Herman's experiments.[29]

Overall significance of problem-solving and language research

While each of the research studies or anecdotes that we've surveyed in this chapter suggests the presence of some sort of cognitive ability in various

---

[29]   Denise Herzing observes:

> That dolphins demonstrate the capacity to operate within an artificial representational and rule-governed system is highly suggestive of the fact that in their own lives they employ a capacity (the details of which have yet to be identified) that is equally as cognitively complex as the human capacity for language without being analogous in structure and form.
>
> (Herzing and White, "Dolphins and the Question of Personhood," p. 75)

Lori Marino expands on this possibility when she notes:

> I think that it is entirely possible that dolphins have something different but analogous to language and that part of the reason why they have such large brains is because they have a very complex communicative system. The reason I think this is because it provides an explanation for their prodigious artificial language abilities. Also, I think a complex social life requires a complex communication system. Additionally, the fact that we are having a difficult time decoding the dolphin communication system hints that there is more there than meets the eye. For instance, the fact that we cannot find a strict correlation between most dolphin whistles and context suggests there could be the property of displacement. To date, no one has figured out what the unit of information is in dolphin whistle repertoires or even if they perceive their whistles in that way. Brenda McCowan has applied information theory to dolphin whistle repertoires and has uncovered interesting evidence that there is more structure there than in many other mammal repertoires.
>
> (Private communication)

dolphins, the picture that arises from the combination of all of them is truly striking. We have seen dolphins use their brains to create novel solutions to problems, invent innovative behaviors, respond imaginatively to life-threatening situations and understand artificial languages. These tasks require a range of sophisticated cognitive abilities: abstract thinking, creativity, understanding symbolic systems, representing the causal structure of their environment, the flexibility to adapt to a foreign cognitive environment, and the ability to reflect on the contents of one's consciousness.

As we saw at the end of our consideration of Lou Herman's research, the performance of Phoenix and Akeakamai even suggests the possibility that wild dolphins use their brains in ways that are closer to how humans do than has been recognized.

It is the task of the next chapter, however, to complete our investigation of what the dolphin brain can do and to explore what "dolphin intelligence" might ultimately amount to in these cetaceans' own domain – the ocean.

CHAPTER 5

Dolphin Social Intelligence

In the fantasy novel, *The Hitchhiker's Guide to the Galaxy*, Douglas Adams makes an amusing observation about differences between humans and dolphins. Adams writes:

> It is an important and popular fact that things are not always what they seem. For instance, on the planet Earth, man had always assumed that he was more intelligent than dolphins because he had achieved so much – the wheel, New York, wars and so on – while all that dolphins had ever done was muck about in the water having a good time. But conversely, the dolphins had always believed that they were far more intelligent than man – for precisely the same reasons.[1]

Adams' book is fiction, but a central truth undergirds his comments. There may very well be fundamental differences in how "intelligence" manifests itself in different, big-brained species when one has evolved on land, the other has evolved in the oceans, and they've had to adapt to dramatically different environments.

In this connection, it's important to note that there's not even universal agreement about what "intelligence" means in humans. For example, for much of the twentieth century, most psychologists took "intelligence" to refer to a single, general cognitive ability that makes possible human skills in mathematics, language, abstract thought and problem solving. This trait supposedly could be measured by "IQ tests." Toward the end of the century, however, it became apparent that these tests had a variety of racial and cultural biases – which

---

[1] Douglas Adams, *The Hitchhiker's Guide to the Galaxy* (New York: Pocket Books, 1979), p. 156.

meant that "intelligence" is more difficult to define, isolate and measure than scientists had first thought. In addition, the idea that "intelligence" is a single, cognitive ability came under fire. Daniel Goleman, for example, has argued that our concept of intelligence should be expanded to include "emotional intelligence" – knowing one's emotions, managing emotions, motivating oneself, recognizing emotions in others and handling relationships.[2] Howard Gardner argues for an even more expansive definition. Gardner claims that "intelligence" is better understood not as a single, general intelligence, but as multiple intelligences that include not simply intellectual abilities, but emotional and physical ones as well. He identifies eight intelligences: linguistic, logical-mathematical, naturalist, musical, bodily-kinesthetic, spatial, inter-personal, and intrapersonal.[3]

With so much debate about intelligence in humans, we can imagine just how difficult and confusing it could get to identify intelligence in dolphins – and then to try to compare it with intelligence in humans. We can also see that if we base our discussion on a definition of human intelligence, we risk coloring our inquiry with anthropocentric prejudice. Gardner and Goleman suggest that a bias in favor of a single, general intelligence has prevented psychologists from seeing important dimensions of *human* intelligence. It's virtually certain, then, that working with a concept of intelligence grounded in human abilities would skew the way we identify and evaluate the intelligence of other species.

The preceding two chapters have been exploring the question of "dolphin intelligence" by examining dolphin cognitive abilities and noting where they're similar to our own. We've seen that, like humans, dolphins apparently have the ability: to experience self-consciousness and emotions; to engage in abstract, conceptual thought; to invent new and creative solutions to problems; to understand the causal structure of their environment; grasp grammar and syntax; and to operate in a foreign cognitive environment. However, by focusing too much on the similarities between our species, we risk suggesting the anthropocentric idea that the extent to which dolphins (or any other nonhumans) have moral standing depends on how much they are "just like us." Moreover, focusing on the similarities between our species downplays the significance of Diana Reiss's suggestion that dolphins may represent an "alien intelligence." Accordingly, it's important at this point to pay attention to some of the critical differences in what it takes to live on the

[2] Daniel Goleman, *Emotional Intelligence* (New York: Bantam, 1995).
[3] Howard Gardner, *Intelligence Reframed* (New York: Basic Books, 1999).

land versus surviving in the ocean. We need to seriously consider the possibility that, in some important ways, intelligence manifests itself differently in
the water than it does on land.

There are a variety of reasons to think that – at least when we compare
humans and dolphins – our definition of "intelligence" may need to be
species-specific. The challenges that need to be met simply to stay alive are
significantly different on the land and in the water. The means available for
solving problems differ. There may even be some anatomical reasons that intelligence looks different in different species. Frank Wilson, a neurologist, has
suggested that the character of human intelligence has been shaped by the
"co-evolution" of the human brain and the human hand.[4] If there is a relationship in intelligent mammals between the brain and external organs that
play a vital role in survival, the fact that dolphins lack hands suggests that we
need to be careful in making straightforward comparisons between human
and dolphin intelligence. It may be like comparing apples and oranges.

Accordingly, given all of the complications in defining intelligence in a way
that will let us make comparisons across species, perhaps the best thing to do
is to use the simplest possible definition. Howard Gardner defines intelligence
as "a biopsychological potential to process information that can be activated
in a cultural setting to solve problems or create products that are of value in
a culture."[5] But his reference to "creating products" presents problems for when
we try to apply this definition to an aquatic species. So instead of thinking
about intelligence as the capacity that lets us invent computers, cure disease
and produce great art and civilizations, let's ratchet things down and focus
on what lies underneath these accomplishments. Let's think about intelligence
simply as the intellectual and emotional abilities that make it possible for both
a species in general and its individual members to survive in their environment and to solve the problems and overcome the challenges that life throws
at them.

Such a basic definition will let us develop a picture of "dolphin intelligence"
that is free of the anthropocentric idea that intelligence is a property that will
manifest itself in the same way no matter what the species, that is, that it will
show itself in the life of any species the way it does in humans. Humans and
dolphins may both have the capacity to reflect on the contents of our consciousness (e.g., perceptions from one's interactions with physical objects and

---

[4]   Frank R. Wilson, *The Hand: How its Use Shapes the Brain, Language, and Human Culture*
(New York: Pantheon Books, 1998) Wilson's thesis will be discussed in Chapter 6.
[5]   Gardner, *Intelligence Reframed*, pp. 33–34.

other beings, and one's own thoughts, emotions, memories, etc.) in a way that lets us use certain cognitive and affective capacities to decide what to do in the situations in which we find ourselves. But because our physical and social environments in which our species operate are so different, we shouldn't be surprised to discover that our large brains may take us in different directions.

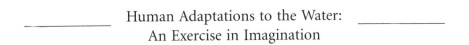

Human Adaptations to the Water: An Exercise in Imagination

Perhaps the best way to approach this issue of "dolphin intelligence" is to focus on the special challenges of surviving in the ocean. So let's try an intellectual experiment. Imagine that all of the discussion about global warming has, in fact, colossally underestimated the problem. In reality, the temperature of the planet is going to climb so high that over the next few centuries the polar ice caps will completely melt and flood the planet. Also assume that, for one reason or another, it's going to be impossible for us to create floating communities that would let us preserve our land-based technologies. However, life in the sea will persist. The bottom line is that ultimately it's going to be just us and the oceans. Humans will have to return to the water if our species is to survive. Obviously, our bodies would change dramatically. The differences between living on land and living in the water dictate that certain bodily designs and sensory abilities enhance the odds of surviving. So we'd end up with a more hydrodynamic design; and, like cetaceans, our auditory abilities might become much more sophisticated. But it's reasonable to imagine that survivability might also be enhanced by particular cognitive and affective abilities. In fact, a new group of scientists has emerged – evolutionary psychologists – who are exploring the question of just how much the physical conditions in which we've evolved have shaped the main lines of our inner world.[6] The claims of evolutionary psychologists remain controversial. But they point to the importance of considering the possibility that, as Robert Wright explains it, "the theory of natural selection, as understood today, reveals the contours of the human mind."[7] And, if this is true of humans, it's likely also true of dolphins.

[6] See, for example, the work of Steven Pinker: *The Blank Slate: The Modern Denial of Human Nature* (New York: Viking, 2002) and *How the Mind Works* (New York: Norton, 1997).
[7] Robert Wright, *The Moral Animal: Evolutionary Psychology and Everyday Life* (New York: Vintage Books, 1994), p. 11.

So, let's speculate about how we'd use our brains to adapt to living in the water. What cognitive and affective adaptations would the challenges of survival dictate for humans? How would *homo sapiens* use our intelligence in order to survive? At the end of this long, evolutionary process, what would we point to as signs that we were an intelligent species?

Life in the ocean

We shouldn't underestimate the creative potential of the human mind, so there's no telling what imaginative ways aquatic humans would cope with their environment. But there's no question that the differences between living on the land and living in the water would present us with major challenges.

Let's start with the basic task of ensuring our physical safety. We'd be at risk from dangerous weather conditions and predators, but we wouldn't be able to construct shelters. We might be able to make some small, crude weapons from, say, the bones or teeth of dead sharks, cetaceans or humans. But carrying them with us all the time would make us less hydrodynamic, and we couldn't build a storage facility for them. And if we assigned some members of our group the job of carrying our tools and weapons, we'd be slowing these people down so much that they'd be easier targets for predators.

Lacking artificial structures or natural barriers against physical threats, we'd be in a very vulnerable situation. Our primary defense against danger, then, would probably have to be each other. We can't control storms or sharks, but we would have a better chance of surviving if we could rely on other people to help us. We'd be safest, then, if we were part of a tight-knit group in which everyone could be trusted to be alert to the presence of predators, to warn others and to help one another when necessary.

If we turn to the problem of finding food, we get a similar picture. What will work best for us is the help of other people. All of us will probably eat better if we cooperate in locating schools of fish and, in particular, in catching them.

Another challenge that we'd face is storing information. It's unlikely that we could find a way to store the vast amounts of information our species stores now. So priority would go to facts about things critical to our survival. For example, we'd need to know: how to recognize predators and food; how to avoid the former and find the latter; how to identify dangerous water and weather conditions; and how to respond to them appropriately. We'd also need to know about one another – the strengths and weaknesses of the people around us, whom we could trust, how to work with one another, and the like.

Once again, the challenges of living in the water recommend that we regard the people around us as a critical resource. As was the case with food and safety, given the technological limitations we'd be facing, we'd probably rely heavily on one another for storing, retrieving and passing on to succeeding generations the facts critical to survival.

Life in the ocean: the importance of other people

The most fundamental fact of life of our transition back to the oceans, then, might very well be that we'd be safer if we lived in close, tight-knit groups. (The corollary to this is that trying to live alone would be tantamount to suicide, and that being thrown out of a group would be the equivalent of a death sentence.) It's no accident that the "school" is a basic social unit in the ocean. What we might call "the dynamics of survival in the ocean" dictates that a highly social, cooperative way of life is the most prudent strategy. That is, we'd probably need the good will of other people much more than we do now.

Returning to the water, then, might encourage humans to develop ways to treat each other differently than we do now. For openers, we'd want to figure out how to avoid killing each other. Strictly in terms of staying alive, it would be both in our own individual interest and in the interest of the group to keep everyone alive, to keep our group as large as our food source would allow, and to find a way to resolve differences without destroying group cohesion. This isn't to say that we'd stop being aggressive, just that we'd have more reason to learn how to be aggressive in a more productive, less wasteful fashion. Expelling people from the group or killing members of our group for any reason other than self-defense could make us more vulnerable to harm. So we'd have strong incentives to discover ways to resolve differences peacefully.

As a result, we might expend no small amount of brainpower on learning how to manage our relationships with the many different people around us. We'd want to concentrate on: what it takes to encourage others to help us, how to cooperate with others, how to project dependability, how to communicate, how to negotiate, how to compromise, how to manage differences with other people so that we weren't seen either as a direct threat or as so uncooperative that other people would want to throw us out of the group. We'd recognize that the more people we had close relationships with, the better. Similarly, the stronger these relationships and connections were, the safer we'd be. The better we could master the dynamics of close relationships with a large number of other people, the more likely we'd be able to handle the challenges to survival.

Accordingly, the personality traits of people who work especially well in groups – cooperative, diplomatic, perceptive of other people's feelings, self-effacing, etc. – could, over time, become the dominant qualities of human beings. The nature of the challenges of surviving in the ocean could give people with these traits an edge over highly individualistic and autonomous people. Natural selection might favor cooperation and punish rugged individualism. It's not unreasonable to think that our species would gravitate in the direction of becoming expert in human relationships. This doesn't mean that we couldn't become expert hunters and predators in our search for food – like orcas, for example. But it might mean that – again, like orcas – we would excel in *group* hunting and not engage in predation against each other.

A complete list of challenges that we'd need to deal with now that we were living in the ocean would obviously be much longer than we've considered. And it's important to keep in mind how speculative this exercise was and how unpredictable natural selection is. However, for our purposes, we don't have to go any farther. The point was simply to ask the question, "Could 'intelligence' look different in the water than it does on land?," and it seems clear that the answer is "Yes."

The combination of the challenges of surviving in the ocean and the strategies available to us dictates that our species would focus our brainpower differently than we do now coping with the problems we face living on land. After millions of years of adapting to life in the oceans, what would aquatic humans use our large brains for? Instead of concentrating on tools, construction and artifacts, we'd might focus on dealing with one another. A sign of our intelligence might be a "social technology" that lets us manage relationships in a way that makes our lives more secure.

In light of these insights, our central question now becomes: When we look at how dolphins behave in their natural environment in the oceans (as opposed to experimental settings), do we see signs of "intelligence"?

Dolphin Intelligence in the Wild

In the last couple of chapters, we've surveyed the scientific research that suggests the strong possibility that dolphins have advanced cognitive and affective capacities. The question now is what those findings mean when we shift our attention away from the laboratory and direct it to dolphins in their natural habitat. Do we see evidence that dolphins use cognitive and affective capacities to solve problems that their environment presents them with? Do we see any signs that they think, plan, feel, choose their actions, relate to each other and/or communicate with each other in a way that is qualitatively different from what we typically expect from "animals"? Do dolphins use their large brains to live their lives in a way that's closer to humans, than, say, lions, tigers and bears?

Tool use

The exercise that we've just completed – imagining how humans would use our big brains to survive in the oceans – makes it plain that we have to adopt a particular perspective if we're looking for signs of "intelligence" in a mammal that lives in the water, as opposed to on land. For example, the difficulty of producing artifacts in the water combined with the fact that dolphins lack hands means that we probably shouldn't expect to find dolphins making tools. However, this doesn't mean that they can't use natural objects as tools – which appears to be the case among some of bottlenose dolphins.

In both Sarasota Bay, Florida and Shark Bay, Australia, scientists have observed dolphins apparently using bubbles to help them capture fish.[8] A dolphin lifts the back part of its body out of the water and then brings it down sharply into the water. This causes a loud splash and creates a trail of bubbles that may keep the fish from getting away. Scientists call the practice "kerplunking" after the sound made by the dolphin's tail.[9] It looks like the dolphins make something like a "bubble net" and use it as a tool in their fishing.

In Shark Bay, some of the dolphins apparently use sponges as a tool. Rachel Smolker, who began studying these dolphins at Monkey Mia in 1982, and whom we've met earlier in this book, observed a number of female dolphins carrying around sponges on their rostra. Because of the difficult water conditions in her study site, Smolker wasn't able to verify conclusively how the dolphins were using the sponges. But she concluded that the most likely explanation was that they were using them for protection as they foraged for food. The floor of Shark Bay is inhabited by scorpionfish, stingrays, stonefish,

---

[8] R. S. Wells, D. J. Boness, and G. B. Rathbun, "Behavior," in J. E. Reynolds III and S. A. Rommell (eds) *Biology of Marine Mammals* (Washington, DC: Smithsonian Institution Press, 1999), p. 361.

[9] John E. Reynolds III, Randall S. Wells, and Samantha D. Eide, *The Bottlenose Dolphin: Biology and Conservation* (Gainesville, FL: University of Florida Press, 2000), p. 130.

and other creatures that could produce a painful, even potentially lethal injury to a dolphin. As Smolker explains:

> All of these nasty creatures could be hazardous to a foraging dolphin, and some are particularly common in this channel. The dolphins are most likely using their sponges to shield themselves from the spines, stingers and barbs of creatures they encounter. They could also be shielding themselves from abrasion. Dolphins sometimes poke their beaks into the sand and bottom debris after burrowing fish. Using a sponge might help them to avoid getting scratched and cut by small sharp bits of shell and stone."[10]

However, the significance of Smolker's discovery doesn't stop there. The scientist also discovered that this behavior is apparently taught by one generation to the next, thus constituting what she refers to as "a cultural tradition of tool use.[11]

Social intelligence

As interesting as these two possible examples of tool use are, however, the nature of an aquatic environment militates against finding many such examples. Our primary evidence for examples of cognitive and affective sophistication in wild dolphins is found in how dolphins deal with each other, that is, in their "social intelligence."

A number of scientists support this idea. Peter Tyack, a senior scientist at the Woods Hole Oceanographic Institution who has studied cetacean communication since the early 1980s, argues that large brains evolved in dolphins to support complicated social functions.[12] Smolker reports her "powerful realization that these dolphins spend most of their time and mental energy sorting out their relationships."[13] She remarks about Nicky, one of the dolphins that she studies, "Her mind is a social mind, her intellectual skills lie in the realm of relationships, politics, social interaction."[14] In essence, these scientists are referring to what Howard Gardner regards in humans as the "intelligences" that make it possible for us to deal effectively with others. Gardner

[10] Rachel Smolker, *To Touch a Wild Dolphin* (New York: Doubleday, 2001), pp. 112–113.

[11] Ibid., pp. 112–114.

[12] Peter L. Tyack, "Communication and Cognition," in John E. Reyholds III and Sentiel A. Rommel (eds) *Biology of Marine Mammals* (Washington, DC: Smithsonian Institution Press, 1999), pp. 317–318.

[13] Smolker, *Touch*, p. 254.

[14] Ibid., p. 242.

calls these "intrapersonal intelligence" ("the capacity to understand oneself, to have an effective working model of oneself – including one's own desires, fears, and capacities – and to use such information effectively in regulating one's own life") and "interpersonal intelligence" ("a person's capacity to understand the intentions, motivations, and desires of other people and, consequently, to work effectively with others").[15]

Dolphin social life

Before we look for specific examples of social intelligence, however, we should have a general idea of the context in which they'll occur – that is, the basics of dolphin social life. There is an extensive research literature about dolphin social life, so a good deal has been discovered.[16]

First, there's no set size of a dolphin community. Groups can be made up of only a few dolphins or hundreds of dolphins. Membership can change in some cases, as dolphin schools aren't "kin groups," but what Ken Norris calls "a society of remarkably cooperative friends."[17] There may be instances of dolphins (primarily males) trying to assert dominance over each other. But there's no evidence of strict hierarchies.[18]

However, the research shows that the basic structure of dolphin societies in the ocean is fairly consistent. The overall group consists of three main types of smaller groups: female and nursery groups, juvenile groups and male groups (usually pairs).

[15] Garner, *Intelligence Reframed*, p. 43.
[16] For some good sources on dolphin social life, see Janet Mann, Richard C. Connor, Peter L. Tyack, and Hal Whitehead (eds) *Cetacean Societies: Field Studies of Dolphins and Whales* (Chicago: University of Chicago Press, 2000); Richard C. Connor and Dawn Micklethwaite Peterson, *The Lives of Whales and Dolphins* (New York: Henry Holt and Company, 1994); Kenneth S. Norris, *Dolphin Days: The Life and Times of the Spinner Dolphin* (New York and London: W. W. Norton, 1991); Kenneth S. Norris, Bernd Würsig, Randall Wells, and Melany Würsig, *The Hawaiian Spinner Dolphin* (Berkeley, CA: University of California Press, 1994); Karen Pryor and Kenneth S. Norris (eds) *Dolphin Societies: Discoveries and Puzzles* (Berkeley, CA: University of California Press, 1991); John E. Reynolds III, Randall S. Wells, and Samantha D. Eide, *The Bottlenose Dolphin: Biology and Conservation* (Gainesville, FL: University Press of Florida, 2000).
[17] Kenneth S. Norris, "Comparative View of Cetacean Social Ecology, Culture, and Evolution," in Kenneth S. Norris, Bernd Würsig, Randall S. Wells, Melany Würsig with Shannon M. Brownlee, Christine M. Johnson, Jody Solow, *The Hawaiian Spinner Dolphin* (Berkeley, CA: University of California Press, 1994), p. 342.
[18] On dominance behaviors, see Reynolds, Wells and Eide, *The Bottlenose Dolphin*, pp. 124–125.

Mothers with babies swim together, as do pregnant females. Sometimes the females are related to each other; sometimes not. However, it's not unusual to see more than one generation of females together: a baby, a mother, and a grandmother. A baby's brother or sister may also be seen with the mother after the birth. However, these female dolphin groups aren't the tight matri-archal pods we see with orcas. Membership may change over time, and the females aren't necessarily related to each other. The baby will also be watched over by babysitters, often the baby's sibling. Sometimes, this even involves dolphins of different species. For example, Denise Herzing has seen cases of young female spotted dolphins babysitting bottlenose calves in the Bahamas.[19] Child rearing is apparently no easier among dolphins than among humans. Mothers have to teach the babies how to fish and the basics of making their way in the group. Sometimes a young dolphin behaves appropriately. But Herzing has observed that sometimes he or she gets so out of line that the only way a mother can discipline it is take it to the bottom, buzz it a bit with sound and hold it down on the bottom until it gets the point.

Calves stay with their mothers three or four years, at which time the mother usually has another baby. Calves nurse throughout this time, but they also learn how to fish. Calves also interact with other young dolphins in "playpens" created by a ring of protective adults.[20]

After leaving their mothers, young dolphins associate mainly with other juven-iles for the next few years. They start learning dolphin social behavior in these mixed sex groups – mating and mock fighting, for example – and they may baby-sit. In fact, the point of babysitting may actually be more to teach the young dolphins how to be parents than to allow the mother to fish more easily than she could with a baby in tow.[21]

At about age 9, the females become sexually mature, generally have their first baby and associate mainly with other females. Males apparently reach maturity later than females, and so remain in the juvenile groups longer. Young adult males begin to form relationships with other males and ultimately form a long-term bond with another male dolphin that can last for decades. These male pairs are usually found on the outer edge of the group, perhaps acting as sentries. Sometimes adult males are also seen overseeing juvenile groups.[22]

---

[19] Denise Herzing, *The Wild Dolphin Project: Long-term Interaction of Atlantic Spotted Dolphins in the Bahamas* (Jupiter, FL: The Wild Dolphin Project, 2002), p. 56.
[20] For example, Reynolds, Wells and Eide report this taking place among the Sarasota Bay bottlenose dolphins. *Bottlenose Dolphin*, p. 121.
[21] Ibid., p. 121.
[22] Norris, *Dolphin Days*, pp. 165–166.

Among the Hawaiian spinner dolphins that marine scientist Ken Norris observed, there was even a daily cycle of activity. The dolphins would enter shallow coves or bays in the early morning. They would transition into rest. They'd rest from late morning to early afternoon. After four to five hours, the dolphins would become more alert and begin a characteristic "zig-zag swimming" which moved the school towards the ocean. Eventually, somewhere between two hours before sunset and one hour after sunset, the school headed out to deep water to hunt through the night.[23]

Cooperative fishing

Even this quick overview of dolphin social life reveals some important areas where we may find examples of social intelligence, that is, dolphins using cognitive and affective capacities to operate more effectively in a group. Let's start with one of the most mundane, but most important, parts of their life – fishing.

We saw in the last chapter that some of the fishing practices of different groups of dolphins (hydroplaning, using mud rings and cooperative herding) suggest an ability to solve problems with novel solutions. However, one of these examples (herding) is a particularly good example of cooperative behavior. Bernd Würsig describes a striking example of complex, cooperative feeding by dusky dolphins in an area of 10 to 20 square kilometers (c. 6–12 square miles) of the South Atlantic. Up to 30 small groups of 6 to 15 dolphins live in this area. When a group finds a school of anchovy, it herds it into a ball against the surface and apparently signals other groups of dolphins. More than 300 dolphins may ultimately get involved and behave cooperatively. Würsig writes:

> [D]olphin cooperation appears to extend throughout the herding and feeding episode. Dolphins apparently take turns going through the fish school to feed, while others keep the fish school tightly packed. I can argue that the prey is never truly secured, for if all dolphins rushed in to take a bite, surely the school would scatter and each individual dolphin would obtain less food than by cooperating. Such cooperation must require a highly refined communication, so that particular individuals do not unduly, either unwittingly or purposefully, take advantage of the situation and try to grab more fish and spend less time herding the fish than others. It is likely that dolphins know each other well enough to control the situation.

[23] Bernd Würsig, Randall S. Wells, Kenneth S. Norris and Melany Würsig, "A Spinner Dolphin's Day," in *The Hawaiian Spinner Dolphin*, pp. 65–102.

Herding and holding prey are not a stereotyped series of actions. At times, the fish school may fragment into smaller balls. When that occurs, a few of the dolphins break off from the group and herd the fish back into the central fish school. It is a dynamic, ever-changing system, which may require organization by these large-brained and communicative social animals. Differential role-playing and premeditation (such as a decision that certain members do particular things in order to meet various contingencies) may be important in this kind of cooperation. The degree of behavioral flexibility to encompass novel situations appears well developed.[24]

Cooperative fishing strategies extend even to working with humans. In Laguna, Brazil, for example, Karen Pryor observed bottlenose dolphins cooperating with local fishermen in a fishing strategy that benefits both sides.[25] About 30 dolphins out of a population of about 200 participate. As a school of fish enters the lagoon, the dolphins herd it and drive it to the fishermen, who are waiting in the shallows. Following the dolphins' cues, the men throw their nets. The dolphins then go after the fish that escape the nets. Pryor testifies to the complexity of this strategy when she notes that "the technique is highly ritualized and involves learned behavior on both sides." Since such cooperation has been going on for perhaps the last hundred years, more than one generation of dolphins has been trained in it.

For groups of dolphins – particularly groups of 200 to 300 – to be successful at handling such fluid situations as herding and feeding off of large schools of fish, it seems likely that the dolphins are using a variety of cognitive and affective capacities. They must know what will constitute an effective strategy in most cases. They must also be able to figure out how to respond appropriately to the way the situation changes from moment to moment. They must organize and coordinate their efforts based on knowledge about each other's

[24] Bernd Würsig, "The Question of Animal Awareness Approached Through Studies in Nature," *Cetus*, 5(1) (1983): 5–6. A similar example of cooperative fishing has also been observed in bottlenose dolphins in the Black Sea by V. M. Bel'kovich, who identified a variety of specific strategies for searching and hunting. V. M. Bel'kovich, E. E. Ivanova, O. V. Yefremenkova, L. B. Kozarovitsky and S. P. Kharitonov, "Searching and Hunting Behavior in the Bottlenose Dolphin (*Tursiops truncatus*) in the Black Sea," in Pryor and Norris, *Dolphin Societies*, pp. 39–57.

[25] K. Pryor, J. Lindbergh, S. Lindbergh and R. Milano, "A Dolphin-Human Fishing Cooperative in Brazil," *Marine Mammal Science* 6 (1990): 77–82. Similar practices have been observed in Mauritania and the Black Sea (R. Wells et al., "Behavior," in Reynolds and Rommell, *Biology of Marine Mammals*, p. 362). Susan Shane reports similar behavior along the shores of Australia and West Africa (*The Bottlenose Dolphin in the Wild* (San Carlos, CA: Hatcher Trade Press, 1988), p. 5.

strengths, weaknesses and dispositions. They're probably communicating with each other during the hunt. And throughout the process, all of the dolphins involved must be patient and show self-restraint.

Such highly cooperative fishing practices also require trust that everyone in the group will perform the way they're supposed to. And we may actually get a glimpse at how dolphins assess one another's trustworthiness in a behavior we sometimes see them do with humans. As Rachel Smolker describes it:

> Zzzzzzzzzzzzz, zzzzzzzzzzzzz, zzzzzzzzzzzzz. Frozen in place, I was standing in knee-deep water in Monkey Mia shallows, recording equipment hanging over my shoulder. Sicklefin had his open jaws poised around the calf of my leg and was emitting a crazy, screeching, cicadalike buzz that I had never before heard coming from any dolphin. In combination with the flash of his many fine, pointed teeth, I was reminded of a chain saw. This was obviously a test. If either one of us flinched, I would end up with a bloody, shredded leg. His teeth, though not particularly long, were sharp and plentiful, and I had developed a healthy respect for them. Bibi approached, attracted by the sound, and joined Sicklefin in his antics. Now both of them, tense and twitchy, eyes wide, ran their open jaws up and down my legs. Zzzzzzzz, zzzzzzzz, zzzzzzzz. They sounded like air-raid sirens. I tried to remain calm, and after a minute or so they moved off, attention diverted by the approach of a tourist. Whew, saved by a bucket of fish.[26]

Smolker was apparently being tested on how much she trusted these two bottlenose, and it's not unreasonable to think that dolphins might use some version of this test to assess one another.

Recognizing the fact that individuals have different traits – and especially that they may differ in terms of trustworthiness and dependability – is surely a sophisticated insight. Managing these differences in a group – as we saw dolphins do in these examples – is an impressive accomplishment.

Helping behavior

Cooperative behavior would certainly be expected among large-brained beings who live in groups. However, the ability to set one's own interest aside apparently even extends among dolphins to behavior that directly assists another.

The most frequently reported example of apparently altruistic behavior among dolphins is when one dolphin supports an ill or injured dolphin at the

---

[26] Smolker, *Touch*, pp. 147–148. A similar behavior has been reported on occasion at the Dolphin Research Center in the Florida Keys.

surface so it can breathe. In some instances, the helping dolphin even compromises its own health by doing this for an extended period of time.[27]
Sometimes dolphins help members of a different species. There are even
stories of dolphins helping humans in this way.[28]

Despite the short-term costs connected with giving serious assistance
to another dolphin, the long-term benefits make it a sensible strategy. It not
only keeps alive a member of the group in a situation where there's safety
in numbers. It probably also increases the likelihood that, at some point in
the future, the dolphin receiving aid will help the dolphin who is providing
it now.

Division of labor

Another area in which we might see evidence of social intelligence is the way
the group organizes its activities to make sure that the community is safe and
cohesive.

At least some dolphin communities appear to rely on a kind of "division
of labor" that members might be expected to perform in order to ensure the
smooth functioning of the group. Ken Norris's description of the way that
Hawaiian spinners approached particular activities almost makes it sound
like their "job." Norris observed that "within the protective school each
school member seemed to have hourly chores to do that helped maintain the
school's integrity."[29] "The dolphins engaging in [these behaviors]," he writes,
"did so with obvious singleness of purpose, shunting aside other behavior in
favor or what seemed almost like a 'duty.' "[30]

---

[27]   "Comparative View," in Norris et al., *The Hawaiian Spinner Dolphin*, p. 340. See also
R. C. Connor and K. S. Norris, "Are Dolphins Reciprocal Altruists?," *American Naturalist*,
119 (1982): 358–374, and M. C. Caldwell and D. K. Caldwell, "Epimeletic (care-giving) behavior
in Cetacea," in K. S. Norris (ed.) *Whales, Dolphins and Porpoises* (Berkeley, CA: University of
California Press), pp. 755–789.

[28]   For examples, see next chapter.

[29]   Norris, *Dolphin Days*, pp. 14–15.

[30]   Christine M. Johnson and Kenneth S. Norris, "Social Behavior," in Kenneth S. Norris, Bernd
Würsig, Randall S. Wells and Melany Würsig, *The Hawaiian Spinner Dolphin* (Berkeley,
CA: University of California Press, 1994), p. 246. Bottlenose dolphins in the Black Sea may also
show division of labor. See V. M. Bel'kovich, A. V. Agafonov, O. V. Yefremenkova, L. B.
Kozarovitsky and S. P. Kharitonov, "Dolphin Herd Structure," in Pryor and Norris, *Dolphin
Societies*, pp. 17–38; and V. M. Bel'kovich, E. E. Ivanova, O. V. Yefremenkova, L. B.
Kozarovitsky and S. P. Kharitonov, "Searching and Hunting Behavior in the Bottlenose
Dolphin (Tursiops truncatus) in the Black Sea," in *Dolphin Societies*, pp. 43–44.

Norris's spinners engaged in three separate types of activities that appeared in what he called cyclic episodes or "bouts" – echolocation, aerial behavior and caressing – that were performed when dolphins were alert and active.[31] Each "bout" lasted between 15 and 40 minutes, at which point a dolphin would cycle to another activity.

Each of these activities apparently has a specific purpose. Echolocation bouts probably help the school navigate, find food and detect predators. The magnificent spins and aerial behaviors of these dolphins produce sounds from the splash and the bubbles that are produced when the dolphins entered the water, and these may define the dimensions of the school. Caressing – the extensive sexual behavior among dolphins of both the same and different sexes – is, according to Norris, "the essential social glue of an extended society of 'dolphin friends.'"[32]

Norris also suggests two other "jobs" performed by specific males in the group. He suggests that certain males may have responsibility to protect the group. He notes that "nearly every time we ventured into a dolphin school we were met by a squad of older adult males, from half a dozen to twelve or more in number. Typically they interposed themselves between us and the remaining school, swimming resolutely, and without the evident *joie de vivre* of other dolphins nearby. They are the oceanic equivalent of what students of primates ashore call male coalitions, and they clearly have a job to do."[33] And he also suggests that some males may have the job of supervising the juveniles.[34]

Like the examples of cooperative fishing we saw above, these methods of organizing central activities in the group probably require a good deal of coordination, communication and cooperation among members.

Alliances: political skills

The fact that hundreds of dolphins cooperate and coordinate their efforts to herd, feed and handle their group's critical tasks certainly suggests a significant level of social intelligence. However, marine scientist Richard Connor has

---

[31] Norris, *Dolphin Days*, pp. 270–276. Christine M. Johnson and Kenneth S. Norris, "Social Behavior," in Norris et al., *The Hawaiian Spinner Dolphin*, pp. 243–287.

[32] Norris, *Dolphin Days*, p. 274.

[33] Ibid., pp. 28–29.

[34] Norris, "Comparative View," in Norris et al., *The Hawaiian Spinner Dolphin*, p. 336. Norris adds that this phenomenon may have been observed in the striped dolphin by Japanese researchers. Some version of this may also have been observed by Denise Herzing among the Atlantic spotted dolphins in the Bahamas.

documented a kind of sophisticated social behavior among the Shark Bay bottlenose dolphins that has been seen in only one other mammal – humans. Connor has observed not merely cooperation among individual dolphins, but the establishment of alliances among small groups of male dolphins. Connor's claim that these alliances are used to herd female dolphins for sex is particularly troubling for anyone who sees dolphins as happy, playful, gentle watersprites. But Connor's discovery does make dolphins look more like humans than like Flipper.

We noted earlier in this chapter that male dolphins regularly develop long-term bonds with other males. Among many dolphin communities, these are pairs. Among the Shark Bay bottlenose, these relationships are pairs or triads, and these small groups will form temporary alliances with other dolphins. Connor writes:

> Male bottlenose dolphins in Shark Bay exhibit two levels of alliance formation. First, males in pairs and trios, 'first-order alliances,' cooperate to form coercively maintained consortships with individual females. Second, teams of two or more alliances, 'second-order alliances,' cooperate in attempts to take female consorts from other alliances or to defend against such attacks.[35]

For example, Snubnose, Bibi and Sicklefin had an alliance with Wave and Shave, while Trips, Bite and Cetus were seen spending time with Chop, Bottomhook and Lamda and then also with Realnotch and Hi. Rachel Smolker describes one particularly dramatic example of these alliances in action.

> It was August 19, 1988, a day that none of us will ever forget . . . Walking down to the beach that morning, Richard [Connor], Andrew [Richards] and I could see from a distance that something was up. Snubnose, Bibi, and Sicklefin [three male bottlenose] were in, and whatever was going on, it was exciting, with lots of splashing and fast action. I could hear dolphins squealing even way up on the beach.
>
> When we got down to the water's edge, Dave Charles, the ranger on duty, filled us in, "Holeyfin [a female] is back, and the guys are pretty keen on her." Indeed, the males were paying no attention whatsoever to the twenty or so tourists who were wading in and out of the water with fish in hand. Instead they were surfacing in a tight, tense, synchronous rank behind Holeyfin . . . Snubnose and Sicklefin followed every move Holeyfin made, staying close to and usually just

---

[35]   Richard C. Connor, Randall S. Wells, Janet Mann and Andrew J. Read, "The Bottlenose Dolphin," in Mann et al., *Cetacean Societies*, p. 111.

behind her. Twice they rushed up toward Holeyfin from behind and tilted sideways as they dove underneath her, both angling their heads toward her genital area and buzzing intently inspecting her genital area . . .

During a momentary lull in the activity, we looked up from our work long enough to realize that two other dolphins were present. It was Trips and Bite, two of the males from the Trips, Bite, and Cetus triplet alliance. This was a rare event. Only once before had we seen Trips and Bite so close to shore at Monkey Mia. They were offshore dolphins, yet here they were, just twenty feet from shore. They floated quietly, oriented directly toward Snubnose, Bibi, Sicklefin, and Holeyfin, who seemed completely oblivious of their presence . . . [A]fter about half an hour, Trips and Bite headed offshore. [Shortly thereafter, we saw] at least five or six dolphins, in a wide rank, surging toward shore like a tidal wave. One or two of the dolphins leapt out of the water as they came rushing in to the Monkey Mia shallows. Then all hell broke loose.

As they swept in to the shallows, I heard horrible nasty growling and grunting sounds, like a group of lions attacking a family of warthogs. Snubnose, Bibi, Sicklefin, and Holeyfin took off at top speed to the west, and the others followed. A huge chase ensured, but they were all moving so fast that it was difficult to tell who was chasing whom. I heard the dull *thwack*ing sounds of dolphins hitting each other, but soon they were out of range of my hydrophone and away down the beach . . . The chase had gone on for quite a while, occasionally breaking down into bouts of fighting, hitting, ramming, and then more chasing. Although it had been hard to keep track of all that had transpired, one thing was clear: At the end of it, Holeyfin was now with Trips, Bite, and Cetus.

Realnotch and Hi had joined up with Trips, Bite, and Cetus to help them abscond with Holeyfin . . . Once Holeyfin was secured with Trips, Bite, and Cetus, the two alliances had parted company, but not too far away, apparently remaining within calling distance. For the first time, we were beginning to understand why alliances formed special bonds with other alliances (what we referred to as second-order alliances). Two alliances working together could overpower a third alliance and steal a female from them or put up a solid defense against attempts from other alliances to interfere with their herding.[36]

Connor even observed what he called a "super-alliance." This was a group of 14 males who, while they often switched "first-order alliance" partners, regularly cooperated with each other to herd females over a two-year period.[37]

[36]   Smolker, *To Touch a Wild Dolphin*, pp. 153–158.
[37]   Connor, Wells et al., "The Bottlenose Dolphin," in *Cetacean Societies*, p. 111.

As uncomfortable as some people find such aggression, this level of co-operation is very significant. Smolker writes:

> Cooperation between alliances added a significant level of complexity to the political world of male dolphins. Males had to sort out relationships not only within their alliances, but also with the members of the other alliance with whom they cooperated in a second-order relationship. This multilevel cooperation in dolphins was perhaps the most important discovery our research team would make. Cooperation among male mammals even on an occasional basis is rare enough, and alliance formation, where males form long-term cooperative bonds, is even rarer. But nothing as complex as long-term alliances among pairs and triplets forming long-term alliances with other pairs and triplets has been found in any other mammal besides dolphins and humans.[38]

Aggression

Smolker's striking account of a clash between two alliances brings up a part of dolphin social life that is typically ignored in popular discussions of dolphins – aggression. Despite the stereotyped image of dolphins as happy, playful beings who spend their days gamboling in the waves, there's no question that male dolphins, in particular, get aggressive with each other. Indeed, given the role of aggressive behavior in the lives of most living things, it would be remarkable if dolphins weren't at least as aggressive as other mammals. It would also be surprising if dolphins didn't use aggression as one of their tools in managing their relationships with each other. For the purposes of our inquiry, the question is whether they use aggression in a way that suggests social intelligence.

Dolphin aggression has been observed by Denise Herzing to take various forms.[39] Sometimes the aggression is more psychological than overtly physical, as when dolphins perform specific behaviors that signal displeasure. Tail slaps, jaw claps, blasts of bubbles, bubble rings, and open mouth behavior are common aggressive behaviors. Certain sounds (squawks) also signal a

---

[38] Smolker, *To Touch a Wild Dolphin*, pp. 158–159. Richard Connor points out that while chimpanzees also cooperate with each other, they do not do so at the level of "second order alliances," as these bottlenose do (Richard Connor, *The Lives of Whales and Dolphins*, p. 126).

[39] For a number of interesting examples of aggressive behavior, see D. L. Herzing, and C. M. Johnson, "Interspecific Interactions Between Atlantic Spotted Dolphins (*Stenella frontalis*) and Bottlenose Dolphins (*Tursiops truncatus*) in the Bahamas, 1985–1995," *Aquatic Mammals*, 23(2) (1997): 85–99.

FIGURE 5.1   S-posture

FIGURE 5.2   Open mouth behavior

warning or threat, as do particular body postures – displaying a penis, and adopting an unusual posture in which a dolphin arches itself into the shape of an S. Ken Norris believes that the point of the S-posture is to make the dolphin look something like a shark. This posture mimics an aggressive posture that sharks take, and Norris's spinners imitate sharks even further by moving their tail from side to side (rather than up and down) and swimming

FIGURE 5.3   Aggressive behavior

in a pattern similar to sharks.[40] Most of the time, these behaviors appear to be enough to get another dolphin to stop doing something annoying.

Herzing has observed that if things escalate, dolphins may face off head to head and make characteristic aggressive sounds.

Sometimes these exchanges escalate to the point where two dolphins will swim rapidly towards each other, rub together and repeat the pattern in what looks like a game of "chicken." And these encounters can even get to the point where one dolphin will tail-slap the other's head.

Males also assault each other sexually. In the Bahamas, for example, it is not unusual for Herzing to observe male bottlenose dolphins mounting the much smaller male spotted dolphins in what is clearly an aggressive episode.

However, in a way not altogether different from the Shark Bay alliances, Herzing observed what appeared to be spotted retaliation against such an attack. The day after the assault, a coalition of spotteds apparently sought out the bottlenose and initiated an aggressive encounter of their own.[41]

[40]   Norris and Johnson, "Social Behavior," in Norris et al., *The Hawaiian Spinner Dolphin*, p. 279.
[41]   Herzing and Johnson, "Interspecific Interactions", pp. 85–99.

FIGURE 5.4   Aggressive behavior

FIGURE 5.5   Aggressive behavior

FIGURE 5.6   Two male bottlenose dolphins with erections attempt to side-mount a
male spotted dolphin
Source: D. L. Herzing and C. M. Johnson, "Interspecific Interactions between Atlantic
Spotted Dolphins (*Stenella frontalis*) and Bottlenose Dolphins (*Tursiops truncatus*) in
the Bahamas. (1997). 1985–1995." *Aquatic Mammals* 23 (2), pp. 85–99

Are there any signs of intelligence in dolphin aggression? Mimicking a shark
as a way to scare either other dolphins, humans or sharks could be a conscious
and clever way to deal with a perceived threat. Another would be the spotted
dolphins' retaliation. As was the case with group fishing and second-order
alliances, getting a group of dolphins together to locate and punish an advers-
ary would seem to take a significant amount of cooperation, coordination and
communication.

However, a more important example of social intelligence in dolphin aggression may be that it's as restrained as it is. As physically rough as dolphin aggression gets, it appears as though dolphins only rarely inflict major or lasting
damage on each other. In short, they generally do not seem to set out to kill.[42]

[42]   There are reports that a community of bottlenose dolphins in the Moray Firth, Scotland,
have attacked and killed harbor porpoises, possibly because they compete for the same fish.
It's also been suggested that this group and bottlenose dolphins off the coast of Virginia may

To some extent, this may be because of what Ken Norris calls "a sweetness of disposition that makes them sweeter than we are" and "an inordinately co-operative streak."[43] However, it may also result from an awareness that killing one another is counter-productive because it removes someone from the group who can help in the daily work of the school. In such a group situation, the best strategy is to use just enough aggression to get one's desired result without doing any major damage – killing someone, making them feel so alienated that they want to leave the group or to stop pulling their weight, or fracturing the group into factions.

When you either directly observe or are on the receiving end of dolphin aggression in the wild, it's easy to conclude that the dolphins measure their reaction. In the Bahamas, I've observed a few angry encounters where a group of as many as 20 spotted dolphins went through bouts of head-to-head squawking among coalitions, and perhaps some aggressive swimming at each other by individuals. But then the dolphins apparently resolved their differ-ences and settled back into calm swimming.[44] In one of these encounters, as I inadvertently drifted towards the action, I heard a jaw clap from behind me directed at one of my fins. Understanding what this meant, I immediately left the area, and the dolphin involved went back to arguing with his compan-ions. On another day, as a few of us were watching some of the Bahamian bottlenose dolphins crater feed, a group of young males who had been physically fighting with the spotteds earlier in the day swam into the area and, about 30 yards away from us, let us know through their posture and sounds

practice infanticide (S. G. Barco, W. A. McLellan, D. A. Pabst, D. G. Dunn, W. J. Walton, H. Fearnback and W. M. Swingle, "Virginia Atlantic Bottlenose Dolphin (*Tursiops truncatus*) Calf Strandings: Dramatic Rise in Numbers and Emergence of Traumatic Deaths," in S. A. Rommel et al., (eds) *Proceedings of the Sixth Annual Atlantic Coastal Dolphin Conference*, 103, Sarasota, FL, May 1998, p. 3; and I. A. P. Patterson, R. J. Reid, B. Wilson, K. Grellier, H. M. Ross and P. M. Thompson. "Evidence for Infanticide in Bottlenose Dolphins: An Explanation for Violent Interactions with Harbour Porpoises," *Proceedings of the Royal Society of London B* 265 (1998): 1167–1170. See also, "Infanticide Reported in Dolphins," *Science News*, 154 (July 18, 1998): 36. There is not widespread documentation of such practices among other communities of bottlenose, and there are no reports of similar violence in communities of other species of dolphins. So it is difficult to know how to interpret these reports.

[43]   Ken Norris, private communication.

[44]   Richard Connor describes the same practice among the Shark Bay bottlenose: "Vexed bottlenose in Shark Bay will line up head to head, squawking in a comical burst of highs and lows that brings Donald Duck to mind. Sometimes these verbal insults escalate into a brawl, but often it seems that the dolphins squawk themselves out and go their separate ways" (*The Lives of Whales and Dolphins*, pp. 113–114).

that we weren't welcome. Again, as soon as we read the signs and left the area, they went about their business (which, one is tempted to speculate, on that day, at least, included threatening anyone smaller than themselves).

In terms of the question of whether dolphin aggression shows signs of social intelligence, in each of these cases, what the dolphins did *not* do is perhaps just as significant as what they did. The dispute among the large group of spotted did *not* escalate to physical violence. I received a verbal warning, *not* a painful poke in the ribs. And the young bottlenose dolphins simply signaled their displeasure; they did *not* come after us.

Similarly, although the bottlenose and spotteds in the Bahamas may have aggressive encounters, Herzing hasn't observed either species going to war against the other. (And it is easy to imagine that the larger bottlenose could wipe out all of the spotteds with little difficulty.) Whatever issues they have, they appear to work them out with limited amounts of aggression.[45]

If the controlled character of dolphin aggression is deliberate, it could be a sign of social intelligence.

————————————— Dolphin Communication —————————————

Communication: acoustic

What we've seen so far strongly suggests that dolphins communicate with each other. Cooperative tasks such as 200 dolphins herding fish imply some kind of communication, as do the variety of signals for aggression. Dolphins clearly communicate, but does dolphin communication involve any higher order abilities?

The complex whistles that dolphins make have been very much at the center of research and speculation about how dolphins communicate. And there's reason to think that dolphins use whistles to communicate. We saw earlier that dolphins have unique "signature whistles" that they apparently use to communicate their identity to each other. Signature whistles are often

---

[45]   Another possible example of limited aggression has to do with what Ken Norris calls "echolocation manners." He notes that during the Hawaiian spinners' "echolocation bouts," "Kehaulani and her schoolmates never sprayed each other with loud sounds, but when they were in an echolocation bout they generally swam below the others, head angled down and away from their tankmates . . . In one hundred passes, our echolocating dolphins never once sprayed the other animals directly with their click trains" (*Dolphin Days*, p. 272).

used as contact calls between individuals, e.g., mother and calves, separated by some distance. Adult dolphins also imitate one another's signature whistles – perhaps as a way of initiating interaction.

However, it appears as though they use signature whistles to communicate not only their identity, but something about their emotional state as well. The signature whistles of dolphins being captured can be warbled or broken into segments.[46] And when mothers and calves are separated in stressful situations, they whistle much more often than usual.[47]

The combination of mimicry and modulation suggests to Ken Norris that the Hawaiian spinners have a communication system that lets them know a good deal about each other.[48] He notes that this could allow a dolphin to say, "I'm so-and-so, I hear you, I'm over here, and I'm frightened."[49] There's even reason to believe that dolphins who know the identity of the whistler recognize the significance of the emotional content of the message. Richard Connor describes an interesting situation in this regard:

A large male pantropical spotted dolphin who was apparently a member of a herd in waters off Oahu, Hawaii, was captured and his nearly continuous whistles recorded. A week later the recording was played back to the animal's herd. When they heard the male in distress, the herd became alarmed and began to flee. The reaction was quite different, however, when the tape was played to a different audience, this time a herd of the same species that inhabited the waters off another island. This herd's response was one of curiosity. The dolphins approached the source of the sound; some even touched the underwater speaker.[50]

---

[46] Norris, *Dolphin Days*, p. 205.

[47] Richard Connor, "The Bottlenose Dolphin," in Mann et al., *Cetacean Societies*, p. 117.

[48] Norris explains:

We began to think of whistles as the basic stuff of what one linguistics scholar names Jakobsen has called a *phatic communication system*. That bit of jargon identifies an important concept, namely that in social animals, some sounds provide a communication matrix, a set of party lines running among all animals, over which the basic state of the school can be assessed by any animal listening in. With our spinners the whistles might be the wires of the party line, and the ways they were modulated carried the messages, whatever they might be. Thus, it seems to me, dolphins in their schools can know the state and identity of each member in the dark, or at considerable distance, and the school as a whole can react appropriately.

(Norris, *Dolphin Days*, p. 206)

[49] Ibid., p. 206.

[50] Richard Connor, *The Lives of Whales and Dolphins*, p. 83. L. S. Sayigh, P. L. Tyack, R. S. Wells, A. R. Solow, M. D. Scott, and A. B. Irvine, "Individual Recognition in Wild Bottlenose Dolphins: A Field Test Using Playback Experiments," *Animal Behaviour*, 57 (1999): 41–50.

Norris claims that this communication system actually makes it possible to communicate enough relevant information for the group to make "decisions." He describes the process by which a group of Hawaiian spinners "decided" to leave the shallows and head for the deeper water. As the spinners got more active after their rest period, they went through cycles of noisy clicks, whistles, squawks and zigzag swimming followed by periods of quiet and calm swimming. Norris characterized this stage as "indecision" that ultimately was resolved by a group "decision" that everyone was prepared to head out to sea to hunt through the night. He believes that the bouts of whistling ultimately established that there was enough group cohesion for the task at hand. And he claims that the dolphins assessed this by measuring the *timing* of one another's responses. When appropriate synchronicity was achieved, the group left the bay.[51]

Norris's claim that the *timing* of the dolphins' responses to one another is an important element in their communication system is particularly important to note because it speaks directly to the issue of the challenge of using sound to communicate in an aquatic environment. Norris explains that, in the oceans, timing is a more dependable factor than pitch:

> [T]he use of precise timing as a means of carrying messages is a feature especially appropriate to dolphins. The ocean is sometimes layered in a complex way by different temperatures and densities of sea water, and this can distort sound in unpredictable ways. What it does not distort nearly so severely is the timing within a series of sounds given close together. So we find dolphins timing each other's reactions when sounds come from a distance, rather than interpreting the variations in pitch.[52]

Peter Tyack's suggestion that some species of dolphins use echolocation clicks in communication adds to the plausibility of Norris's suggestion.[53]

Norris even suggests that the whistles are complex enough to serve as a tool to organize the whole school. He believes that whistles given by dolphins throughout a school define the boundaries of the school. And modulations in the whistles communicate information about "emotional state, level of alertness, hierarchy, the presence of food or danger, and similar information."[54]

---

[51] Norris, *Dolphin Days*, pp. 78–80, 207–208.
[52] Ibid., p. 208.
[53] Peter Tyack, "Functional Aspects of Cetacean Communication," in Mann et al., *Cetacean Societies*, p. 304.
[54] Norris writes:

> We propose that whistles are the basic organizational and structural signals class that regulates school organization and function, as Tyack's . . . work seems to support. We suggest that whistles given by

The system of communication that Norris proposes surely requires cognitive skills. Dolphins need to be able to recognize not only the pattern of other dolphins' signature whistles. They also need to understand the significance of the modulations and the timing of the sounds from other dolphins – factors which seem to communicate important information about members of the school and its environment.

Communication: non-acoustic

Whistles may be a good tool for communicating in the water because sound travels so far, but this very fact also makes sound a problematic medium. Being heard could put dolphins at risk because it alerts predators to their location. In testimony to this fact, groups of wild dolphins can be surprisingly quiet. Indeed, in the Bahamas, Denise Herzing has observed that when baby spotteds break into a characteristic, excited squawking, an older dolphin immediately comes over and calms them down until they're quiet. In addition, Ken Norris has noted that dolphins always make body movements when they generate sounds. He hypothesized that these movements are "packets of information" which are part of dolphin communication.[55] Indeed, Norris speculates that wild dolphins combine both acoustic and non-acoustic means to constitute a "sensory integration system" that communicates vital information throughout a school very efficiently and maximizes a school's ability to remain safe.[56] Body movements and posture, then, become critical elements of how dolphins communicate.

dolphins scattered throughout a school can define the limits and disposition of the school. Variations in how whistles are emitted can carry graded or analogic information about emotional state, level of alertness, hierarchy, the presence of food or danger, and similar information . . . Such a signal system can be modulated in intensity, frequency, and frequency pattern through time to produce a complex system of great potential information-carrying capacity.

(Sharon M. Brownlee and Kenneth S. Norris,
"The Acoustic Domain," in Norris et al.,
The Hawaiian Spinner Dolphin, p. 180)

[55]   Private communication.

[56]   Norris explains:

We came to suspect that the spatial disposition of animals within dolphin schools, in particular the interdolphin distance and the fluid geometry of echelons, was in part an expression of a crucial signaling system that allows organization of information transmission and response throughout the school . . . a *sensory integration system*.

Sensory integration means that the individuals of a school swim as parts of a supraindividual signaling system that allows sending and receipt of information and the passage and amplification

For example, Norris sees the ways that spinners display their body coloration to be part of how they may communicate. He writes:

> Spinners are very different from the robust, nearly unicolor gray dolphins we are used to in oceanarium shows. Their slim six- to nearly seven-foot body is patterned with a glistening dark gray cape laid over their backs from tip of snout to their flukes. Their flanks are paneled with exquisite pearl gray, sharply demarcated from the dark cape above and the immaculate white belly below. . . . Their eyes are ringed with a small black mask that extends as a dark band to their black flippers.
>
> This pattern, we found, is a complex signal system sending messages about position, intent, and activity to other dolphins. Some patterns send signals quite long distances through the clear water. For example, as one spinner rolls toward another in a passing school, the observer sees the flash of bluish-white bellies even beyond the range where the animal's body form may be easily discerned. The dolphins may use this flash as a signal of affirmation, because when it occurs they tend to move toward one another and often begin to caress.[57]

We've already seen how dolphins use certain postures and behaviors to signal aggression: tail slaps, open mouth behavior, adopting an S-shaped posture. Norris has also identified other postures that apparently communicate something: *belly-tilts* (a dolphin tilts its belly toward another dolphin) initiates or continues interaction; *tilt-aways* (a dolphin tilts its belly away) stops contact; *belly-ups* (one dolphin swims under another with its belly up) invite or request genital contact; *tilting the pectoral fin* signals diving; and *jerking the rostrum in a particular direction* suggests a turn.

Signals can even be found in *patterns* of behaviors. Norris claims that there are specific series of behaviors that initiate a caressing episode among the Hawaiian spinners. There are also patterns that signal the end of such an episode. For example, the two dolphins oscillate their swimming – cycling a few times from

of environmental information from the collective sensory windows. Very faint environmental information can be amplified so that all schoolmembers can receive it if a schoolmember receives a signal from the environment and then initiates its own signal through the school. The SIS can provide early warning of predators, and food or other environmental features can be localized. Mimicry among schoolmembers can "initialize" a communication between specified individuals and thereby indicate such things as relationship and hierarchy.

(Kenneth S. Norris and Christine Johnson,
"Schools and Schooling," in Norris et al,
The Hawaiian Spinner Dolphin, p. 235)

[57] Norris, *Dolphin Days*, p. 27.

very close contact, to moving slightly farther away, moving close again, moving away, coming close – then head for the surface, breathe and then separate.[58]

And then there are a variety of behaviors that, because they're observed so frequently, probably mean something. And because of how these behaviors look in context, they're most likely affiliative in some way.[59]

Communication: overview

Between whistles and body movements, then, dolphins can apparently communicate a good deal of vital information to each other. Some of the information is probably about specific facts, for example, the boundaries of the school, and the presence or absence of predators or food. But much of the information is probably about the physical condition or emotional state of individual dolphins. From these different pieces of information communicated throughout the group, each dolphin apparently constructs a mental representation of a critical, but abstract concept – the state of the school.[60] Such a system of communication surely requires a fair degree of cognitive ability.

────────── Social Intelligence and Group Cohesion ──────────

Norris's "sensory integration system" probably handles one of the major problems that dolphins face in the wild – how to communicate information

[58] Ibid., pp. 270–272; Norris and Johnson, "Social Behavior," in Norris et al., *Hawaiian Spinner*, pp. 246–247.

[59] For example, rubbing pectoral fins appears to communicate some kind of reassurance. Herzing has observed mothers doing this with young dolphins after disciplining them. Rachel Smolker reports that after Snubnose, Bibi and Sicklefin lost in their encounter with the other alliance, "Bibi and Sicklefin were petting each other furiously. It was as though they needed to reassure each other after such a defeat" (Smolker, *Touch*, p. 160).

[60] Norris claims that the spinners' "sensory integration system" allows each dolphin

to sense the spatial disposition of its comrades and thus to define the school's protective envelope for its members. This implies the capabilities that underlie the emergence of animal culture. That is, each dolphin must construct in its own mind a gestalt of the shape of the school at any instant from just a few data points. It must mentally fill in the spaces in three dimensions. At the same time, it must also make predictions about the immediate future. Receiving information that some members are indicating the imminence of a turn tells the dolphin what it must do. The dolphin is not following a leader *seriatim* but is instead behaving in terms of a more abstract conception – the state of the school.

(Norris, "Comparative View," in Norris et al., *Hawaiian Spinner Dolphin*, p. 334) to one another in a way that doesn't endanger the group. However, dolphins also face the challenge of ensuring that the group is cohesive. So if dolphins possess a high degree of social intelligence, we should be able to find mechanisms designed to build strong relationships. Dolphins appear to use a variety of ways to build such bonds. Some play and synchronized behavior are similar to ways that we ourselves foster a sense of connection with others, but one mechanism in particular – their sexual practices – is very different.

Like a number of mammals, dolphins engage in "play" behavior as a way of teaching young dolphins some adult behaviors. However, some of their play looks like "games" that aim simply at letting all of the players have a good time together. Herzing has observed that the Bahamian spotteds, for example, play what looks like a dolphin version of a combination of "catch" and "keep away" with a strand of sea grass.[61] The game involves only a few dolphins at any time, and the dolphin with the sea grass swims around, moving the strand around to different parts of its body (pec, fluke, rostrum) while being chased by the others. He or she ultimately drops it for another dolphin to pick it up, who then takes the lead. Interestingly, the game apparently has rules, such as, "you must wait until the dolphin with the grass drops it; you may not snatch it away."

Another way that dolphins build feelings of connection may be in bouts of synchronized swimming and breathing. Watching dolphins swim together is sometimes like watching a ballet, such is the precision with which dolphins move in concert with each other. In fact, in the male bottlenose triads in Shark Bay, if the surfacing of one of the dolphins is slightly out of synch with the other two, this signals that he's the "odd man out" in the group.[62] Dolphins have great capacity for imitating movements. Perhaps this ability facilitates social bonding. Even among humans, mimicking someone's posture is a way to establish rapport with them. For beings as social as dolphins, mirroring one another's movements may be a powerful device for establishing and communicating a sense of connection.

---

[61] Norris describes something similar among the Hawaiian spotteds (Norris and Johnson, "Social Behavior," in Norris et al., *Hawaiian Spinner*, pp. 272–273). Dolphins sometimes invite human swimmers into the activity. Terry Maas describes one such interaction in Terry Maas and David Sipperly, *Freedive!* (Ventura, CA: Blue Water Freedivers, 1998), pp. 120–122.

[62] Connor et al., "The Bottlenose Dolphin," in Mann et al., *Cetacean Societies*, pp. 104–105, 113.

──────────────── Dolphins and Sex ────────────────

As important as play, synchronous behavior and reassurance may be for building group cohesion, however, the most important way that dolphins affirm
their relationships is most likely through sex.

Sexual activity is an important part of dolphin social behavior. Norris observed
that the Hawaiian spinners might spend as much as a third of their day in
caressing bouts with many other members in the community.[63] And the
frequency with which captive dolphins have sexual contact is legendary.
Dolphins in captivity reportedly have about 10 sexual encounters a day. Dolphins appear to be bisexual by nature, they have numerous partners, and
sexual behavior can be observed even in very young dolphins.[64] In addition
to copulating between males and females, there is copulation between males,
caressing, buzzing another dolphin's genital area and pushing another dolphin
around by placing a rostrum against the genital area.

Sexual activity has such a variety of functions in dolphin society that some
scientists label it "socio-sexual behavior."[65] Unlike virtually all other mammals
(except such primates as humans and pygmy chimps), dolphin sexual activity is not tied to female estrus cycles. Dolphin sex takes place all year and is
affiliative, aggressive and recreational, as well as reproductive.[66]

There is general agreement among dolphin researchers that sex plays a
central role in forging and maintaining relationships among group members.
Norris describes it as "the essential social glue of an extended society of
'dolphin friends'" and "a means of assurance for them that they were in that
'society of friends.'"[67] Similarly, other scientists note that all of the touching
and rubbing among dolphins may serve the same function that social grooming does in primates – establishing and maintaining strong relationships

[63] Norris, *Dolphin Days*, p. 40.
[64] Reynolds, Wells and Eide mention a young male copulating with his mother, *Bottlenose Dolphin*,
p. 116.
[65] Connor, Wells et al., "The Bottlenose Dolphin," in Mann et al., *Cetacean Societies*, p. 104.
[66] Connor points to differences in copulation when he implies that males may not ejaculate
during social sex. He writes, "Bottlenose dolphins, it turns out, can produce prodigious ejaculate with highly concentrated sperm, but only during the mating season. The rest of the year,
sperm production drops off markedly, suggesting that the production of sperm is energetically
expensive, so dolphins don't waste it during times when sex is mostly social." (Connor, *Lives
of Whales and Dolphins*, p. 154).
[67] Norris, *Dolphin Days*, p. 274.

with other members of the group.[68] Primatologist Robin Dunbar argues that the equivalent of social grooming in humans is "gossip" – which, he argues, probably amounts to about 60 percent of how we use language.[69] Viewing dolphin sexual behavior as having a similar function certainly differentiates it from human sexual behavior and puts it in an interesting light. Ken Norris reportedly claimed that sex to dolphins was like a handshake to humans.[70] If we think of dolphin sexual behavior as "social grooming," it may be more accurate to see it as the dolphin equivalent of hanging around the water cooler chatting.

The Cognitive and Affective Skills Involved in Group Living

When we look at how dolphins spend their days in the wild and at the challenges that they face, the picture that emerges is dominated by the group. They live in groups, belong to different subgroups as they mature, fish in groups, play in groups, even have sex with many members of the group. They establish long-term, close relationships with some members of their community. They appear to maintain at least a decent relationship with most, if not all, members of the group. Tending to these relationships appears to be a central facet of life for dolphins – taking up as much as a third of their day.

When we step back and ask how dolphins may be using their brains in their daily lives, then, it appears that, as many scientists suggest, "dolphin intelligence" is most likely "social intelligence." But this means that they may draw more on *affective* than *cognitive* skills.

It's important to note that we do see evidence of some level of cognitive sophistication in such abilities as: using some natural objects (bubbles and sponges) as tools; carrying out complex fishing strategies; organizing the group's activities; using alliances; and understanding the acoustic and non-acoustic signals of their communication system. However, the challenges that they face in managing their numerous relationships are more likely *affective* than *cognitive*, and this is probably where they apply their brainpower. If we recall

---

[68] Wells et al., *Bottlenose Dolphin*, p. 116.

[69] Robin Dunbar, *Grooming, Gossip, and the Evolution of Language* (Cambridge, MA: Harvard University Press, 1996).

[70] Reynolds et al., *The Bottlenose Dolphin*, p. 116.

Howard Gardner's definition of intelligence as "a biopsychological potential to process information that can be activated in a cultural setting to solve problems or create products that are of value in a culture," we're reminded that the vast majority of information that dolphins need to process in order to solve problems may have to do mainly with *how to deal with each other*. Similarly, the most important instruments or "products" that they can create to help them solve problems are most likely their *relationships* with other members of their group. The dangers and limitations of living in an aquatic environment create strong evolutionary pressures to live and function well in schools. Principles of natural selection mean that aquatic beings with large brains who can develop capacities to live well in groups will survive while their autonomous fellows will not. We might say that, in the ocean, nature may select for specialists in relationships, not tools – for emotional sophistication perhaps more than for cognitive sophistication.

Consider the demands of dolphin social life. Forging and sustaining long-term relationships (such as the male pairs), managing first-order and second-order alliances, maintaining good relations with everyone else in the school, fishing cooperatively with hundreds of other dolphins, and being appropriately aggressive in a group situation probably require a variety of sophisticated skills that make the ability to use natural objects as tools look simple by comparison.

We saw in the last chapter, for example, that in order to solve the problems presented by John Gory and Stan Kuczaj, the dolphins had to grasp "the causal structure" of their environment. That is, they had to have a working knowledge of how gravity, cause and effect, and necessary and sufficient conditions apply to objects in the physical world. In order to come up with novel solutions to the problems they were presented with, the dolphins also had to be able to develop a mental representation of their environment.

As demanding as all of that is, however, now think about how much more challenging it is to understand one's environment when we add intelligent beings. The behavior of physical objects may be predictable once we understand the laws of nature, but things aren't so simple with beings with emotions and the power of choice. It takes much more for me confidently to say that I truly *understand a friend* and that I know how he or she will behave in certain situations than it does for me to say that I *understand gravity* and that I know what will happen if I drop a glass onto a concrete floor. To understand someone else, I need to recognize their emotional strengths and vulnerabilities, to learn how they see themselves, to identify their likes, dislikes and "quirks" (irrational fears, neuroses, etc.), to figure out how to approach them on sensitive issues, to know how to express anger at them without hurting the relationship, and the like. In short, I need to know what "makes them tick" emotionally.

To understand another person, I need the cognitive capacity to produce a mental representation of someone else's "inner world." In particular, I need to be able to fashion and grasp a mental representation of the critical differences between my friend's inner world and my own. When my friend and I have, for example, different emotional reactions to the same event, I need to be able to use my imagination to put together two things that are intimately connected in my friend's mind (fear and water, for example) that have no connection whatsoever in mine.

Such a mental picture of someone else's inner world will help me decide how to behave towards them so that we sustain our relationship and benefit from it. For example, if I want to enlist my friend's help for something, I will know the appropriate way to approach him. Of course, in order for my friend and me to have a mutually satisfying relationship, he must also be able to develop a mental representation of my inner world and to understand me well enough to deal with me in ways that preserve and strengthen the bond between us. And if my friend and I want to cooperate in accomplishing some task together, we need to approach it in light of our mutual understanding of one another. If not, odds are we'll fail at the task.

However, the kind of *understanding* of one another that we're talking about here can't be reduced to a series of factual statements. In some fashion, my friend and I have to be able to say either, "I know how you feel" or "I can imagine how you feel." To manage relationships with others, in addition to needing the cognitive ability to represent the inner dynamics of other people's inner worlds, I also need a variety of sophisticated affective capacities – respect, patience, acceptance of differences, trust, emotional honesty, emotional self-knowledge, a willingness to set aside my desires in favor of someone else's, pleasure at helping someone else, the ability to defer my own gratification when appropriate, the strength and self-respect to assert my own needs when appropriate, cooperativeness, compassion and affection.

It is obviously impossible to know which of these affective capacities dolphins have. However, dolphins are self-conscious beings with the ability to reflect on the contents of their consciousness. They should thus be able to reflect on their own emotional states, to understand those of others and to use this information in deciding how to act. They appear to be able to form strong bonds with other members of their school and to manage a wide range of relationships. In their socio-sexual behavior, they even seem to be able to manage a far greater amount of intense physical (and perhaps emotional) intimacy than the average human handles. Therefore, it seems reasonable to infer that they have a significant level of affective capacity.

Dolphin "social intelligence" and their "relationship brain"

The behavior of dolphins in the wild strongly suggests that they have sophisticated affective capacities. However, it's important to remember that this possibility is also suggested by what we saw earlier in this book about the dolphin brain. That is, evolutionary pressures may have created a brain designed primarily to process information relevant to managing the large number and varied character of relationships they have in a community.

Recall the distinctive traits of the dolphin brain:

- In comparison with the human brain, the dolphin limbic system may be stretched out over more of the brain, and limbic (that is, emotional) information may be more integrated into a variety of brain functions.
- The structure of dolphin neocortex suggests that higher brain functions in dolphins may be located more in emotional activities.
- Dolphin brain architecture could lead dolphins to have deeper emotional attachments than humans experience.
- The fact that the sensory and motor regions interlock with each other ("cortical adjacency") may give dolphins a more integrated perception of reality than we have. That is, they may be able to process information simultaneously more richly than we can from sight, sound and touch – something that would enhance their ability to use multiple senses to communicate with and to understand each other.

It is possible, then, that the dolphin brain evolved to support social intelligence – that is, that it is designed to allow dolphins to solve the problems they face *primarily* by working with other members of their community.

Indeed, Robin Dunbar suggests that the main use of big brains in mammals is to handle living in groups. Dunbar explains that living in large groups increases the amount of information that a social animal must process. Accordingly, he writes, "the evolutionary pressure selecting for large brain size and super-intelligence in primates did seem to have something to do with the need to weld large groups together." More specifically, Dunbar claims that "the principal purpose for which so much computing power was needed was, it seemed, to enable primates to form long-lasting, tightly bonded coalitions."

Dunbar has advanced the controversial thesis that language evolved in humans "as a kind of vocal grooming to allow us to bond larger groups than was possible using the conventional primate mechanism of physical grooming." In short, he says, "language evolved to allow us to gossip."[71]

Dunbar's thesis suggests an interesting line of speculation. Dunbar argues that the ratio of the neocortex (where thinking goes on in our brains) to the volume of the rest of the brain predicts the size of the group and social complexity that primates can handle. Humans have an impressive neocortex ratio of 4:1; however, dolphins may exceed that.[72] We have not yet seen any evidence of language in dolphins, so the large percentage of neocortex suggests that dolphins have developed a nonlinguistic, but highly sophisticated mechanism for managing their communities. Ken Norris alludes to something like this when he comments that, "The fact that [dolphins] can understand symbols and syntactic arrangements when trained must have its origins elsewhere in their lives than in anything like a language. I suspect it lies deep in the cultural level of organization itself."[73] Again, it appears that "dolphin intelligence" lies in "social intelligence."

Conclusion: Dolphin Intelligence

The passage from Douglas Adams that we started this chapter with is not as flippant and irrelevant as many people might think. Most of us would probably argue that the distinctive character of human intelligence expresses itself largely in what we create. Adams lists "the wheel, New York, wars and so on." Scientists and philosophers would surely also insist that we add "language" to that list. When we observe dolphins, we don't see any of these things. As Adams puts it, "all that dolphins had ever done was muck about in the water having a good time." Yet in Adams' story, this was enough to allow the dolphins to see themselves as the more intelligent species.

Setting aside for a moment the issue of intellectual superiority, what is clear is that the problems of living in the water faced by dolphins are dramatically different from those faced by humans trying to survive on land.

---

[71] Dunbar, *Grooming*, pp. 64–79.
[72] Ibid., p. 69. See Lori Marino, "Brain-Behavior Relationships in Cetaceans and Primates," pp. 209–210.
[73] Norris, "Comparative View," in Norris et al., *Hawaiian Spinner Dolphin*, p. 342.

"Intelligence" is ultimately just about the brain's ability to process information in ways that solve problems and enhance the survival of both individuals and species. So in dramatically different environments, "intelligence" will look different. As suggested at the start of this chapter, we should, then, regard the distinctive traits of "intelligence" as being "species-specific," and be open to Diana Reiss's idea that the intelligence of dolphins might be so different from ours as to be "alien."

Our examination of dolphin social behavior shows that their lives are more complex and more difficult than "mucking about." And it's important to appreciate how effectively dolphins have used the cognitive and affective capacities of their large brains to deal with the problems of survival. Their societies appear to be organized. They can handle the most important tasks of survival – finding food and protecting themselves against predators. They cooperate with each other – even forming second-order alliances in some communities. They keep aggression from getting out of hand. They appear to have both acoustic and non-acoustic ways to communicate vital information to members of their school. And they devote a good deal of time and energy to developing and maintaining strong relationships with other members of the group. Indeed, the centrality of relationships in their lives probably means that on a daily basis they process more emotional information and are called on to use emotional skills more than humans do. It is difficult to look at all of this and not conclude that there is an impressive level of intelligence behind it.

Dolphins have not produced what humans have. But their intelligence appears to have let them discover how to live within the limits of their environment and how to deal with each other. The way that dolphins live maximizes the odds that not only individual dolphins but entire species will have long and successful lives in the water. Since the same cannot yet be said of humans, asking which species is "more intelligent" may not be such a silly question after all.

CHAPTER 6

What Kind of Beings Are Dolphins?

Dolphins don't always fare well at the hands of humans. Dolphins in the eastern tropical Pacific Ocean are daily harassed, sometimes injured and even die in connection with the human fishing industry. Hundreds of captive dolphins are used for our entertainment and research. The fact that dolphins have sophisticated cognitive and affective abilities, however, implies that these cetaceans are a "who," not a "what." And this means that there's a serious question about whether human behavior towards dolphins is ethically justifiable.

As I explained in Chapter 3, the basic reason that humans expect other members of our own species to treat us in particular ways (to respect our dignity, for example) comes from the kind of consciousness that our brains produce. We are self-conscious, unique individuals who are vulnerable to a wide range of physical and emotional pain and harm, and who have the power to reflect upon and choose our actions. Because we can experience pain so intensely and because we value our ability to choose our own actions so deeply, we neither accept nor minimize it when other people hurt, coerce, threaten or manipulate us. We object to such actions so strongly that we label them not just as "inconvenient" or "unpleasant," but as "wrong." Ethics – our labeling actions as "right" or "wrong" – is grounded in the idea that the type of consciousness that we have gives us special capacities and vulnerabilities. When we label something as "wrong," then, we're saying that it crosses the line with regard to not respecting some fundamental feature that makes us human.

Humans have traditionally assumed that we are the only beings on the planet with this type of consciousness – and, hence, this combination of capacities and vulnerabilities. This book challenges this assumption by describing the relevant scientific research that suggests that dolphins also have this kind of consciousness.

This book is ultimately about only two questions: "What kind of beings are dolphins?" and, "What does our answer to the first question tell us about the ethical character of how humans behave towards dolphins?" Now that we've surveyed the major scientific research on dolphins – particularly the research on dolphin intelligence – we're in a position to try to answer these questions. This chapter will handle the first. The next chapter will tackle the second.

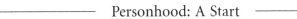

Personhood: A Start

The easiest place to begin an inquiry into what kind of beings dolphins are is to ask whether dolphins are "nonhuman persons." Recall from the first chapter that philosophers use the concept of "person" to refer to any being with certain advanced traits. The point of using a concept like this is to avoid the danger of anthropocentric bias. We'll see later in this chapter that even a concept like personhood is not as free of species bias as we'd like. But, for our purposes, the question, "Are dolphins nonhuman persons?" is a reasonable place to start.

You might be surprised to read the question, "Are dolphins *persons*?" It might not even make sense to you. "Of course they aren't *people*," you might say, "they're dolphins not humans." Yet despite the fact that many of us use "human" and "person" as synonyms in common parlance, the terms actually mean different things. "Human" is a biological concept, denoting membership in *Homo sapiens*. "Person," however, is a philosophical concept, indicating a being with capacities of a particular sort.

Although philosophers debate the appropriate criteria for personhood, there is a rough consensus that a person is a being with a particular kind of sophisticated consciousness or inner world. Persons are aware of the world of which they are a part, and they are aware of their experiences. In particular, persons are aware of the fact that they are aware, that is, they have self-awareness. And the presence of such a sophisticated consciousness is evident in the actions of such beings.

If we translate this general idea into a more specific list of criteria, we arrive at something like the following:

1 A person is alive.
2 A person is aware.
3 A person feels positive and negative sensations.
4 A person has emotions.
5 A person has a sense of self.

6 A person controls its own behavior.
7 A person recognizes other persons and treats them appropriately.
8 A person has a variety of sophisticated cognitive abilities. It is capable
   of analytical, conceptual thought. A person can learn, retain and recall
   information. It can solve complex problems with analytical thought. And
   a person can communicate in a way that suggests thought.[1]

Let's go down our list of criteria, then, and see how dolphins fare.

1. A person is alive

This one is easy. Dolphins are animals, so they are alive.

2. A person is aware

Dolphins are certainly aware of their external environments. Dolphins are universally placed high on the biological ladder, and the fact that they are aware
of the external world and able to interact with it is apparent from the way
that they handle the demands of living in the ocean and from the simple fact
that they can be so easily trained. When we get farther down the list, we'll
try to judge how complex a dolphin's awareness is. But there's little doubt that
their behavior suggests a significant level of awareness.

[1] I believe that this list captures the major traits that philosophers identify in various discussions of the characteristics of "persons." For example, D. C. Dennett lists: being rational,
being intentional and being perceived as rational and intentional, perceiving others as rational
and intentional, capable of verbal communication, self-consciousness ("Conditions of
Personhood," in *Brainstorms: Philosophical Essays on Mind and Psychology* (Cambridge, MA:
Bradford Books, 1976–1978), pp. 267–285). Joseph Fletcher offers 15 "positive propositions"
of personhood: minimum intelligence, self-awareness, self-control, a sense of time, a sense of
futurity, a sense of the past, the capability of relating to others, concern for others, communication, control of existence, curiosity, change and changeability, balance of rationality
and feeling, idiosyncrasy and neocortical functioning ("Humanness," in *Humanhood: Essays in
Biomedical Ethics* (New York: Prometheus, 1979), pp. 12–16). In addition, see A. C. Danto,
"Persons," in Paul Edwards (ed.) *The Encyclopedia of Philosophy*, vol. 6 (New York: Macmillan
and Free Press, 1967), pp. 110–114; David DeGrazia, *Taking Animals Seriously* (Cambridge:
Cambridge University Press, 1996), W. R. Schwartz, "The Problem of Other Possible Persons:
Dolphins, Primates and Aliens," *Advances in Descriptive Psychology*, vol. 2 (1982), pp. 31–55;
the essays in *What Is a Person?*, edited by Michael F. Goodman (Clifton, NJ: Humana Press,
1988). Also see the various essays in Paola Cavalieri and Peter Singer (eds) *The Great Ape Project:
Equality Beyond Humanity* (New York: St. Martin's Press, 1993) and Paola Cavalieri (ed.) *Etica
& Animali: Special Issue Devoted to Nonhuman Personhood*, 9/98. I owe "recognizes other
persons and treats them appropriately" to Professor Karen Bell.

3. A person feels positive and negative sensations

Most nonhumans react to cuts, bruises and broken bones as we do – with behaviors that suggest these beings feel pain. Dolphins, too, clearly act in ways that suggest they experience "positive and negative sensations."

4. A person has emotions

Among scientists and dolphin trainers, there is also little doubt that dolphins have emotions. But this is not surprising, since a growing number of humans seem willing to concede that many nonhuman species have some kind of emotional life.[2]

We've seen evidence for the idea that dolphins have emotions at a variety of points in our earlier discussion.

- As we saw in Chapter 2, the dolphin brain has a limbic system – the part of the brain that generates emotions. We also saw that emotional information may play a bigger role in the dolphin brain than in the human brain.
- When we discussed the basic traits of dolphin consciousness in Chapter 3, we saw Ronald Schusterman's account of an episode in which a dolphin expressed aggressive feelings and Denise Herzing's description of a grieving dolphin in the wild. Dolphins also show fear of predators and can become despondent after the death of a calf or companion.[3]
- As we saw in Chapter 5's discussion of dolphin social intelligence, a variety of dolphin behaviors are understood by scientists to communicate anger or displeasure.

Perhaps the most interesting point about dolphin emotions is that the emotional traits of dolphins appear to combine into the equivalent of our "personalities," what researcher Carol Howard calls "dolphinalities."[4] Trainers

---

[2]   For a popular account of such an outlook, see Jeffrey Moussaief Masson and Susan McCarthy's *When Elephants Weep: The Emotional Lives of Animals* (New York: Delacourt Press, 1995).

[3]   Susan Shane writes:

> Captive dolphins have been known to refuse food and starve themselves to death when a tank companion dies. Mother dolphins have carried the decomposing bodies of their stillborn calves for two weeks and longer. Such behavior indicates that social bonds between individual dolphins are very strong and emotional attachments are deep.
>
> (Susan Shane, *The Bottlenose Dolphin in the Wild* (San Carlos, CA: Hatcher Trade Press, 1988), p. 28)

[4]   See Carol Howard, *Dolphin Chronicles* (New York: Bantam, 1995), Chapter 5, "Dolphinalities."

see differences in curiosity, timidity, playfulness, aggression, speed of learning and patience. Some captive dolphins enjoy swimming with humans more than others. Some like learning new behaviors more than others. Even mothers differ; some refuse to cut the apron strings, while others encourage their young to become independent. Dolphins also seem to have what we call moods. Captive dolphins can be eager to work some days, lackadaisical on others, and stubbornly uncooperative on still others.

5. A person has a sense of self

It's one thing to experience physical pleasure, pain and a variety of emotions. But it's quite another to be aware that one is having these experiences and to be able to reflect on them. And so, we come to one of the most important requirements for personhood – self-awareness. Can a dolphin look inside and say, "I"?

There are a variety of grounds for believing that dolphins have some concept of self:

- As we saw in Chapter 3, dolphins may have a unique whistle called a "signature whistle." They reportedly use these whistles to initiate interaction, to stay in contact with each other when separated from a distance, and to communicate information about themselves.
- As we also saw in Chapter 3, dolphins can recognize reflections of themselves in mirrors as just that, reflections. To date, only humans and other great apes have demonstrated this capability. All other non-humans – and human children before a certain age – ignore the image or mistake it for another animal or child. For dolphins to join us in this group, they would clearly need the capacity to say the equivalent of, "The image in this surface is a representation of me. It is not some other dolphin."
- Dolphins can do things that appear to require a sense of self. Most importantly, in order to do the kind of problem-solving that we saw in Chapters 3 and 4, dolphins would probably have to be able to reflect on the contents of their consciousness – something that surely requires self-awareness.

6. A person controls its own behavior

By "self-controlled behavior" we mean actions that are generated from within the person, not by irresistible internal or external forces. In the case of nonhumans, this means at least a noteworthy ability to act independently of instinct, biological drives or conditioning. The capacity of a person to be the author of his or her own actions is important for two reasons. First, it demonstrates that a being's cognitive and affective states are sophisticated enough to control its actions. In addition, such control leads us to hold a person responsible for what he or she does.

Do dolphins control their actions sufficiently that we can say they *choose* them? Do they show any evidence of understanding and using a concept of *responsibility*?

Choice and control over behavior   We have seen evidence that suggests that dolphins control their behavior on a number of fronts:

- In Chapter 3, we saw examples of feeding strategies (the use of mud rings, hydroplaning and herding) that appear to be the product of deliberation and choice.
- In Chapters 3 and 4, we saw fascinating accounts of two unusual events: Rachel Smolker's lost tool kit being found by one of the Monkey Mia dolphins, and Wayne Grover's encounter with dolphins who solicit his aid to remove a fishing hook from a baby. Both appear to result from deliberation and choice.
- Most impressive from a scientific perspective is John Gory and Stan Kuczaj's research on dolphins' ability to solve problems, which we saw in chapter 4. There seems little question that the behavior or the two dolphins involved in this research resulted from thinking and choice.

Choice and responsibility   The ability of dolphins to choose their behavior is also suggested in the actions of a community of wild Atlantic spotted dolphins that has interacted with humans since about 1980 in the Bahamas. The dolphins initiated this contact, which typically takes place in shallow waters (about 20–30 feet deep) approximately 50 miles offshore. The dolphins appear to be motivated simply by a desire for social interaction – perhaps some combination of curiosity, socializing or recreation. (There's no food involved, and spending time with humans doesn't give them more protection from predators in their environment.) These dolphin/human encounters can last from 5 minutes to 4 hours involving anywhere between 1 and 50 dolphins. Given a dolphin's superior speed and agility in the water, the dolphins obviously control the duration and character of these interactions. Cetaceans are the only wild animals known to actively seek out contact with humans in the wild. It's difficult to imagine any other explanation for this behavior than conscious choice.

More interesting than the fact that these interactions give us more examples of choice, however, is an incident that raises the possibility that dolphins may both understand and utilize a concept of responsibility. This community of spotted dolphins has not only sought out human interaction, but it has allowed humans to observe aspects of its culture. Since 1985, marine scientist Denise Herzing has observed and recorded these interactions with the aid of a changing group of volunteer assistants. (I have been part of this group since 1990.) Over time, two distinctly different encounters have emerged. In the one, the dolphins desire a high degree of social interaction with the humans. In the other, the humans are expected simply to watch, as the dolphins go on with aspects of their lives. To date, these dolphins have shown: hunting and feeding; sexual behavior; disputes and the resolution of disputes; adult dolphins teaching the young skills like fishing; baby-sitting; disciplining the young; juvenile behavior; and both peaceful and aggressive interactions between different species of dolphins (spotteds and bottlenose). In one of the "observing" encounters that I was part of, a mother dolphin was teaching its calf how to fish. One of the human swimmers mistook this encounter as one in which interaction was appropriate, and her attempt to engage the calf distracted the youngster from its task at hand. The mother then swam in front of Herzing, performed a tail-slap (a sign of displeasure or attention getting), gathered her calf from the swimmer and returned to teaching its offspring how to fish.

What is striking about this action is that the mother dolphin tail-slapped in front of Herzing, *not the offending swimmer*. Given the context of this encounter and the history of Herzing's interactions with the community, it is likely that the mother targeted Herzing, and not the swimmer, because the dolphin recognized Herzing from years of encounters as the individual who was dominant in the hierarchy of humans and held her "responsible" for the actions of the other swimmers. Moreover, this is consistent with the way dolphins deal with each other because Herzing reports that this is exactly the way this signal is used when directed to a responsible party of a juvenile subgroup of dolphins. It is likely, then, that the mother dolphin's message had something to do with her sense of Herzing's *responsibility* for her group.

7. A person recognizes other persons and treats them appropriately

Do dolphins act in ways that suggest not only that they have a sophisticated inner world, but that they can recognize it when they encounter this trait in others? That is, do they recognize other persons and then respond appropriately?

Specifically, do dolphins act towards humans in ways that suggest that they recognize us as the type of beings whom we are?

We have two reasons to think that they do. First, dolphins seek out contact with humans, and they do so apparently only for the social contact. Second, they treat us appropriately, even generously.

Social interaction   Dolphins appear to be the only beings other than humans who will go out of their way to seek out social contact with another species. The community of wild Atlantic spotted dolphins that Denise Herzing studies is probably the best example of this. These dolphins began seeking out human interaction since about 1980, and they have continued, with varied levels of interest and enthusiasm, to interact with members of Herzing's research team and with passengers on dive boats.

The significant issue is why these encounters take place. The interactions satisfy none of the dolphins' basic survival needs. They receive no food or protection. The dolphins aren't touched or rubbed by the humans. There's no sexual stimulation. Moreover, the interactions themselves don't seem to be that rich from the dolphins' perspective. Even the best human swimmers aren't as fast or agile in the water, so we don't represent a challenge for them to swim with. As mentioned in the last chapter, these interactions occasionally consist of playing a kind of "seaweed keep away" with humans. But it seems unlikely that humans are amusing or interesting enough as play-mates to sustain the dolphins' long-term interest. So the dolphins' primary motivation in engaging in these encounters is most likely some kind of gratification that comes solely from social interaction with humans. It's certainly possible that they recognize us as beings who are similar to themselves – that is, "intelligent" – and they're curious about us in the same way that we're curious about them.

Appropriate treatment   The second reason to think that dolphins recognize us as persons is that they behave in ways that suggest that this recognition matters to them. That is, they behave towards us in a way that's similar to how we behave towards each other.

The most basic sign that we recognize someone else as a person is that we treat that individual as "some one," not "some thing." We appreciate their intrinsic worth, and we act accordingly. Surely, one sign that we recognize other persons and treat them appropriately is that we go out of our way to help them.

Recall that our survey of dolphin social behavior in chapter 5 showed that they engage in a fair amount of behavior that helps one another. For example, they assist ailing dolphins for no apparent reward. The dramatic story from chapter 4 about two dolphins at the Dolphin Research Center helping a sick dolphin new to the facility suggests that they value one another's life. Dolphins also appear to limit the amount of aggression they use against each other. Ken Norris even claimed that the dolphins he studied "have a sweetness of disposition that makes them sweeter than we are."[5] On balance, dolphins treat each other pretty well – probably better than how humans treat each other.

In general, dolphins also treat humans well. There are relatively few incidents of dolphins harming humans. And in a number of those cases, there's reason to believe that the humans involved had engaged in behavior that they did not realize was provocative.

However, the most intriguing aspect of how dolphins deal with humans is the fact that, for centuries, stories have been told about dolphins helping humans who have gotten in trouble in the ocean. These tales range from dolphins helping sailors navigate through dangerous waters to supporting people who have fallen overboard. During the 1998 South Caribbean Ocean Regatta, for example, a sailor fell into the ocean while moving forward on his boat to drop a sail. Because the seas were so rough, the rest of the crew lost sight of him. As boats in the race searched for a couple of hours, the swimmer found himself surrounded by a group of dolphins. At the same time, one of the boats saw two dolphins swim towards it, swim away, and then repeat the pattern. Even though the boat had searched the area that the dolphins were swimming towards, the crew felt that the dolphins were trying to tell them something. They followed the dolphins and were led to the swimmer.[6]

If dolphins recognize that we and they are both aware and intelligent, it wouldn't be unreasonable that they might value our lives and well-being as they do their own.

> *8. A person has a variety of sophisticated cognitive abilities.*
> *It is capable of analytical, conceptual thought. A person can learn,*
> *retain and recall information. It can solve complex problems*
> *with analytical thought. And a person can communicate in*
> *a way that suggests thought*

To most humans, the most important criteria for personhood are intellectual. Persons must be able to think analytically and conceptually. Their behavior must demonstrate cognitive capacities. They must be "intelligent."

We have seen a great deal of evidence in this book to suggest that dolphins have significant cognitive abilities:

---

[5] Private communication.
[6] "Dolphins Find Missing Sailor," *Cruising World*, March 1998, 10–12.

- In our discussion of the dolphin brain in Chapter 2, we saw that there is reason to think that it can support advanced cognitive and affective operations. It has a large cerebral cortex and a substantial amount of associational neocortex. Anatomical ratios that assess cognitive capacity place it second only to the human brain.

- The research we surveyed in Chapter 3 showed that dolphins appear to have not only consciousness, but self-consciousness. Their performance on the pointing and gazing experiments suggest that they can also recognize other minds.

- Research that uses television screens shows that dolphins understand representations of reality – something that requires conceptual thought.

- The dolphins' performance on John Gory and Stan Kuczaj's experiments on problem solving is particularly impressive. The dolphins demonstrated an array of cognitive skills needed to solve new and complex problems. They were able to "create a novel and appropriate solution in advance of executing the solution." They could represent the causal structure of their environment. And, perhaps most notable, the dolphins were able to operate in a foreign cognitive environment.

- Karen Pryor provided further evidence about dolphins' abilities in problem solving, innovative thinking, learning and cognitive flexibility.

- Lou Herman's research into whether dolphins can understand artificial languages is particularly striking. He showed that the two dolphins he studied can understand and work with the basic elements of human language (vocabulary, grammar, syntax, complex sentences, etc.). Herman's research provides additional examples of a cetacean ability to think abstractly and to operate in a foreign cognitive environment.

- On balance, however, the most significant evidence that we've seen for higher-order abilities in dolphins comes from what we saw in Chapter 5 about dolphin social intelligence – that is, the way that dolphins use their large brains in their natural environment rather than in controlled experimental conditions. We saw examples of tool use, social organization, cooperative fishing, political alliances, limited aggression, acoustic and nonacoustic communication and managing relationships.

Are Dolphins Persons?

Dolphins, then, do quite well at measuring up against a fairly traditional set of criteria for personhood – even without taking into account the distinctive features that emerge from the fact that they are aquatic mammals. They seem to have all of the traits that philosophers traditionally require for persons. The idea of a "non-terrestrial intelligence" is no longer in the domain of science fiction. Such beings apparently have been living in the Earth's oceans for millions of years.

Problems with personhood

As significant as our conclusion is that dolphins are nonhuman persons, it is important to consider whether the label *nonhuman person* reveals the full significance of the scientific research on dolphins. A major reason that philosophers use the concept of personhood in discussing nonhuman animals is to avoid the danger of anthropocentric bias.[7] However, if we look closely at the distinctive traits of personhood, it becomes apparent that the way we usually define the concept isn't as neutral as we'd hope. Accordingly, if we stopped our investigation here, our findings would be both incomplete and colored by unintentional species bias. And, if Diana Reiss is correct that dolphins represent an "alien intelligence," our inquiry, then, would be fatally flawed.

The easiest way to appreciate the point that the standard definition of "person" may not be "species neutral" is to consider a comment that Lou Herman once made in defending his use of certain terms to describe the linguistic abilities of Phoenix and Akeakamai. He explained,

> Some feel that you should use a term [that describes linguistic abilities] only if you can demonstrate that the animal uses it in all the ways a human does. That's obviously unduly restrictive. A dolphin might think that humans don't demonstrate swimming ability until we've demonstrated all the things a dolphin can do, like leaping fifteen feet from the water, staying underwater for fifteen minutes, swimming at twenty knots, and so forth.[8]

Herman's observation should be sobering. If we take the way that dolphins move in the water as the standard for "swimming," even the performance of the best human swimmers doesn't come close. Yet surely we wouldn't say that this means that humans were unable to swim. In other words, when we specify the criteria for complex abilities, it's important to recognize how

---

[7] See, for example, Paola Cavalieri and Peter Singer (eds) *The Great Ape Project: Equality Beyond Humanity* (New York: St. Martin's Press, 1993) and Paola Cavalieri (ed.) *Etica & Animali: Special Issue Devoted to Nonhuman Personhood*, 9/98.

[8] "Interview with Lou Herman," *Omni*, June (1989): 86.

differently things might look from the perspective of other species. In our investigation, it's important to recognize the significance of the dramatic difference in the environments in which humans and dolphins evolved – and yet, this is precisely what standard definitions of personhood fail to do.

If we go back and look at our list of traits of a "person" with these cautions in mind, we will see that our criteria are not as unbiased and "species-neutral" as we first think they are. The problem lies both in what our definition of personhood places most emphasis on and in what it leaves out.

The problem with personhood: what we're emphasizing, or, the tyranny of "language"

Thinkers often discuss the question of whether dolphins are the kinds of beings who deserve special consideration in a way that, in effect, commits the human equivalent of the very mistake that Lou Herman's "swimming" comment warns us of. Where we set the bar extremely high, however, is in terms of the cognitive traits that our species excels in – particularly language. Worse still, this mistake is made even by individuals who are consciously committed to avoiding it.

Steven Wise, for example, is a pioneer in the field of animal rights law who has been trying for years to get courts to extend legal personhood to include at least some nonhuman animals.[9] He is sensitive to the problem of speciesism, and he even recognizes that "we mustn't think human intelligence the only intelligence."[10] However, Wise's discussion of dolphins focuses almost exclusively on their *linguistic* capabilities.[11] In addition, on a "practical autonomy" scale that Wise has developed to show how much some nonhumans deserve legal recognition, dolphins fall below bonobos, gorillas and orangutans.[12] Wise's explanations of the higher level of "mental abilities" evidenced by the primate research subjects described in the scientific literature he examined – Chantek (orangutan), Koko (gorilla) and Kanzi (bonobo) – primarily detail how well these three primates perform on *human* tasks (human intelligence tests, tests related to assessing the developmental progress of human children, the ability

[9]   Steven M. Wise, *Rattling the Cage: Toward Legal Rights for Animals* (Cambridge, MA: Perseus Publishing, 2000) and *Drawing the Line: Science and the Case for Animal Rights* (Cambridge, MA: Perseus Publishing, 2002).

[10]   Wise, *Drawing the Line*, p. 45.

[11]   See Wise, "Phoenix and Ake," Chapter 8 of *Drawing the Line*.

[12]   Wise, *Drawing the Line*, p. 241.

to use elements of human language, etc.). In other words, other primates rank higher than dolphins because they're *more like us* – which, given our biological relationship, is no surprise.

The problem with language

Such a criticism of thinkers like Wise may seem unfair. Isn't it reasonable to think of "language" as simply the tool that any being with thoughts and beliefs would use when it reflects on the contents of its consciousness, when it manipulates its own ideas, and when it tries to communicate those thoughts and beliefs to other intelligent beings? And if we don't see any evidence of this kind of tool, wouldn't it be reasonable to conclude that such a being lacks the kind of sophisticated inner world that most humans would insist on before accepting the idea that such beings have moral standing, that is, that they deserve special consideration when we interact with them?

A rudimentary definition of "intelligence" can apply across species.[13] Why can't we think of language as just a particular facet of higher intelligence – the basic tool that's used in processing and working with information? Why is it anthropocentrism to insist that dolphins (or any nonhuman species) demonstrate at least elementary linguistic abilities before they "count" in a moral calculation? The answer to this question is that "intelligence" is best understood as a *species-specific* trait. That is, there is good reason to accept the possibility that large-brained species who evolved in dramatically different environments adapted to these conditions in very different ways – both externally and internally.

Language is not some magic, ethereal gift of the gods. Language (in the form that we use it) is a biological adaptation by humans. It arose and evolved because language was useful to our ancestors in dealing with the challenges in their environment. Yet language – at least in the form that it's developed in humans – may not be useful in every set of evolutionary conditions. If dolphins lack language, it may be because it's not a particularly helpful tool in the oceans, not because dolphins lacked the intellectual capacity for developing it had it been useful.

[13]   We saw in the preceding chapter that Howard Gardner's definition of intelligence as "a biopsychological potential to process information that can be activated in a cultural setting to solve problems or create products that are of value in a culture" was something that we could use as at least a reasonable point of departure in discussing dolphins' cognitive capabilities. Howard Gardner, *Intelligence Reframed* (New York: Basic Books, 1999), pp. 33–34.

The adaptive character of language in humans

Part of the problem here is that many humans generally do not fully understand what we use language for. Many of us see language as the tool that lets
humans use our rationality in solving the problems that our environment has
thrown at us over the centuries. Language lets us develop science, medicine,
philosophy, art, law and all of the other achievements that are part of human
civilization.

While there's no denying what language has let us accomplish, there are
also, however, some alternative perspectives about language that deserve
consideration. First, as noted in the preceding chapter, primatologist Robin
Dunbar has argued that language evolved primarily as a way for us to handle
living in groups. Dunbar has advanced the controversial thesis that language
evolved in humans "as a kind of vocal grooming to allow us to bond larger
groups than was possible using the conventional primate mechanism of
physical grooming." In short, he says, "language evolved to allow us to gossip"
– something which, according to Dunbar, amounts to about 60 percent of
how we use language.[14]

Dolphins are also highly social, and, as we saw in the preceding chapter,
they may use their large brains mainly for social intelligence – that is, to
manage their relationships. However, from the perspective of Dunbar's
theory, if dolphins found nonlinguistic ways to build social cohesion, there
would have been less evolutionary pressure to develop something analogous
to human language. And dolphins unquestionably have ways of reinforcing
relationships and building social cohesion.

Second, Dunbar's idea that language's primary function has to do with
managing our relationships is supported by research suggesting that how we
use language has less to do with truth than with lies. University of Massachusetts
social psychologist Robert Feldman has found that all of us may lie more than
we realize. In one study 60 percent of Feldman's subjects lied, with an average of 2 to 3 lies per 10-minute period; both men and women lied, but the
two sexes told different types of lies: women told lies that made someone else
feel better, while men lied in ways that made themselves look better.[15] In another
study, Feldman found that males lied 2 to 3 times more than women, but women

[14]   Robin Dunbar, *Grooming, Gossip, and the Evolution of Language* (Cambridge, MA: Harvard
University Press, 1996), pp. 78, 79.
[15]   R. S. Feldman, J. A. Forrest, and B. R. Happ, "Self-presentation and Verbal Deception: Do
Self-presenters Lie More?" *Basic and Applied Social Psychology*, 24 (2002): 163–170.

were likely to be better at it.[16] That is, at least in our culture, we may use language more to bend the truth than to tell the truth. While most of us would dismiss the lies that Feldman is talking about as harmless "white lies," the fact remains that we may use language more to smooth out our dealings with other people (more of a social and emotional task) than to state the truth (more of a cognitive task).

We even regard the capacity to deceive to be a sign of intelligence, because it requires the ability to have intentions and to make inferences about the mental states of other people. When we lie, we try to get someone else to accept as true a belief that we know to be false. The ability to deceive is even a kind of benchmark in human development. When children reach the point where they're able to lie, it's taken to be a sign that they've grown to a stage where they have what child psychologists a "theory of mind."[17] Similarly, the claim that some nonhumans can deceive is offered as a sign of that species' intelligence.[18]

Language clearly makes it easier to deceive others, and deception of other humans must have been a useful (that is, adaptive) strategy in the course of our species' evolution. In the ocean, however, deception may not be as useful. Deception of natural predators is helpful – which is probably why dolphins mimic sharks. But given the importance of trust, cooperation and dependable relationships in dolphin communities, deceiving other dolphins may lead to little, if any, benefit.

It's even possible that dolphins may actually be incapable of successfully deceiving each other. In humans, there are many physical signs that someone's lying. Outward signs include everything from avoiding eye contact to increased swallowing and face touching.[19] Less obvious are changes in

---

[16] R. S. Feldman, J. Tomasian and E. J. Coats, "Adolescents' Social Competence and Nonverbal Deception Abilities: Adolescents with Higher Social Skills Are Better Liars," *Journal of Nonverbal Behavior*, 23 (1999): 237–249.

[17] That is, the child recognizes that: people have different mental states (beliefs, intentions, desires, etc.); the fact that a child knows something doesn't mean that someone else does as well; there's a connection between these states and what people do; and if you can manipulate the contents of someone else's consciousness (e.g., their beliefs), you can influence their actions.

[18] For example, Donald Griffin writes, "In fact, deceptive communication may be more rather than less likely to require conscious thinking that accurate expression of what an animal feels, desires or believes" (*Animal Minds*, Chicago: University of Chicago Press, 1992, p. 196). Also see Marc D. Hauser, *Wild Minds: What Animals Really Think* (New York: Henry Holt and Company, 2000), esp. Chapter 7, "Tools of Deceit."

[19] Psychiatrist and neurologist Alan R. Hirsch, M. D. claims that there are 23 verbal and nonverbal signs that can help determine whether a person is lying. A. R. Hirsch, "Physical and Verbal Signs of Lying," *Directions in Psychiatry*, 23(2003): 15–19.

breathing, heart rate and perspiration – which is what polygraphs track. There's even evidence that certain parts of our brain are more active when we lie than when we tell the truth.[20] Since dolphin communication may require considerable sensitivity to posture and body movements, the average dolphin may be more perceptive at reading the nonverbal signals of deception than the average human is. In addition, dolphin echolocation might be able to detect any internal signals of deception, such as, increased heart rate. That is, to dolphins, signs of deception might be as noticeable as changes in the length of Pinocchio's nose.

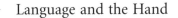

Language and the Hand

The idea that dolphins lack language because their ancestors didn't experience pressures to develop such an adaptation leads us to another reason that making the equivalent of human language a necessary condition of higher intelligence is anthropocentric – the relationship between human language and the human hand.

One of the most intriguing sources of support for the idea that "intelligence" does not mean precisely the same thing when we talk about humans and dolphins comes from an unlikely source – the unintended implications of a physician's speculations about the relationship between the brain and the hand. Frank Wilson, a neurologist who has specialized in the rehabilitation of hand injuries, became interested in paleoanthropology – the study of ancient human origins – and he has put forth a fascinating theory about the relationship between the human hand and the brain. In his *The Hand: How Its Use Shapes the Brain, Language and Human Culture*, Wilson argues that the character of human intelligence – and particularly the character of human language – are largely a function of, what Wilson calls, "the logic of the hand." Wilson argues that the hand and the brain "co-evolved," with the development of the former driving the development of the latter.[21] He argues that "any theory of human intelligence which ignores the interdependence of

[20]   D. D. Langleben, L. Schroeder, J. A. Maldjian, R. C. Gur, S. McDonald, J. D. Ragland, C. P. O'Brien and A. R. Childress, "Brain Activity during Simulated Deception: An Event-Related Functional Magnetic Resonance Study," *Neuroimage*, 15(3) (March 2002): 727–732.

[21]   Frank Wilson, *The Hand: How Its Use Shapes the Brain, Language and Human Culture* (New York: Random House, 1998), p. 169.

hand and brain function, the historic origins of that relationship, or the impact of that history on developmental dynamics in modern humans, is grossly misleading and sterile."[22]

If Wilson is correct, another reason that dolphins may lack some precise analog to human language is that *they lack hands*. And this gives us still more reason to refrain from thinking about language (in the way that humans construct, use and understand it) as a trait that we can assume is universally a feature of higher intelligence.

Because this issue is so important, it deserves to be discussed in detail.

Wilson, the brain, the hand and language

Wilson bases his claim on the fundamental Darwinian point that the character, abilities and organs of all living beings result from the interaction between an organism and its environment. Wilson's view of human evolution proceeds from the ideas of anthropologist Sherwood Washburn who argues that the brain was the last organ to evolve in humans and that this evolution was driven by the increase in tool use among our earliest ancestors. More importantly, Wilson sees this process as shaping the character of human intelligence and, specifically, as resulting in the origins of human language. Wilson writes, "It is a virtual certainly that complex social structure – and language – developed gradually in association with the spread of more highly elaborated tool design, manufacture and use." Wilson notes that anthropologist Peter C. Reynolds claims that stone tool manufacture may very well have been done by small groups of people working together, and that this activity would have required some means of communication – "In other words, cooperative tool manufacture could have provided a crucial precondition for the evolution of language."[23]

Wilson also finds backing for this hand–brain–language perspective in the position of three prominent linguists, David Armstrong, William Stokoe and Sherman Wilcox who argue that human language may have been created first in the hands. They write:

Hominid hands did shape tools for striking and piercing and cutting, did ignite and control fire, did fashion clothing and habitation, and did domesticate animals and cultivate plants. But with their hands and developed brain and greatly

[22] Ibid., p. 7.
[23] Ibid., pp. 15–34.

increased eye-brain-hand neural circuitry, *hominids may well have invented language* – not just expanding the naming function that some animals possess but finding true language, with syntax as well as vocabulary, *in gestural activity*.[24]

Wilson argues that because of the interrelationship between hand and brain, the ongoing development of mechanical skills mapped the brain's circuitry regarding how it represents reality. He argues, "There is growing evidence that *H. sapiens* acquired in its new hand not simply the mechanical capacity for refined manipulative and tool-using skills but, as time passed and events unfolded, an impetus to the redesign, or reallocation, of the brain's circuitry."[25]

The impact of the hand on the brain's organization means, according to Wilson, that we construct *sentences* the same way we construct *objects*. Wilson cites the work of psychologist Patricia Greenfield who claims to have shown that

the human brain organizes and oversees the child's interactions with objects almost exactly the same way it organizes and oversees the production of speech. These two specific skills (manipulating objects and manipulating words), and the developmental chronology associated with the child's mastery of those skills, proceed in such transparently parallel fashion that the brain must be: (a) applying the same logic or procedural rules to both; and (b) using the same anatomic structures as it does so.

Wilson claims that Greenfield's work argues that "evolution has created in the human brain an organ powerfully predisposed to generate rules that treat nouns as if they were stones and verbs as if they were levers or pulleys." In other words, "we humans are instructed (or constrained) by our genes to build sentences the way we build huts and villages."[26]

Brain follows body

The main lines of this approach – the idea that what ancient humans were doing with their bodies could have such a profound impact on the organization and capacities of the brain – are also supported by scientist Robert Ornstein's explanation of the evolution of the brain. He writes:

---

[24]   David F. Armstrong, William C. Stokoe, and Sherman E. Wilcox, *Gesture and the Nature of Language* (Cambridge: Cambridge University Press, 1995), p. 197; emphasis added; cited in Wilson, *The Hand*, p. 204.

[25]   Wilson, *The Hand*, p. 59.

[26]   Wilson, *The Hand*, pp. 165, 169.

Although [our evolutionary ancestors] left the trees, our adaptations for forest life did not leave us. Moving in the trees required sequences of actions and the ability to coordinate series of movements. This "neurological grammar" for the talented arboreal acts of our primate ancestors begins in those areas of the brain that later enlarged in early humans and were still later "recruited" for language.[27]

The brain evolved according to the logic of survival, not our desire to chat. Nature selects according to superior abilities at surviving, not doing philosophy. "Although it might seem cynical to think of the intellect as anything but a primary evolutionary goal," notes Ornstein, "it was at best a side benefit of another adaptation."[28] The outer world shaped our inner world.

The significance of the hand–brain–language connection: intelligence

The significance of this perspective cannot be overstated. In essence, Wilson claims that the hand, the brain and language are intimately connected – with the hand enjoying logical primacy. In other words, the brain's abilities were determined by the hand's need. Human "intelligence" then, refers to a set of cognitive abilities that developed in response to a combination of: (1) the specific conditions that early humans were living in; (2) their successful response to the challenges in this environment; and, specifically, (3) the manual abilities that humans developed (the capacity to make and use increasingly complex tools) that increased the likelihood of their survival. From this point of view, all sophisticated human cognitive operations are driven by the "logic of the hand." Consequently, all the products of human intelligence – technology, culture, art, etc. – are colored by the "logic of the hand."

For the purposes of our investigation, Wilson's thesis has two powerful implications. First, it explains why discussions about "intelligence" in nonhumans put so much emphasis on "language." That is, Wilson's theory gives us a paleontological explanation for the fact that philosophical discussions of the possibility of intelligence in nonhumans are dominated by a preoccupation with language and the linguistic abilities of nonhumans. Wilson argues that:

> The partnership of language and culture is so deeply woven into human history, and so compelling a force in our own personal development and acculturation, that we quite naturally come to regard language as the trait that both explains and defines our intelligence.[29]

[27]   Robert Ornstein, *Evolution of Consciousness* (New York: Prentice Hall, 1991), p. 47.
[28]   Ibid., p. 56.
[29]   Wilson, *The Hand*, p. 37.

Ornstein reinforces this general perspective when he claims that: "The mind is the way it is because the world is the way it is. The evolved systems organize the mind to mesh with the world."[30] Wilson stresses the central role of the biological instrument through which this response is mediated. The *human mind* developed in response to specific environmental conditions and survival imperatives. Our brains responded as they did because of our nature as handed, land mammals. The dolphin brain, however, developed in response to the dramatically different evolutionary pressures of the ocean. Their response was mediated by a different sort of biological instrument – one that evolved to be as hydrodynamic as possible. Their brains responded as they did, then, because of their nature as aquatic mammals.

The more important implication of Wilson's line of thought, however, is what it has to say about nonhumans such as dolphins, who have big brains but no hands. If the picture that Wilson and Ornstein paint about the dynamics that drive the evolution of a large brain, is correct, the idea that *dolphin intelligence* and *human intelligence* are dramatically different isn't merely possible, it's probable. Indeed, given the vast differences in the conditions in which the two species were evolving and in the challenges they were facing, it would be hard to believe that "intelligence" would look the same in the two of them. To do so would be a naïve denial of the fundamental forces that drive the world of nature and, particularly, the evolution of the brain. The question is not, "Could human and dolphin intelligence be different?" but "How could they possibly be the same?" The differences, moreover, might be so great that – to echo Reiss – these intelligences would seem "alien" to each other.

The bodies of ancient dolphins adapted to their environment, acquiring traits that would increase the likelihood of survival. Presumably, the dolphin brain responded in concert with these adaptations. If there is a "neurological grammar" imprinted by the co-evolution of the dolphin brain and central aspect(s) of the dolphin body, it is not based on "the logic of the hand." At this point, we can only speculate on the logic of dolphin brain evolution, but it seems virtually certain that this would lead to "intelligence" that is very different from what we find in humans.

Before we can even hazard a guess at what all of this means in terms of our question of what kind of beings dolphins are, we must first return to our definition of personhood and see what it's missing.

[30]   Ornstein, *Evolution of Consciousness*, p. 11.

*The problem with personhood: what we're
missing – or, "Where's everyone else?"*

I remarked earlier that the traditional definitions of personhood have two weaknesses. We've just seen the way that they overemphasize a capacity for human language. Perhaps even more serious, however, is that these definitions underemphasize social intelligence.

When we look at our definition of personhood from the point of view of what we saw in the preceding chapter about dolphin social intelligence, the first thing that is apparent is how "rational" and "cognitive" our definition is. Although there's reference to emotions, feeling is generally considered a more primitive activity than thinking. We've seen in our discussion of dolphin social intelligence, however, that dolphin intelligence is probably closer to Howard Gardner's "interpersonal" and "intrapersonal" intelligences or Daniel Goleman's concept of "emotional intelligence" (with its emphasis on relationships) than to the type of intelligence involved in language, tools and technology. Therefore, a traditional set of criteria for personhood leaves out consideration of a being's level of emotional sophistication and skills in handling relationships with others.

Reference to social and emotional intelligence reveals another important gap in our definition – it is almost completely devoid of reference to other people. Virtually all of the traits that we identify (being alive, being aware, feeling pleasure and pain, having emotions and a sense of self, controlling one's behavior and having sophisticated cognitive abilities) can be demonstrated by solitary individuals. The only traits that require the existence of other people have to do with recognizing other persons and the ability to communicate.

The idea that a *person* is best described as a solitary, autonomous individual may not strike you as being at all problematic. After all, one of the most important traits of personhood is *self*-awareness. And isn't that a completely solitary process? When the French philosopher René Descartes makes his famous pronouncement, "I think, therefore I am," isn't he expressing the idea that his own existence as a solitary being is the one thing that he is unshakably certain of? Doesn't the very concept of the "self" – what we're aware of when we look inside and say "I" – refer to an essentially independent and autonomous being?

Not necessarily – or, at least, it's a more complicated matter than it first appears. Although modern Western cultures virtually deify the free, autonomous individual, other cultures place more emphasis on the individual's relationship to his or her family, group or community. The ancient Greek philosopher Aristotle thought that our nature is so much to be members of a community that he regarded someone designed to live alone to be either a beast or a god – but not really human.[31] Certain Native American cultures stress the close connection between the individual and the community so much that one story tells of a Navajo man who, when asked what he thought about some important issue at hand, said that he wouldn't know until he discussed the matter with his community.[32]

Even in contemporary Western societies, there's evidence suggesting that some individuals' sense of self is fundamentally social. In one study, people answered the question, "How would you describe yourself to yourself?" in two distinctly different ways. One group referred to physical characteristics (tall), athletic skills (good runner), intellectual abilities, tastes or preferences, and the like. What emerges is a picture of a solitary, autonomous individual with specific characteristics. The other group, however, answered the question by referring to other people, or to traits that at least required the existence of other people (being trustworthy, friendly or married, for example). What we see here, by contrast, is a picture of someone who is part of a web or network of relationships. The psychologist conducting the study claimed that the different self-descriptions showed that the former group had a "separate self," while the latter had a "connected self."[33]

Perhaps the dolphin definition of "self" might be more social and connected than individual and autonomous.

A Social Self

The idea that dolphins might have a sense of self that is qualitatively different from what we experience as humans – and one that is fundamentally social – has been proposed by brain specialist, Harry Jerison.[34]

---

[31] "A man that is by nature and not merely by fortune cityless is either low in the scale of humanity or above it" (Aristotle, *The Politics*, I. i. 9).

[32] As reported to me by David Ozar, members of the Navajo community would never decide a matter of life and death on their own, viewing the wisdom of the community together to be an essential basis for such decisions.

[33] Nona Plessner Lyons, "Two Perspectives: On Self, Relationships and Morality," in Carol Gilligan, Janie Victoria Ward and Jill McLean Taylor, with Betty Bardige (eds) *Mapping the Moral Domain* (Cambridge, MA: Harvard University Press, 1988), pp. 21–48.

[34] Jerison writes:

> In the human species, the most remarkable of the constancies created by the brain may be the constancy of the self as observer. For us, the self is the firm, permanent object to which external events

Jerison regards "the self" in humans as something that the brain constructs from information that it processes. Some of the information is external; some is internal.[35] However, since dolphins get so much of their information about the external world through echolocation, Jerison thinks that this could lead to the construction of a different type of self.[36] (Indeed, he thinks that the way that dolphins experience reality in general could be fundamentally different from human experience.[37])

Jerison describes a fascinating possibility. He starts with how rich a source of information dolphin echolocation is, and he claims that "For the dolphin

are referred. There is integrity of the body image, and only rarely (in the absence of neuropathology) is there a serious question of what is and is not part of the self . . . The self is constant in time as well as space: We change as we age, of course, and yet we "know" that we remain the same. This and other intuitions about the self are so strong that it is difficult to imagine a creature with information processing capacity comparable to ours, equal to us in intelligence, as it were . . . , that has a differently constructed self. However, if we accept the constructed nature of the self, and the likelihood that it is this kind of construction that is one of the benefits of (and explanations for) an enlarged brain, we should consider the possibility that it might be on such a dimension of a model of reality that other large brained species might have evolved significantly. Unless there were remarkably parallel evolution, it is also on such a dimension that dolphins are most likely to be dramatically different from us, because they are likely to use their processing capacity in species-typical ways, just as so much of the processing capacity of the human brain is used in controlling species-typical human language.

   (Harry J. Jerison, "The Perceptual World of Dolphins," in Ronald J. Schusterman,
      Jeanette A. Thomas and Forrest G. Wood (eds) *Dolphin Cognition and Behavior:
      A Comparative View/* (Hillsdale, NJ: Lawrence Erlbaum Associates, 1986), p. 148)

[35]   Jerison explains:

The construction of the self as one of the objects in the brain's "real world" undoubtedly requires a very large investment in neural processing machinery. Like all objects, the self is based on information processed by the brain. External information about reference axes of space and time, with the self as center, and internal information about the position and orientation of the head and body, are obvious elements in the construction. Memories, expectations, plans, and so forth are additional elements.

   (Jerison, "Perceptual World," p. 144)

[36]   "Were this kind of construction [of the self] part of the dolphin's world, perhaps the most unusual features might arise from the role of echolocation as a source of information about the external world" (Jerison, "Perceptual World," p. 144).

[37]   He writes:

There are surely different possible worlds that would be consistent with the same neural data about the external world. In imagining the world built by a species with unusual sensory adaptations, living in an exotic environment, and having an unusually enlarged brain, there are different constraints on speculation than in the analysis of smaller brained species that live in environments similar to our own. The "a priori categories" that organize experience in dolphins could be significantly different from the ones that Kant proposed as universal because he identified them in the human species.

   (Jerison, "Perceptual World," p. 149)

an object is apparently more of an object when it is heard than when it is seen."[38] (He believes that dolphins are more auditory than visual – the opposite of what he sees with humans.[39]) However, dolphins apparently can "eavesdrop" on one another's echolocation clicks.[40] The result is the idea that, by listening to someone else's echoes, one dolphin can actually share another dolphin's experience. Jerison writes,

> Intercepted echolocation data could generate objects that are experienced in more nearly the same way by different individuals than ever occurs in communal human experiences when we are passive observers of the same external environment. Since the data are in the auditory domain the "objects" that they generate would be as real as human seen-objects rather than heard-"objects," that are so difficult for us to imagine. They could be vivid natural objects in a dolphin's world.[41]

There's nothing analogous to this experience of in humans. The closest thing that Jerison imagines is if we could share neural data in a way that would let us see what something looked like through someone else's eyes.

Jerison thinks that such "social cognition" might even lead to a different sense of self. He proposes the possibility that "the processes underlying decisions might be shared by several dolphins as a group when facing the same task" and that this "communal experience might actually change the boundaries of the self to include several individuals."[42] He suggests, for example, that

---

[38] Ibid., p. 158.

[39] Jerison writes, "The human brain may be better organized to impose structure on visual data than on auditory data, and in the dolphins the reverse may be true," ("Perceptual World," p. 159). Jerison published this essay in 1986 and, to support this point, refers to research from 1953 and 1980 that is possibly out of date. Jerison cites a 1980 study by Lou Herman that suggests that dolphins are much more adept at handling auditory than visual information. However, as we saw in Chapter 2, Lou Herman's 1998 cross-modal "match to sample" experiment using both vision and echolocation showed that dolphins did equally well whether they saw the object, and then matched it with echolocation, or whether they used sonar first, and then matched the object with vision. However, there's little question that dolphins are able to get much more of a sense of an object through sound than humans can. And this probably results in the qualitatively different experience of reality that Jerison suggests.

[40] H. E. Harley, M. J. Xitco Jr., and H. L. Roitblat, "Echolocation, Cognition, and the Dolphin's World," in R. A. Kastelein, J. A. Thomas, and P. E. Nachtigall (eds) *Sensory Systems of Aquatic Mammals* (Woerden, The Netherlands: De Spil Publishers, 1995), pp. 529–542.

[41] Jerison, "Perceptual World," p. 160.

[42] Ibid., p. 160.

this gives us a new way to interpret examples of dolphins helping each other that typically get labeled "reciprocal altruism" – that is, when one being does a favor for another being in the understanding that the favor will be returned in the future. Jerison proposes that "the 'individual' (at least during the altruistic episode) [is] not one animal but a group of dolphins sharing communally in the experience as well as the behavior."[43] That is, because of the intimate connection that exists among such dolphins as a result of social cognition, there's a sense in which they're helping *themselves* in these cases. Or, to put it slightly differently, such dolphins may not experience as much of a sense of separation and difference between themselves and another dolphin as we humans do in such a situation. This possibility is made even more likely by Jerison's opinion (that we noted in Chapter 2 on the dolphin brain) that the architecture of the dolphin brain suggests that dolphins may form stronger social attachments than humans do.

Jerison's speculation does not include all of the details of this proposed extension of the boundaries of the self. Nonetheless, the general idea of a highly social sense of self makes sense given what we've seen already about dolphin social intelligence – and it, too, reinforces Reiss's idea that the differences between human and dolphin cognitive processes might be so profound that we should properly consider them to be "alien" intelligences.

Suppression of individuality

The idea that dolphins have a highly social self is also indirectly supported by Ken Norris's belief that individuality is suppressed in dolphin personalities. Norris writes that when the Hawaiian spinners that he studied were confronted by something unfamiliar, or when the school was under attack, "individuality is reduced close to zero."[44] Norris notes that the impulse to act primarily for what's good for the group is so strong that it pervades their lives.

The suppression of individuality is so strong that Norris's research even suggests the possibility that in certain fearful situations, dolphins will respond only in ways that are available to the entire group. That is, a sense of the group is so strong that individual dolphins will not take advantage of options that might save themselves – because those same options aren't available to "the group" to take *en bloc*. In the course of looking for ways to reduce the deaths

---

[43]   Ibid., p. 161.
[44]   Norris, *Dolphin Days*, p. 186.

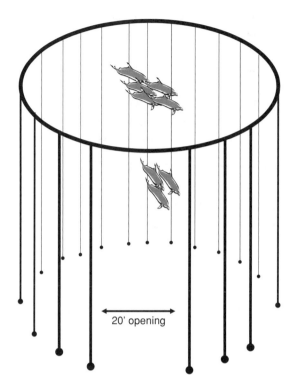

20' opening

FIGURE 6.1   Norris's hukilau

of dolphins in connection with the tuna fishing (something that we will discuss next chapter), Norris discovered that it was disturbingly easy to keep a dolphin school trapped. Using his own version of a Hawaiian fishing device called a *hukilau* (see figure), Norris realized that trapped dolphins wouldn't try to escape separately as individuals, even though the option was readily available.

In one case, Norris's research team encircled a school of 40 to 60 spinners with the *hukilau*, reduced the surface area to about 20 × 30 feet, and the crowded dolphins remained inside – even when strands of the *hukilau* were removed to create a "door" 20 feet wide.[45]

---

[45]   Ibid., pp. 137, 139.

Social self explained

The idea of a "social self" may at first seem difficult to accept, but it's not all that implausible. Jerison's speculation doesn't suggest that dolphins can't recognize the boundaries between their bodies, the outside world and the bodies of other dolphins, or that dolphins have shared emotional experiences. Rather, it implies that an integral part of a dolphin's experience of "self" (who he or she is) is connection with other dolphins.

Think of it this way. Imagine that you describe yourself as a "football player" to a friend. He or she then asks, "What team are you on? What position do you play?" And you reply, "I'm not on any team, and I don't play a specific position." You'd surely get a puzzled look back from your friend because your answer doesn't make any sense. Football is fundamentally a team activity, with different individuals taking different roles. You can't be a "football player" by yourself. You may throw or kick a ball around, but that doesn't make you a "football player." Your answer suggests that you don't understand the concept.

It's possible that the dolphin answer to the question, "Who are you?" would always include reference to the group to which it belongs. This sense of connection with others could be so strong that the notion of the solitary and autonomous individual might seem like an incomplete aberration to them. This could be an even stronger sense of connection with others than we see in humans who are so deeply in love (or in some other way attached to one another) that they can't imagine life without their partner. In such cases, if one partner dies or chooses to end the relationship, the other can feel so devastated that they have great difficulty functioning in life. They feel as though they have lost a part of themselves.

A sense of self that includes relationships with others as an essential element might even explain dolphins' limited physical aggression against each other and point up an important difference between these cetaceans and humans. If dolphins have such a social self, there's a good chance that this reduces the amount of *fear* they might feel towards each other. After all, a strong sense of connection and identity with other dolphins would increase the likelihood that dolphins involved in a dispute would be motivated to find a resolution short of hurting or killing each other. They would be aware of just how much their interests were the same and how much their welfare depended on each other. They would probably be able to see each other just as individuals who disagreed, not as adversaries who were a threat to each other. Less of a sense of threat would mean less fear, and this would probably translate into less serious physical aggression. This, of course, stands in marked difference with humans whose senseless level of violence against members of our own species implies lethal levels of fear and distrust.

Personhood Redefined

While there may be other ways that the traditional definition of personhood has an unintentional anthropocentric bias, it should be clear that, at least when it comes to applying it to dolphins, it has major weaknesses – both in terms of what it emphasizes and what it excludes.

Some thinkers have argued that "personhood" is so flawed a concept that we shouldn't use it. And, as we've seen, it does have its problems. However, the fact that dolphins do so well when measured by such a flawed standard makes an even stronger case for recognizing them as beings entitled to moral standing. And our recognition of the differences between our species in matters as fundamental as self-concept and the nature of intelligence should make us sensitive to the complexities of the question (which we will take up in the next chapter) of how we determine what counts as ethical behavior when it involves two such different, intelligent species.

However, the flaws that we've been examining in the traditional definition of personhood raise the interesting question of what things would look like if we revised our criteria accordingly. That is, when dolphins are evaluated by traditional human standards of intelligence that stress linguistic ability, for example, dolphins fall short. Just out of curiosity, let's ask how humans would do if we define the traits of personhood according to how we might speculate dolphins would define them.

While there are a number of directions in which we could speculate, looking at just a couple of traits will make the point. For the sake of this exercise, let's take *self-awareness* and *recognizing and treating other persons appropriately*.

Self-awareness *revised*

A dolphin-designed test for self-awareness would probably start the same way a human-designed test would. It would look to see if there was a basic sense of self. However, the dolphin test would probably be looking for more than a simple sense of "I." It might look for indication of a social sense of self – something of the sort that we saw above in Nona Lyons' research on self-definition in humans. That is, the test would look for evidence of a sense of "I-connected-with-others." To highly social beings, an autonomous self-definition might actually be regarded as "pre-self-awareness." An autonomous self-definition would show promise – but it would probably be seen as a sign of only a primitive and elementary stage. It would most likely be found lacking because it didn't demonstrate the essential perception that to be a person is to be integrally connected to other persons.

More complicated is the fact that a dolphin test for self-awareness would probably be auditory, not visual. As we saw in Chapter 3, human researchers use the mirror test in looking for self-awareness in nonhumans. This may make sense in testing other great apes, but dolphins are more auditory than visual. It is difficult even to imagine what a purely auditory test of self-awareness would be like. Perhaps it would be based on the ability to identify the echo of one's own voice. (However, since dolphins read echoes for information about the objects they're bouncing off of, it might not involve echoes at all but something to do with what dolphins would assume is a human equivalent of a signature whistle.) But whatever the design, it would probably be more difficult for most humans to demonstrate self-awareness on such a test than we do through a visual mirror test. Presumably, humans who are blind would probably do better than the rest of us.

On balance, then, the evidence that many of us would give for self-awareness according to dolphin-defined traits might not be especially convincing.

Recognizing other persons and treating them appropriately *revised*

As problematic as human behavior might be on a dolphin-designed test of self-awareness, the degree to which we demonstrate an ability to "recognize other persons and treat them appropriately" would probably be even more questionable. The criteria that we use for this capacity in a traditional definition are fairly minimal. Do we recognize enough of a difference between a cattleman and the cattle he's selling us that we dine on the latter, not the former? However, beings hard-wired for social intelligence and managing relationships might place the bar a good bit higher. "Treating another person appropriately" would probably start with treating them in a way qualitatively different from inanimate objects or animate nonpersons. But it could also include such things as: behaving in a way that recognizes the potential value of a person in advancing the good of the group; assisting other persons when they need help; forming authentic relationships with many other persons; demonstrating the ability to resolve disagreements with other persons in a way that preserves a mutually satisfying relationship; and, certainly, refraining from killing other persons. These capacities should, of course, be evident in dealing with other persons no matter what their species. Realistically, however, persons of one species may find it difficult to recognize and treat persons of another species appropriately. But, unquestionably, persons should readily evidence these traits when dealing with other persons of their own species.

Although some humans demonstrate these abilities, it's fair to say that an objective observer would maintain that, overall, our species lacks them. As in the case of self-awareness, we might be seen as a species that could – at some point in the future – develop the capacity to recognize and treat other persons appropriately. That is, *Homo sapiens* might some day achieve personhood. But at this point in our history, we'd probably be seen as falling short.

——— Conclusion: What Kind of Beings Are Dolphins? ———

Our attempt to answer the question, "What kind of beings are dolphins?" gives us a variety of things to ponder. It should also give us pause.

First, according to even a traditional definition of personhood and a conventional set of criteria for the various traits of a person, the scientific research that's currently available about dolphins suggests a strong case for recognizing them as nonhuman persons. It appears as though dolphins are self-aware beings with complex cognitive and affective capabilities. A dolphin appears to be a "who," not a "what" – a being, not an object – with a sophisticated, individual awareness of the world.

Second, close consideration of the traditional definition of persons – particularly the traits that humans typically associate with intelligence – reveals that elements of the standard definition are subject to anthropocentric bias.

Third, the problems with personhood that we examined all suggest fundamental differences in the inner worlds of our different species. In short, in many ways, dolphins are beings who are in many ways truly alien to us. While our species are similar in many ways, the differences between humans and dolphins are both deep and difficult to grasp.

In view of the fact that so much evidence suggests that dolphins are intelligent beings who are, at the same time, very similar to and very different from us, we now face the ethical implications of our investigation. Dolphins are injured and die at our hands. We use them for our entertainment and to satisfy our curiosity. Are we doing anything wrong?

CHAPTER 7

Ethics and Human/Dolphin Contact

- Dolphins are harassed, injured and even die in connection with the human fishing industry.
- Captive dolphins are used to entertain and educate us.
- Dolphins are also used for therapy and by the military.

The fact that some (if not all) of these practices would be considered seriously unethical if they involved humans should indicate the gravity of the situation we have in front of us. In light of the fact that dolphins are intelligent, self-aware beings – and have fundamentally the same grounds for moral consideration as humans do – are we doing anything wrong in any of this? Are there grounds for thinking that practices that humans do every day with a clear conscience might actually be wrong? Are there solid reasons for thinking that we need to change the way we act towards dolphins?

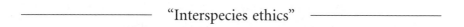 "Interspecies ethics"

It would be an understatement to say that most humans have given relatively little attention to "interspecies ethics." In general, most humans probably think that only two things count as being morally questionable when it comes to how we deal with other animals: "inhumane treatment" (deliberate cruelty, needless pain, neglect, and the like) and the extinction of an entire species. Otherwise, virtually everything else is considered defensible. This means that when it comes to trying to prove that some human practice that affects non-humans is *wrong*, the bar is set quite high.

Our discussion of the ethics of human/dolphin contact, however, will be governed by three important points.

- One of the most important philosophical implications of the scientific research we've examined is that individual dolphins have moral standing.
- Accordingly, from an ethical perspective, we have a situation in which we don't need to prove that a particular way that humans deal with dolphins is unquestionably *wrong*. We just need to cast "reasonable doubt" on the claim that it's ethically acceptable. And that lowers the bar a good deal.
- In assessing the ethical acceptability of human practices that affect dolphins, we need to make sure that we use "species-appropriate" standards. That is, I believe that whether something is *right* or *wrong* is in large measure grounded in the defining, biological traits of a species. And this is where the fundamental differences between humans and dolphins come to play.

Why do dolphins "count" in an inquiry about ethics?

The first point governing our investigation of human/dolphin contact is why dolphins are entitled to consideration.

Recall from Chapter 3 that the main reason humans believe that *we* deserve special treatment is that we possess a particular type of consciousness. We are self-conscious, unique individuals (with distinctive personalities, life-long memories and personal histories) who are vulnerable to a wide range of physical and emotional pain and harm, and who have the power to reflect upon and choose our actions. As a result, to echo Immanual Kant, we have "intrinsic worth" and "a dignity" (as opposed to "a price"). We have "moral standing" as individuals. Traditionally, debates about whether nonhumans should also have moral standing ended here, because the assumption was that only humans possessed these traits. However, scientific evidence suggests that, like humans, dolphins are also self-aware individuals with a sophisticated consciousness. Therefore, from an ethical perspective, they would share with us the right to some kind of special status and protections. That is, because dolphins appear to have a consciousness that makes them vulnerable to a wide range of physical and emotional pain, and that gives them the power to reflect upon and choose their actions, they should be seen as having intrinsic worth and moral standing as *individuals*.

Intrinsic worth, moral standing and "reasonable doubt"

Given what we now know about dolphins, we don't need to prove conclusively that a particular practice is *wrong* in order to argue that humans shouldn't do it. We can challenge the ethical acceptability of an action simply by generating "reasonable doubt" that it's right.

The reason we can lower the bar in this way has to do with one of the implications of recognizing someone's intrinsic worth and granting them moral standing. Consider the following situations.

- You're driving your brand new car at night along a road that bicyclists also use. Most cyclists have lights on their bikes so that drivers can spot them, but not all of them do. You want to see how quickly you can go from zero to 60 in your new car, and you notice something ahead that's either a cyclist crossing the road or a shadow caused by the wind blowing some tree branches around. You aren't sure which it is. Do you floor it?
- You and a friend are doing some electrical work in your home, and you've had the power turned off. You've finished installing a light fixture, and you want to turn the power back on to see if it works. You don't know where your friend is, however. You thought he said something about going for coffee. Maybe he's out, but maybe he came back and is working on another fixture. You really aren't sure. Do you turn on the power?

Unless you're someone without a conscience or a shred of decency, in both cases you'll hesitate doing something that could hurt someone. You'd probably agree that if you roar down the road or flip the switch, you'd have acted in such a callous and negligent way that you've done something seriously wrong. In situations where there's *reasonable doubt* about whether we can proceed without hurting anyone, we have a moral responsibility to refrain from acting.

The key here, of course, is that your action might harm another person – someone with intrinsic worth and moral standing. The cyclist and your friend have their own rights and interests – the least of which is to remain alive and unharmed – that are entitled to be respected. When we're in situations where it's not clear whether our actions will hurt others or not – but where there's a reasonable chance that they will – most of us recognize that we should err on the side of caution. That is, if there's reasonable doubt about the impact of our actions, the benefit of that doubt should go to those who could be harmed if we proceed. Maybe you believe that a shock won't kill your friend. And perhaps you figure that you can handle your car well enough so that the worst that the cyclist experiences as you go speeding by is a close call or a fall. But respecting the rights, interests and dignity of others means that you aren't entitled to take those chances.

If this is how we're obliged to act when it involves another individual human, then we're also obliged to act the same way if it involves individual dolphins.

In view of the fact that dolphins and humans have the same grounds for claiming moral standing – being self-aware individuals with a sophisticated consciousness – we have the same moral obligation about how to behave in an uncertain situation. If some of our actions might seriously harm individual dolphins or treat them inappropriately, we have a moral obligation to refrain from doing them until we can clarify the situation.

Accordingly, the question we're facing isn't, "Can we prove conclusively that certain human activities harm dolphins in a way that means that these practices are without a doubt ethically unjustifiable?" Instead, it's, "Is it reasonable to think that certain practices could harm individual dolphins or treat them inappropriately?" Or, "Is there *reasonable doubt* about whether certain practices harm dolphins or not?" From an ethical perspective, if the situation is uncertain, we don't have the right to proceed when it involves individuals with moral standing.

Note, too, that the same logic means that we stand under the same moral obligation even if there is only a *reasonable possibility* that dolphins are the kind of beings I argue that they are. In a questionable situation – whether the doubt is over whether the harm counts as serious or whether the victim has moral standing – our moral obligation is clear. The "benefit of the doubt" requires us to "do no harm" and respect a being's likely dignity and intrinsic worth.

Basic dolphin needs and conditions for dolphin well-being

To say that individual dolphins have intrinsic worth, a dignity (as opposed to a price) and moral standing for the same reasons that humans do, however, does not mean that the same actions – when done by or to members of our respective species – are automatically right or wrong. Recall that our ethical standard is essentially based in biology – the basic needs that we have simply by virtue of being members of a particular species. Therefore, before we make judgments about the ethical character of actions involving both humans and dolphins, we need to recognize the implications of the fundamental differences between our species. That is, we need an understanding of "basic dolphin needs" equivalent to our sense of "basic human needs," and we need to understand the significance of the similarities and the differences.

The easiest place to begin this discussion is with the obvious areas in which humans and dolphins have similar basic needs. We both need: life, freedom from physical and emotional pain, and a sense of physical safety and security. Children (human and dolphin alike) need protection because of their vulnerability. The young also need access to someone who can teach them the skills and knowledge that will let them survive and function in their society. As highly social beings, we both also need the conditions necessary for developing and preserving the relationships on which we depend.

There are, however, some significant differences between our species. *Homo sapiens* is characterized by a high degree of autonomy, a strong sense of individuality and a powerful need for individual liberty. Throughout recorded human history, there is a consistent theme of individuals asserting a need for self-determination and personal freedom. The personality of dolphins, however, is likely characterized by a stronger social sense than we find in humans. Life in the ocean may require a stronger network of social relationships than it does on land. As we saw in the preceding chapter, the dolphin brain appears to specialize in social intelligence, Ken Norris believes that individuality is suppressed among dolphins, and Harry Jerison even suggests the possibility that dolphins have a social sense of self.

From an ethical perspective, the implications of this difference between humans and dolphins are profound. If dolphins are hard-wired to be as social as appears to be the case, the most fundamental condition for their emotional growth and well-being is membership in a dolphin community. If relationships and group membership are as central to dolphins as freedom and autonomy are to humans, this reveals a significant difference in what might count as *harm* in dolphins and humans. Being deprived of significant relationships and the opportunity to perform the roles of a meaningful group member could be as serious as denying humans individual liberty.

The seriousness of depriving dolphins of meaningful group membership should not be underestimated. For such social beings, the life of the community is probably the arena in which dolphins develop and refine their cognitive and affective abilities. Being deprived of this could have a major, negative effect on how much an individual dolphin is able to develop and flourish.

Consider a couple of human parallels. The experience of freedom is one of the most fundamental and necessary conditions for human flourishing. Similarly, without education, humans would be unable to develop critical skills and traits. As a result, depriving humans of liberty and preventing them from receiving education are universally regarded as serious harms – even when accompanied by comfortable physical conditions.

If dolphins lack meaningful group membership, there may be no opportunity to develop the social intelligence that is so central to their nature. Similarly, disruptions that play havoc with these relationships probably also have a major negative impact on such social beings. "Dolphin nature" is such that any significant compromise in the social conditions that are necessary for the well-being of such individuals would constitute serious harm.

We thus have an interesting first glimpse into the world of interspecies ethics. Because humans are so autonomous, individuality and personal freedom are probably more central to human flourishing than a rich life of relationships and varied social roles. Humans traditionally rebel more against "tyranny" than "emotionally sterile communities" or "meaningless group functions." For dolphins, on the other hand, rich and varied relationships are probably more important for their well-being than individuality is. In terms of the basic needs set down by the nature of each species, suppressing a human's individuality is probably more ethically problematic than suppressing a dolphin's individuality. By the same token, compromising a dolphin's social needs is probably more seriously wrong than doing the same to a human.

There are other basic needs that dolphins probably have that we could explore, as well as more similarities and differences between humans and cetaceans. However, since we have at least a general idea of the ethical standard we're using, and a basic understanding of how to proceed in a way that takes into account fundamental differences between the species in question, we can now proceed to the specific controversies surrounding human/dolphin interaction.

The Dolphin/Tuna Controversy

The most dramatic ethical issue that arises from human/dolphin contact comes from the fishing industry in the Eastern Tropical Pacific and has been a subject of controversy since the 1960s. Since the late 1950s, an estimated 6–7 million dolphins have died because of a particular fishing practice: purse seining.

Years ago fishermen discovered that dolphins and yellowfin tuna in this part of the world often school together. By looking for dolphins, the boats could easily find large schools of yellowfin, the very profitable type of fish used in light canned tuna. As long as fishermen used hook and line, there were no casualties among the dolphins. Yet as the industry introduced a new technology – purse seining – dolphins became encircled in the nets and drowned. The death rate was dramatic and soared to hundreds of thousands of dolphins each year; in 1972, for example, 350,000 dolphins died. The species involved are primarily spotted and spinner dolphins. However, common dolphins, striped dolphins, Fraser's dolphins, rough-toothed dolphins and bottlenose dolphins are sometimes also caught.

The fishing procedure is as follows. A helicopter from the fishing boat will spot a school of dolphin with the tuna below. Speed boats are launched to herd the dolphin towards the seiner – a chase that can easily last more than an hour. When the school is close enough, a skiff is launched to lay out a net of nearly a mile long that encircles the dolphins and tuna. While the top edge of the net remains at the surface, the rest of it sinks down, forming a wall. A cable running through the bottom edge is then winched in and closes it. That is, it "purses the net" – which is why the procedure is called "purse seining".

After the high death rate became known to scientists and consumers, a series of actions produced a dramatic decrease in the number of deaths. The US Congress passed the Marine Mammal Protection Act in 1972; fishermen adopted a new "back down" procedure designed to let dolphins escape from the nets; a consumer boycott against tuna was launched in the mid-1980s; in 1990, the world's three largest tuna companies (StarKist, Bumblebee, and Chicken of the Sea) agreed to stop purchasing, processing, and selling tuna caught by intentionally chasing and netting of dolphins; and non-encirclement became the legal standard in the US for labeling tuna "dolphin-safe." In the 1980s, hundred of thousands of dolphins were dying each year, but by the 1990s, the number had dropped to about 2,000.[1] Many non-US boats still catch yellowfin by encircling dolphins, although the Inter-American Tropical Tuna Commission claims that the death rate per set is negligible.[2] Earth Island Institute, the environmental organization that spearheaded the "dolphin-safe" movement, claims that because of a monitoring program and agreements with import associations, fishing fleets, canners and brokers, "dolphin-deadly" tuna has been eliminated from 90 percent of the world's canned tuna markets.

Because the US tuna market is so large, and because US consumers have come to expect "dolphin safe" as the norm, attempts are regularly made to re-define the phrase so that all of the non-US fleet can sell to American

---

[1] In the process, however, the tuna fleet went from 70 percent American to 1 percent American, as ships re-flagged to avoid US regulations. And the remaining US ships focused on fishing for skipjack tuna (which doesn't school with dolphin) in the western tropical Pacific. The Inter-American Tropical Tuna Commission (IATTC), an industry trade association, reports that in 2006 the majority of the tuna fleet flew under the flags of: Ecuador (87), Mexico (67), Panama (26), Venezuela (21), Columbia (12), Nicaragua (6), Honduras (4), El Salvador (5), Spain (3), Guatemala (3), Vanuatu (2) and Bolivia (1). Only three ships were US flagged.

[2] The IATTC reports that there were 11,783 sets on dolphins in 2004, with a mortality rate of 0.12 dolphins per set. The IATTC reports that the total number of dolphin deaths for 2004 was less than 1,469, which, they say, represents about 0.015 percent of the dolphin population.

consumers. The IATTC, for example, prefers an interpretation of "dolphin safe" that would mean that even though the tuna were caught by encircling dolphin, no deaths or serious injuries were observed during the set.

The overall dolphin population is the area in question is about 1.2 million individuals, and groups of dolphins are chased and encircled from 7,500 to 10,000 times each year. No one knows how often any individual dolphin experiences being chased and captured. Depending on the species of dolphin and location, estimates range from being chased 2 to 10 times each year and being caught 1 to 3 times. However, some groups are chased more than once during the same day, and some dolphins may be captured more than others.

The driving force behind purse seining, of course, is that this is a good way to catch tuna – a healthy source of protein and profitable commodity. Fishing on dolphin, however, is not the only way that the seiners catch tuna. In fact, only about half of the 15,000 to 20,000 annual sets involve dolphin. Nets are also set around schools of tuna that aren't schooling with dolphins, or around tunas that are underneath logs or other objects floating on the surface. Indeed, catching tuna by chasing and encircling dolphins isn't necessarily even the most profitable method.[3]

Ethical issues of purse seining

The controversy over purse seining raises stark ethical issues. Some dolphins die. Some are seriously injured. The health of still others is compromised.[4]

---

[3] It is possible that alternative strategies of fishing for tuna produce a higher yield per set. The IATTC reports that in 2004, for example, 11,783 "sets associated with dolphins" yielded 148,375 metric tons of yellowfin (95%) and skipjack (5%) tuna. The 2004 dolphin sets, then, produced a wholesale value of roughly $227M (or *$19,000 per set*). The 5,640 "sets on fish associated with floating objects" yielded 171,539 metric tons of yellowfin (14%), skipjack (49%) and bigeye (37%), or, roughly $200.9M (or *$35,600 per set*). The 10,133 "sets on unassociated schools" yielded 212,298 metric tons of yellowfin (49%), skipjack (50%) and bigeye (1%), or, roughly $271.1M (or *$26,800 per set*). Determining the precise value of the catch obtained by each strategy, however, also requires taking into account such factors as: how far ships need to travel and the cost of fuel, the size of the tuna caught, search costs and other set costs. In addition, alternate strategies appear to have a bigger by-catch, which is a problem from the standpoint of conservationists.

[4] Researchers from the Southwest Fisheries Science Center contend that "it is plausible that stress resulting from chase and capture could compromise the health of at least some of the dolphins involved" ("Report of the Scientific Research Program under the International Dolphin Conservation Act," prepared by the Southwest Fisheries Science Center, NOAA Fisheries, National Oceanic and Atmospheric Administration, 23 August 2002, p. 6).

Death can come from drowning or cardiac arrest. The stress connected with the chase and capture may release potentially harmful hormones and enzymes. Some scientists suggest that a surge of hormones (catecholamines) during particularly stressful sets can lead to fatal heart damage and death hours or even days after dolphins are released. Dolphins who are injured, weakened or separated from their school because of being chased and/or encircled are probably at greater risk of shark attack. Young dolphins separated from their mothers during the chase are at particular risk.

The emotional experience of being chased and trapped is surely negative. Ken Norris, who observed dolphins inside the tuna nets, describes them as being "deep in the grip of fear."[5] We don't know if such an experience is so disturbing as to be traumatic – although it certainly could be. It wouldn't be unrealistic to suggest that dolphins experience the event as an emotional assault.[6]

Less dramatically, dolphin communities are harassed by the chases and captures. No one knows for certain what the impact is. However, in such a highly social species, it's reasonable to conclude that it could affect everything from rates of reproduction to their social structure.

Given the kind of beings that dolphins are, it's difficult to imagine how fishing for tuna "on dolphin" can be defended as ethically acceptable. If humans were dying as a result of such a practice, it would be denounced as morally wrong. Given the similarity between humans' and dolphins' advanced cognitive and affective traits, it is no less wrong when individual dolphins die. Even if only a tiny percentage of dolphins caught by the nets die, it doesn't change the fact that individual dolphins have moral standing. To defend purse seine fishing on those grounds would be like defending a particular practice used by a business in Honolulu, Hawaii that annually kills 3,000 innocent victims because this amounts to only a quarter of 1 percent of the city's population.

Regrettably – but predictably – the discussion of the impact of purse seine fishing on dolphins focuses only on "stocks" and the viability of the different species involved. The IATTC, for example, argues that

> the best available scientific evidence supports the conclusion that the purse-seine fishery is not having a significantly adverse impact on any depleted dolphin stock

[5] Kenneth S. Norris, *Dolphin Days: The Life and Times of the Spinner Dolphin* (New York: W. W. Norton, 1991), p. 130.

[6] The fact that dolphins experience this event as threatening is reinforced by Ken Norris's observation that the formation that dolphins adopt during capture "could well be the functional unit that the dolphins used to defend their societies at sea," that is, that it mimics a formation observed during an attack on a group of dolphins by sharks (Norris, *Dolphin Days*, p. 121).

in the eastern tropical Pacific Ocean, specifically that the intentional deployment on or encirclement of dolphins with purse seine nets is not having a significant adverse impact on any dolphin stock in the eastern tropical Pacific Ocean.[7]

Even scientists who oppose the tactic of encircling dolphins talk only about "stocks." A study by the Southwest Fisheries Science Center contends that "concerns remain that the practice of chasing and encircling dolphins somehow is adversely affecting the ability of these depleted stocks to recover."[8] As I hope I have shown through my explanation of the implications of the research we've looked at in this book, the traditional focus on the viability of cetacean species, not the state of individual dolphins is indefensible – both scientifically and philosophically. Such a perspective is a holdover from an anthropocentric prejudice that only humans can be self-aware individuals with a sophisticated consciousness.

Even if fishing "on dolphin" could be conducted without deaths, this would still not make it ethically acceptable because dolphins are still seriously harmed in the process. The chase can separate mothers and babies; the stress of the chase and capture can have a variety of negative effects; and the young and weak become at greater risk of shark attack.

It is true that the fishing practice in question produces both nutritional and financial benefits for millions of humans. However, because yellowfin can be caught in other ways, these same benefits are achievable without seriously harming any dolphins. Even if this is a more expensive process, this is surely a more acceptable cost from an ethical perspective. Moreover, the fact that the benefits of purse seining flow entirely to one group (humans) while the harms are borne by another group (dolphins) suggests a fundamental unfairness that can't be ignored. In addition, because dolphins strenuously try to avoid capture, there is no reason to think that communities of dolphins consent to such harassment. It's worth recalling that there are instances of human/dolphin cooperation in fishing in some parts of the world. It is fair to say that the eastern tropical Pacific dolphins, however, do not consent to their treatment.

Accordingly, the practice of fishing "on dolphin" fails to pass muster from an ethical perspective:

---

[7]   Letter of October 30, 2002, p. 1.

[8]   "Report of the Scientific Research Program under the International Dolphin Conservation Act," prepared by the Southwest Fisheries Science Center, NOAA Fisheries, National Oceanic and Atmospheric Administration, 23 August 2002, p. 3.

- Our species can achieve exactly the same benefits with less harm.
- Despite clear signals that the dolphins do not consent to such treatment, we subject them to it anyway.
- In our actions towards dolphins, we use these beings simply as objects to advance our own interests. That is, we demonstrate no respect for the moral standing of the other beings. To use Kant's terms, we treat dolphins as though they have only a price, not a dignity.
- Given the fact that humans and dolphins share the traits that bestow moral standing, the death of each individual dolphin in connection with purse seine fishing is as ethically unacceptable as if it were the death of an individual human.

In effect, from an ethical perspective, dolphins are being treated in a way not unlike how Black slaves were in the United States. Slaves were considered to be "property," not "persons," and treated accordingly. Dolphins in the eastern tropical Pacific are being treated the same way.

Tuna/dolphin: postscript

It is likely that some readers at this point may be tempted to offer the comment, "If dolphins are so smart, why do they get caught in the first place? Why don't they just escape by swimming underneath the purse seine net before it's closed or by jumping over the net once they're surrounded?" I hear such remarks most frequently when they're supposed to be a clever way of suggesting that dolphins actually are not especially intelligent and, therefore, deserve whatever fate befalls them. Strictly speaking, this comment is irrelevant because it doesn't change the fact that human actions still cause so much harm in this situation. So, the ethical problem remains. However, the comment is an instructive error that – even if unsophisticated – is disturbingly persistent.

Not surprisingly, this comment is built on a kind of ignorance and anthropocentric bias that are important to recognize. The challenges to survival and the strategies that have proved themselves effective over time are very different on the land and in the oceans. A glib comment of the sort "Why don't dolphins do what humans would do in such a situation?" is a sad failure to grasp a fundamental fact of nature – just how much both the outer and inner worlds of all living things are the products of the relationship between a species and the environment in which it has evolved.

Dolphins are caught and act as they do in the nets for a variety of reasons. It's no surprise that the dolphins are successfully herded in the first place because the speedboats move so much faster than the cetaceans. However, the primary reason that the dolphins are overwhelmed is that they are, in effect, acoustically blinded. The process produces what Ken Norris describes as "a deep spiraling wake of bubbles and turbulence around the fleeing animals . . . [which] to the dolphin's sonar, was an impenetrable wall."[9] Second, being crowded together apparently disables a defensive social mechanism that the dolphins use in the open ocean.[10] Third, it's also important to remember Norris's claim about how much individuality may be suppressed in dolphins and Jerison's idea that dolphins have a more social sense of self than humans do. The idea of abandoning other members of the group in a threatening situation may be so alien to them as to be inconceivable.

The dolphins in the Pacific have been faced with purse seining only since the 1960s. They have adapted to some degree (which is a factor in the decreasing number of deaths), even if they have not completely mastered the challenges. Nonetheless, the process of chasing and encircling is inherently dangerous to them, so we should never expect it to be conducted with no dolphin deaths at all.

Finally, cynics who still believe that a truly "intelligent" being could easily solve the problem of escape should reflect on any of the countless number of questions that could be posed to challenge the claim of intelligence in humans.

---

[9]   Norris continues:

Unlike storm waves at sea, which simply punctuate the sea with deep cascades of bubbles with long stretches of clear sea in between, this wall was continuous, though it did dissipate slowly as the bubble veil rose toward the surface. I suppose a dolphin could "see" no way around it, especially as it became a spiral and the animals found themselves inside a maze as escape-proof as those of any English garden. The dolphins did not dive beneath the veil. I suppose that might be because fleeing dolphins travel shallowly, using long leaps in the air to increase their speed.

(Norris, *Dolphin Days*, pp. 111–112)

[10]   Norris writes, "Something fragile in the dolphin's social organization had been blasted by encirclement in the net" (*Dolphin Days*, p. 129). In particular, see Norris's discussion of survival strategies that work for schooling, aquatic beings in Chapter 9, "The Magic Envelope," pp. 179–192. He adds:

I suspect that the backdown channel of the tuna seine destroys the dolphin's magic envelope by crowding the individuals of its school so close together that their signal systems no long function. Bereft of their protection, they sink in those pathetic ranks. This is another indication of how deeply they are schooling animals. Much of their place in nature is lost without their magic envelope functioning.

So when we think of releasing dolphins from a tuna seine, we must contrive not to destroy the magic envelope, and then, I predict, they will stream out of the net, their social arrangements and their psyches intact.

(Norris, *Dolphin Days*, p. 192)

For example, if humans are so smart, why can't they drive their cars in a way that doesn't kill tens of thousands of them each year? If humans are so smart, why do they foul their air, land and water with toxic substances, making their own survival – and that of their children – more problematic? Better still, if humans are so intelligent, why can't they resolve conflicts without killing each other?

The deaths of dolphins in connection with other human fishing practices

Purse seining, however, is not the only fishing practice that kills dolphins. Indeed, from an ethical perspective, it's not even the worst practice.

Thousands of dolphins are killed each year in drift nets – monofilament, nylon nets that are usually about 30 feet (10m) deep and 20 miles (30 km) long. These nets are typically deployed at night, carried by the currents throughout the night, and hauled in the next morning. They're nicknamed "walls of death" because they sweep up everything in their path and are a particularly wasteful way to fish. Up to half of the catch may be lost as the net is gathered, and the "by-catch" (take of unwanted types of fish that are then thrown away) is significant.

In some countries, dolphins are legally hunted for food, as an economic commodity or as part of a cultural ritual. For example, in the Solomon Islands, dolphins have been hunted for meat and for their teeth (which is used as money by some tribes).

Especially controversial are "drive hunts" that take place in some parts of Japan that prominent marine scientists consider to be "astonishingly cruel." Beginning in fifteenth-century Japan and now occurring annually from September to April in the villages of Taiji and Futo, the hunts are conducted by small groups of Japanese fishermen and are regulated by the Japanese Government. During the hunts, fishermen herd hundreds, sometimes thousands, of dolphins and other small cetaceans into shallow bays by banging on partially submerged rods that create a sonic barrier. Once there, the dolphins are cor-ralled into nets and then speared, hooked, hoisted into the air by their tail by cranes. The dolphins are then slaughtered, eviscerated alive, and many are left to die a long and painful death. While bottlenose dolphins make up the bulk of the annual take, the hunts also kill striped dolphins, spotted dolphins, Risso's dolphins and short-finned pilot whales. The slaughtered dolphins are used for fertilizer, pet food, and for human consumption. In some cases, live dolphins are procured from the drives for aquariums, marine parks and swim-with-a-dolphin programs in Japan and China, a practice that violates the Code of Ethics maintained by the World Association of Zoos and Aquariums. The

Japanese government defends the hunts by citing competition between fishermen and dolphins for fish and squid – a claim the scientists reject.[11]

It should come as no surprise that, from an ethical perspective, there is little difference between the highly mechanized purse seiners, drift nets or individual hunters. The end result is still the unnecessary and preventable death of a self-aware being with sophisticated cognitive and affective abilities. When boats cast out their drift nets, they may not set out to kill dolphins. However, these nets kill more dolphins each year than purse seine fishing does. The Japanese and Solomon Island hunts may be part of their islands' cultural heritage, but – given what we know about the kind of beings dolphins are – this is not enough to justify them. The end result of these practices is still the deliberate, often brutal killing of nonhuman persons that have the same moral standing as humans. Any defense that ignores this is guilty of anthropocentric bias. Indeed, any defense of such practices based on cultural tradition sounds sadly like the justification of the use and abuse of slaves in America as part of the "peculiar institution" of the southern colonies.

Dolphins in Captivity

The fact that various human fishing practices lead to such obvious harm – death, physical injuries, emotional assault, social disruption – actually makes the ethical issue easy to resolve in that case. Given the similarities between humans and dolphins, if it would be wrong to subject humans to these actions, it's wrong to subject dolphins to them. There's no question about the ethical status of such actions. However, the second major ethical issue that our species faces in our interaction with dolphins – the use of captive dolphins – is more difficult to resolve. The possible harm is less dramatic or obvious. In addition, proponents claim that captivity produces significant benefits for not only for humans, but for some dolphins as well.

There are captive facilities on virtually every continent. Approximately 100 facilities in about 30 different countries house roughly 1,200 dolphins and 50 orcas. Facilities vary considerably. Most common is the aquarium or marine theme park (like Sea World) where dolphins are trained to perform in shows. At some of these places there are also "petting pools," where humans can

---

[11]   This account depends heavily on Diana Reiss and Lori Marino, "Japan's Dolphin Drive Hunts from a Scientific and Animal Welfare Perspective" (2006): www.actfordolphins.org

sometimes interact with dolphins by feeding them. Recently, particularly in Asia and Latin America, there has been an increase in "dolphin-swim" programs that provide human swimmers the opportunity for direct interaction with dolphins. More than 30 aquatic parks have opened in the Caribbean since 1990. Most of these facilities are operated for profit, but some are devoted exclusively to research and/or education.

With the exception of a few facilities that use natural settings, the pools in which captive dolphins live are made of artificial materials and have a homogeneous, if not sterile, design.[12] In addition, compared to the territory that an average dolphin might cover in the course of a day, even the largest facilities are small. Satellite tracking of the movements of three offshore bottlenose dolphins in the waters of Bermuda showed that, in approximately one week, each dolphin ranged over a territory of *1,000–1,500 square miles*. Daily traveling of these three dolphins varied from just a few miles to more than 40 miles.[13] The territory covered by dolphins in the course of a day varies widely depending upon species and habitat, but even the least itinerant dolphins would cover a much larger area than is available in the largest facilities.

The quality of the facilities varies tremendously. Some are well-funded and show considerable care for their cetaceans. Others allegedly show a scandalous disregard for the fact that dolphins are sentient beings, and treat them as commodities whose sole purpose is to generate profit for the owners.[14]

Given what we've seen already in this book, there is little question that facilities in which dolphins experience physical harm, neglect or conditions that shorten their lives are not operating in a way that is ethically defensible. Like purse seine fishing, the ethical shortcomings of such operations are obvious.

The most difficult ethical question in this context, then, is not raised by the worst facilities, or by the average facility. Our question is whether even the *best* facilities operate in a way that is ethically defensible. That is, given what we have seen in this book about what kind of beings dolphins are, it should be apparent that dolphins are sophisticated beings with a complex set of needs. Can captive facilities provide the conditions that would have to be met so that dolphins who inhabit them are able to meet the fundamental needs of their

---

[12]   Exceptions include the Dolphin Research Center, UNEXSO in the Bahamas, and some of the Dolphin Quest facilities.

[13]   Bermuda Bottlenose Dolphin Tracking Project, Leigh Klatsky, Jay C. Sweeney and Randall S. Wells; Affiliate Organizations: Dolphin Quest Bermuda, Quest Global Management (http://www.dolphinquest.org/learningquest/researchquest).

[14]   For an excellent source of information about alleged cases of abuse or neglect, see the Whale and Dolphin Conservation Society.

species? Can dolphins grow and develop fully in these situations? Even when our species is trying our best at running captive facilities, is our best good enough?

The ethical standard: basic needs/flourishing

It is important at this point to remember that when we take up issues of inter-species ethics, *right* and *wrong* can ultimately be grounded in the defining traits of the species involved. Recall that *human well-being* is a traditional foundation for philosophical ethics. That is, from the philosophical perspective we're using, the ethical character of our behavior towards each other is determined by the extent to which actions respect or prevent the fulfillment of one another's basic needs. These are the conditions that must be met in order for any member of our species to remain alive and healthy, to grow, develop fully, achieve our potential and flourish. These conditions are determined by the very nature of our species. *Dolphin well-being*, then, is the parallel concept that implies what these cetaceans require in order, similarly, to remain alive and healthy, to grow, develop fully, achieve their potential and flourish. And when we defined this idea above, we saw that the conditions that dolphins need for their physical and emotional well-being include not only freedom from physical and emotional pain and a sense of physical safety and security, but probably also membership in a dolphin community, significant relationships, and the opportunity to perform the roles of a meaningful group member. When we take the fundamental differences between humans and dolphins into account, I believe that depriving dolphins of meaningful group membership is the equivalent of denying humans individual liberty. Accordingly, providing meaningful group membership is probably going to be the major challenge for any captive facility.

Defense of captivity

Captivity is so controversial because it provides such a mixed picture of possible benefits and harms. Defenders of the best facilities point to a number of ways that they do things well. At this point, most dolphins living in captive facilities are the result of breeding programs, not capture in the wild – so wild communities are left largely undisturbed.[15] Facilities stress the physical care

---

[15]   The Alliance for Marine Mammal Parks and Aquariums (AMMPA) claims: "For all dolphins and whales, those born in zoological facilities were 8 percent in 1979, 26 percent in 1990, and 90 percent in 1995" ("An Introduction to the Missions of Zoological Parks and Aquariums and How They Help Conserve Marine Mammals," November 12, 2002, p. 5).

that the dolphins receive. Dolphins are fed daily with high quality fish. They receive medical attention when they need it. They interact with other dolphins and humans. In addition, to combat boredom, dolphins participate in research, and they are taught behaviors which they perform in shows.

Claims are also made that the dolphins who live in such facilities receive major benefits. Captive dolphins are kept free of the parasites that are virtually ubiquitous in wild dolphins and can compromise their health. They receive food and are protected from predators, "thus escaping," notes Karen Pryor, "the two biggest problems of life in the wild, going hungry and being eaten."[16]

However, the main beneficiaries of captivity are generally seen to be other cetaceans and humans. Most of the scientific research done on dolphins is done at captive facilities. And facilities claim that this research forms the basis of the message they communicate to their visitors. They emphasize that "public display" is a crucial tool for encouraging people to care about marine mammals, to learn about humanity's impact on the oceans and to appreciate the importance of conservation. Accordingly, this supposedly benefits wild dolphins who otherwise might be harmed by human activities based on ignorance.

Captive facilities are often part of stranding networks, they provide medical care for stranded cetaceans, and research on captive dolphins is said to help treat strandees. The research is also claimed to help with the conservation of wild populations and the protection of endangered species.[17]

Defenders and detractors disagree on the question of whether dolphins live for a shorter period of time in captivity than they do in the wild.[18] However,

---

[16] Karen Pryor, "The Domestic Dolphin," in K. Pryor and K. Norris (eds) *Dolphin Societies: Discoveries and Puzzles* (Berkeley, CA: University of California Press, 1991), p. 345.

[17] At least one researcher questions the applicability of findings about captive dolphins to wild dolphins. In a report written for the Whale and Dolphin Conservation Society, Sue Mayer, Executive Director of GeneWatch UK, claims, for example, that "there is significant individual variation in haematology" and that "captivity itself affects haematology" ("A Review of the Scientific Justifications for Maintaining Cetaceans in Captivity," A Report for the Whale and Dolphin Conservation Society, February 1998, pp. 5–6). She expresses similar reservations about research on blood chemistry and social structure.

[18] The AMMPA writes:

A study focusing on the bottlenose dolphin by Drs. Deborah Duffield of Portland State University and Randall Wells of the Chicago Zoological Society shows that the average age of dolphins in marine life parks, aquariums, and zoos is similar to that of dolphins in their natural environment. The study is based on comparative demographic census data for dolphins in public display facilities and a wild Sarasota dolphin population studied by Dr. Wells (IMATA Conference Proceedings, 1990). This work corroborates a study published in 1988 by DeMaster and Drevenak who pointed out that survival of dolphins in aquariums 'may be better than or equal to survival in the wild.' (*Marine Mammal Science*, 4: 297–311, 1988).

as serious as that matter is, I believe that it is not the most important issue before us. Given what we know about the complexities of these cetaceans, mortality rates will never settle the question of whether captivity either harms dolphins directly or is in some other way inappropriate. Even if captive dolphins live longer than wild dolphins, there is still the matter of whether the kind of life that captive dolphins experience is satisfying, appropriate and free from harm.

Voluntary captivity?

The best place to start our discussion of captivity is with facilities that claim that dolphins remain there of their own choice. Some facilities operate in natural settings that allow the dolphins living there easy access to the ocean. This raises an interesting question: "Can we infer from the fact that the dolphins remain that they freely consent to their situation?" If the dolphins have the option to leave at any time, but choose to say, this would seem to imply that, at least in these situations, there are few ethical problems.

The strongest statement of this position comes from Karen Pryor, a founder of Sea Life Park in Hawaii and veteran dolphin researcher. Pryor suggests free consent on the part of dolphins in more than one situation. She refers to "wild-caught dolphins [at the Kewalo Basin Marine Mammal Laboratory and Naval Ocean Systems Center laboratories] that have become willing, even dedicated co-workers in extremely complex research tasks."[19] She also notes:

> [F]or some months, at the Oceanic Institute in Hawaii, we kept a pair of bottlenose dolphins in a pen next to a pier in the ocean, a pen they could jump in and out of at will. They spent most of the day loose, playing at the bows of boats coming in and out of the little harbor, but they spent the nights in the pen, jumping back in at 5:00 P.M. when a trainer showed up with their suppers. And they were once seen to jump hastily into their pen when a large hammerhead shark cruised under the pier.[20]

Similar stories are told about other locations where dolphins apparently elect to live in captivity rather than leave for the ocean.

The WDCS, however, believes that the picture is less clear. See Sue Mayer, "A Review of the Scientific Justifications for Maintaining Cetaceans in Captivity," in A Report for the Whale and Dolphin Conservation Society, February 1998.

[19]   Pryor, "Domestic Dolphin," p. 345.

[20]   Ibid., pp. 345–346.

However, it's not clear what we're able to conclude from the behavior of such dolphins. The issue here is that among humans the standard that we expect for a situation to be ethically acceptable is that people choose to be involved by virtue of *free and fully informed consent*. This is not a simple notion, however. Among humans, we recognize that there are more possibilities than "freely choosing to do something" (which is morally acceptable) and "being forced to do something" (which is morally unacceptable). For example, misrepresentation, lies, deliberate omissions, pressure and threats all undermine free choice, as does the perception of danger. So the absence of physical force doesn't necessarily mean that a situation is the result of free choice.

Similarly, it is not unusual for humans to select what is simply the best of a series of bad options. And what we might call "grudging acceptance" is not the same as "free consent." For example, it is estimated that more than 25,000 people live in slave-like conditions in remote areas of Brazil. Often, only the jungle keeps them from leaving. Escaping into the jungle means that they'll probably die sooner rather than later, so it's no surprise that most laborers choose to stay. We'd hardly say, however, that remaining in bonded servitude instead of escaping means that they freely consent to this situation. They just don't have an option that gives them reasonable odds at something better.

Given our claim that dolphins have moral standing, "free and fully informed consent" seems to be a reasonable standard to use when dolphins are involved. However, captive facilities have some critical difficulties to overcome to meet this standard. First, because of the success of captive breeding programs, we don't know how much dolphins born in captivity understand about life in the wild. Second, we don't know if captive dolphins have the requisite hunting skills that would make leaving for the wild a practical option. Captive dolphins are fed dead fish. Dolphins born in captivity are not taught how to find and catch live fish. The hunting and echolocation skills of dolphins who lived in the oceans probably atrophy. Third, we don't know if captive dolphins have the requisite social skills that would make leaving for the wild a practical option. Compared to many dolphin communities in the wild, captive dolphins live in very small social groups. Groups of captive dolphins might behave differently than wild dolphins, so we don't know how well formerly captive dolphins can integrate into wild societies.[21] Fourth, we also don't know how receptive wild communities are to new members.

[21]   Sue Mayer claims that there is evidence to suggest that captive groups may establish dominance hierarchies, which seem to be absent in the wild. She argues that captive dolphins may also behave more aggressively towards each other. Mayer, "A Review of the Scientific Justifications for Maintaining Cetaceans in Captivity," passim.

Indeed, the difficulty of releasing captive dolphins into the wild is legendary in the field of marine science. The number of challenges that must be overcome are considerable.[22] The U. S. National Oceanographic and Atmospheric Administration (NOAA) considers the matter to be so difficult and the risks of harm so high that it recommends that a scientific research permit issued under the Marine Mammal Protection Act be required.[23] Historically, dolphin releases fail.[24] The most noteworthy success has been the release of two bottlenose dolphins (Echo and Misha) who were captured in 1998 at 6 or 7 years old, kept in captivity for only two years, and released back into the same waters from which they were taken.[25]

[22] For discussion of the difficulties, see, for example, R. L. Brill and W. A. Friedl, "Reintroduction to the Wild as an Option for Managing Navy Marine Mammals," NRaD TR 154 9, 75 pp. with appendices (1993); and R. L. Brill, "Return to the Wild as an Option for Managing Atlantic Bottlenose Dolphins," American Zoo and Aquarium Association Conference, September 18–22, 1994.

[23] NOAA's position is as follows:

> Releasing captive marine mammals to the wild can be hazardous to both the released animal and wild marine mammal populations if conducted improperly and without appropriate safeguards. Issues of concern include: (1) the ability of released animals to adequately forage and defend themselves from predators; (2) any behavioral patterns developed in captivity that could affect the social behavior of wild animals, as well as the social integration of the released animals; and (3) disease transmission and/or unwanted genetic exchange between released animals and wild stocks. According to NOAA Fisheries, any marine mammal release should be conducted with a MMPA scientific research permit to protect the health and welfare of marine mammals. The MMPA scientific research permit is required to ensure that humane protocols be in place that maximize the release's chance of success, and provide for long-term follow-up monitoring and emergency contingency plans in case it is necessary to rescue a released animal.
>
> (NOAA 99-R134, June 10, 1999)

[24] See K. C. Balcolm III (1995) "Cetacean Releases," prepared for the Center for Whale Research, Friday Harbor, WA.

[25] R. S. Wells, K. Bassos-Hull and K. S. Norris, "Experimental Return to the Wild of Two Bottlenose Dolphins" Marine Mammal Science, 14 (1998): 51–71. For a more complete account of this project, see Carol Howard, Dolphin Chronicles (New York: Bantam, 1996). Less well documented is the release of two bottlenose dolphins (Joe and Rosie) in Savannah, Georgia, in 1988 by the Oceanic Research and Communication Alliance. These dolphins also had been in captivity for only a limited amount of time (seven years), and they received retraining for the transition. However, not even careful preparation guarantees success. In 1992, nine Atlantic bottlenose dolphins formerly from Atlantis Marine Park near Perth, Australia, were released under scientific supervision. After six weeks, three of the dolphins were recovered; at least one calf probably died; and the fate of the rest was unknown.

Given the obstacles faced by programs designed to release dolphins into the wild, it's difficult to think that leaving for the ocean is a realistic possibility for the average captive dolphin. Accordingly, when captive dolphins apparently have the option to leave, it's difficult to take their remaining to be a sign of free choice. Therefore, even facilities that apparently give dolphins the option to leave may still be morally problematic.

Harm and social life

Perhaps the most important question is whether the social conditions in which captive dolphins live are sufficient to provide a satisfying and appropriate life. Given what we have seen already about a social sense of self among dolphins, significant relationships and meaningful group membership may be as critical to the well-being and development of dolphins as individual liberty and a sense of autonomy are to humans. For dolphins to lack meaningful group membership, there would be little opportunity to develop the affective abilities and social intelligence that is so central to their nature.

The differences between the social conditions in the wild and those in captivity are so different that it is difficult to believe that the social opportunities in captivity are rich enough to meet the conditions necessary for development of their social nature.

It's important to keep in mind just how social wild dolphins are. Wild dolphins spend a significant portion of their day making direct physical contact with other members of the community. They play active and important roles in their groups: hunting, scouting, raising the young, caring for the sick and injured, protecting the vulnerable, mating, and participating in group play and recreation. Solitary dolphins in the wild are a rarity. Wild dolphins develop strong, long-term relationships.

Important implications about captivity flow from the richness of dolphin social life. First, the complex social interaction that we find in the life of a dolphin in the wild may be necessary simply for dolphins to feel safe. It seems likely that dolphins, far more than is the case with humans, ensure both individual and communal welfare by means of managing a large number of relationships on a daily basis. Simply put, in order for dolphins to feel safe, they may need to live together in a complex web of relationships. Indeed, since humans have so many other ways to help us feel safe and secure (e.g., we can build physical structures), dolphins may need this network of relationships far more than humans do. That is, the absence of a rich social network may leave captive dolphins with a significant level of uneasiness about how safe their world is.

Relationships, self, safety and danger

The possibility that captive dolphins may be vulnerable to anxiety about how safe their world is relates directly to Harry Jerison's suggestion that dolphins have a highly social sense of self. If a being's sense of self is defined in relation to other individuals with whom it has strong connections, the fewer of these connections there are, the greater the possibility that such a being would feel increasingly alone and unprotected. Indeed, this phenomenon has been documented in humans.

In Chapter 6, we saw one study that suggests that humans have either an "autonomous" or "connected" sense of self. However, another study points to significant differences in what evokes unconscious feelings of safety and danger in these two ways of experiencing the self. People with an autonomous sense of self appear to find close relationships with others potentially threatening. That is, situations in which their autonomy is at risk of being compromised by entrapment, rejection or betrayal undercut their sense of strength and safety. On the other hand, people with a connected sense of self find just the opposite threatening – situations in which they're isolated from others. Another way to describe this is that people with an autonomous self experience the world as a *ladder* or *hierarchy*. The higher up they are on the ladder – that is, the farther away they are from other people – the more secure they feel. However, the more that they feel encroached upon by others, the more that life feels insecure or dangerous. In contrast, people with a connected self experience the world as a *web* or *network of relationships*. The more that they feel that they're in the center of a strong web, the safer life feels. However, the more that they find themselves on the edge of the web, or in a web with few strands or weak strands, the more dangerous life feels.[26]

At this point, it is relevant to recall the central place of sexuality in dolphins – and the differences between dolphin and human sexuality. Dolphins are naturally bisexual and far more active sexually than humans are. As we saw in chapter 5, dolphin researchers generally agree that sex plays a critical role in forging, maintaining and managing relationships among group members. Sometimes sexual behavior expresses affiliation, sometimes aggression; sometimes it's reproductive, sometimes it's a matter of instructing the young

---

[26] Susan Pollak and Carol Gilligan, "Images of Violence in Thematic Apperception Test Stories," *Journal of Personality and Social Psychology*, 42(1) (1982): 159–167. See also, Carol Gilligan, *In a Different Voice: Psychological Theory and Women's Development* (Cambridge, MA: Harvard University Press, 1982).

in sexual behavior. However, sex is so important that Ken Norris describes it as "the essential social glue of an extended society of 'dolphin friends'" and "a means of assurance for them that they were in that 'society of friends.'"[27] In captivity, dolphin heterosexual behavior is limited to pairings arranged by facilities for the sake of breeding offspring. Even homosexual contacts are limited only to the dolphins with whom they share a pool. It is hard to believe that this would not have a negative effect on such a sexual being, who presumably gets more than physical pleasure from so much sexual contact with so many members of the community. Following Ken Norris's comment that sex is the "glue" of dolphin societies, it is not unreasonable to think that dolphin sexual behavior is a central vehicle for determining the extent and strength of the "web" of relationships that may be the psychological foundation of a dolphin's world. While celibacy is not unusual in humans (indeed, it's frequently regarded as a virtue), it is virtually unheard of in dolphins. Accordingly, as important as sexuality is as a dimension of the human personality, it is probably even more important in dolphins – potentially serving as a critical vehicle for the emotional development and peace of mind of such social beings.

It is, of course, impossible to know anything for certain about the details of the dolphin psyche. However, as we've seen in our earlier discussions, there is good reason to believe that evolutionary imperatives would encourage these intelligent marine mammals to form strong relationships with one another. The stronger their web, the safer they'd be. It's not unreasonable to speculate, then, that millions of years of surviving in the ocean would hard-wire into modern dolphins: a social self, an inclination to form strong bonds, and a direct connection between the number and strength of such bonds and feelings of safety and security.

If this line of speculation is plausible, then, it's reasonable to suggest that captive dolphins – whose "webs" of relationships are virtually always either small, weak or atypical in comparison to what we find in the wild – are vulnerable to no small amount of anxiety about a very fundamental matter – how safe life is. That is, captive dolphins may experience a relatively fragile sense of life. In short, there is good reason to speculate that, no matter how well captive dolphins are cared for physically, the limited social conditions in which they live might leave them in an emotionally deprived state. Seen in this light, captivity could easily have more of a negative impact on dolphins than it would on humans.

[27] Norris, *Dolphin Days*, p. 274.

Personality development: emotional capacities

Another implication of the rich social lives of wild dolphins is that the extent to which dolphin personalities can develop may very well depend on multi-faceted social interaction. That is, managing a complex "web" of relationships may also be a primary means by which dolphins grow emotionally. The question is whether captivity provides the appropriate conditions for such development.

At least in humans, emotional potential develops into sophisticated emotional abilities only through experience. That is, we learn how to develop and manage relationships only by having different types of interactions with a variety of people. We learn about being family members, colleagues, friends, lovers, competitors and enemies only through trying out a variety of social roles. Through these experiences, we develop certain traits, and we learn how to recognize them in others. We learn about qualities like trust, fidelity, honesty and dependability – as well as their opposites. We learn about both healthy relationships and unhealthy ones. But we acquire such insights and traits only through our contact with other people. However, if we have relationships with only a small number of people, or if we have only the same type of relationship, or if we have only limited or unhealthy relationships, it is unlikely that our emotional capacities will grow and develop appropriately.

There's reason to speculate that the same process applies to dolphins. Dolphins appear to have significant affective capacities, and we've seen that wild dolphins appear to develop sophisticated emotional abilities. For example, they manage many and varied relationships, and they're less aggressive with adversaries than humans are. It's likely that they develop these abilities through experience, that is, through their relationships and through the roles they adopt in these relationships.

Captive situations, however, typically provide dolphins the opportunity for many fewer relationships of a more restricted character than the average wild dolphin would experience. Most captive dolphins interact with only a small number of other dolphins in limited sorts of situations. Pool mates and sex partners are usually determined by the staff.

Captive dolphins also interact with humans, so forming and managing these relationships do provide some opportunity for emotional development. The relationships between humans and dolphins in captive facilities, however, are very restricted. Moreover, while many relationships between trainers and dolphins are positive and characterized by mutual respect, this is not always the case. Some facilities prefer a distant and impersonal relationship based on the positive reinforcement of selected behaviors. I have been told that, although it is not usually the case, some trainers have even been known to see the situation as one in which the human ultimately has to assert dominance over the dolphin, and "break" him or her in the same way that a horse trainer deals with a wild stallion.

On balance, it is difficult to imagine how such conditions could allow for the full development of a captive dolphin's emotional capacities.

Personality development: cognitive capacities

The limited roles that captive dolphins play in their lives also raise the question of whether captivity allows for the full development of another dimension of dolphins' personalities – their cognitive capacities. Again, consider the lives of wild dolphins and how the challenges of living in the ocean (and the roles that dolphins must adopt) would encourage cognitive development. Wild dolphins have to learn, at the very least: echolocation; identifying and hunting for food; navigation; recognizing and avoiding predators and other threats; the verbal and nonverbal features of dolphin communication; group strategy; and the ability to respond to unexpected situations and solve a variety of problems. Captive dolphins, by contrast, lead a much less challenging life. They're supplied with food, and their physical environment is largely constant, free of predators and absent of challenges that would be important in the natural world. However, the main cognitive challenges in the lives of most captive dolphins probably have to do with learning behaviors for public performances. Some dolphins do get involved in child-rearing, but captivity hardly approximates the challenges in a natural setting. Some captive dolphins encounter important cognitive challenges in scientific research that they might be involved in, and these dolphins have shown themselves to be apt students. But it is unclear exactly how much this kind of learning benefits them.

Given the fact that both humans and dolphins have significant emotional and intellectual abilities, the notion that our internal abilities are shaped by our activities in life – that is, that "we become what we do" – may be true for both species. Humans who face challenges, work hard, acquire skills, apply themselves to meaningful tasks, overcome fears and engage in authentic relationships with others will become well-developed, strong specimens of our species. On the other hand, humans who spend their days doing nothing of consequence, shun learning, never push themselves beyond existing limits, and rely on others to take care of their needs will become lazy, self-indulgent, weak, dependent people – a shadow of what they could be. If individuals choose such lives, we may simply lament the lost opportunity. However, if we came upon a situation where these conditions were imposed on a group of people, we'd surely consider this to be seriously wrong. Even if the group were given luxurious physical comforts, if they were nonetheless deprived of meaningful challenges, opportunities and authentic relationships, we'd recognize that they were barred from some of the most important conditions necessary for the growth and development of their personalities.

Something analogous may, then, be the case with dolphins in captive facilities. Captive dolphins live limited lives. They simply do not do much that is especially meaningful or challenging in the course of a day. As a result, captive facilities may very well be producing a class of passive, dependent and acquiescent cetaceans with limited social intelligence. Such dolphins may not be subject to physical abuse or deprivation – indeed, physically, many of them may be living pampered lives. However, particularly for beings who apparently have significant cognitive and affective abilities, it is difficult to think that captivity provides dolphins with the conditions necessary for the growth and development of *their* personalities.

It's important to recognize that looking at captivity from this perspective expands what counts as *harm* to dolphins. From an ethical perspective, harm is not simply physical abuse, neglect, or shortened life-spans. In the case of self-aware individuals with considerable cognitive and affective capacities, it also includes depriving them of the conditions necessary for the development of their personalities. Among humans, the healthy development of emotional and intellectual abilities produces a variety of strengths and a sense of well-being and satisfaction with life. Given the cognitive and affective capacities of cetaceans, the same is probably true with dolphins. Accordingly, depriving either humans or dolphins of necessary conditions for the full development of their personalities would seem to relegate the individuals involved to a lesser quality of life and a weaker sense of well-being and satisfaction with life than their native potential would allow. And whether we're talking about humans or dolphins, such actions are ethically indefensible.

Captive breeding and reduced needs

It might be argued, of course, that after enough generations of captive dolphins, we might actually have the equivalent of a new type of dolphin that has a different set of basic needs than the wild dolphin. After all, the success of captive breeding programs not only lets facilities replenish their dolphin populations without capturing dolphins from the wild, it allows for the possibility of breeding for certain traits. Is there anything ethically problematic about trying to breed a species of dolphin that is designed for captivity? Could this resolve the *quality of life* issue we've just been discussing?

Breeding dolphins for specific traits is possible. In at least one program (the Naval Ocean Systems Center), the goal of the breeding program is "to breed and raise 'in house' . . . dolphins, ensuring healthy animals with desirable characteristics, including trainability, adaptability to captivity, and known breeding lineage."[28] It's important to note that such breeding programs would aim to breed for not only physical traits, but emotional ones as well. Trainability and adaptability to captivity are largely psychological traits. Therefore, the goal of breeding essentially includes an attempt to increase the likelihood of a personality that is: passive; docile; willing to follow instructions; highly tolerant of boredom; and, compared to wild dolphins, has lower needs for social interaction.

So, once again, we're faced with a dilemma that is raised by the similarities between humans and dolphins (both being self-aware individuals with advanced cognitive and affective capacities). Among humans, eugenics in general and forced eugenics in particular are highly questionable from an ethical perspective. Even if the prospect were good that such programs would have only positive tangible results (increased resistance to disease, for example), a program that manipulated genetic material and reproductive processes for the sake of an outcome designed by someone other than the donors of the egg and sperm (and without the consent of the donors) hardly seems to respect the dignity of the human person. Since dolphins have fundamentally the same claim to moral standing that humans do, it is difficult to imagine how such programs can be defended as intrinsically acceptable and as appropriate treatment for beings of this nature.

Slavery revisited?

The idea of treating a species of self-aware beings with a sophisticated consciousness as "property" not "persons," and breeding them with an eye toward the traits that will make them most useful commercially has chilling similarities with the practice of human slavery. Again, the similarities between

---

[28] Sue Mayer, "A Review of the Scientific Justification for Maintaining Cetaceans in Captivity," in A Report for the Whale and Dolphin Conservation Society, February 1998, p. 17, quoted from J. P. Schroeder, "Reproductive Aspects of Marine Mammals," in L. A. Dierauf (ed.) *CRC Handbook of Marine Mammal Medicine: Health, Disease and Rehabilitation* (San Diego, CA: Academic Press, 1990), pp. 353–369.

humans and dolphins on this score are central, because they raise the question of whether capturing, selling, buying and/or breeding is consistent with the dignity due a self-aware being. The economic incentives driving this business are large – as was the case with the African slave trade in the New World. A captive dolphin can be sold for something on the order of $15,000 to $50,000. Its new owner can charge about $100 for a dolphin swim, rapidly recover his initial investment and quickly move to profitability. Even if dolphins are used only to perform in shows, they can still generate sizable revenues. Defenders of dolphin-related businesses argue that the benefits are so considerable that they can even boost local economies in both the source and destination countries.

Captivity: the ethical bottom line

It should be clear that captive facilities have some serious problems from the perspective of philosophical ethics. And this is the case whether we look at the consequences that flow from captivity or at the more narrow issue of whether dolphins are being treated appropriately.

Does the good of captivity outweigh the harm? As in the case of the fishing industry, the primary benefits from captivity flow to humans, not the dolphins involved. The owners of "for profit" captive facilities in the entertainment industry receive financial benefits. Employees who work at such facilities get paychecks. Humans who watch dolphin shows or who swim with the dolphins get enjoyment. The dolphins do receive food and physical safety, but they live in uninteresting physical conditions. More importantly, they live in social conditions that would seem to allow for only a limited amount of development of their personalities. To compound the problem, the traits that captive dolphins are encouraged to develop (e.g., passivity, high tolerance for boredom) hardly seem like strengths. In short, it is difficult to believe that the conditions under which captive dolphins live – even in the best facilities – produce a strong sense of satisfaction with life. While captive dolphins in the best facilities are in good physical health, there is reason to speculate that captive dolphins live in an emotionally deprived state. In short, captivity is probably more detrimental for dolphins than it would be for humans.

Proponents of captivity, however, argue that one of its chief contributions is that it educates humans and makes them more sympathetic to environmental issues, in general, and the fate of wild dolphins, in particular. Accordingly, some might offer the following argument:

- Without captive facilities and television shows like *Flipper*, consumers would never have responded to the deaths of dolphins in the eastern tropical Pacific. That is, without places like Sea World, we would never have gotten "dolphin-safe" tuna.

- Saving the lives of millions of wild dolphins who otherwise would have died in the tuna nets surely counts as a very important benefit.

- Unless captive facilities continue providing humans with first hand experience with dolphins, most people will become less sympathetic to the impact of human actions on wild dolphins. The average human may even revert to the idea that dolphins are no different from any other non-human animal. And this could lead to dolphins losing protections that they currently enjoy.

- Captive facilities are major sites for scientific research. Such research provides us with information about both the nature of dolphins and the conditions under which they flourish. Indeed, the claims of this book are largely dependent on research done in just such facilities. More research is only going to increase our knowledge about dolphins. Through education, this will presumably also create understanding and sympathy for dolphins by future generations of humans.

- Captivity, then, provides long-term, important benefits to present and future generations of wild dolphins (and, possibly, to other nonhumans) by encouraging popular attitudes and scientific research that will increase the likelihood that future generations will take the welfare of wild dolphins seriously.

- Accordingly, when we compare the negative consequences experienced by captive dolphins against the benefits experienced by humans and wild dolphins alike, there is no comparison. Over the long term, the good far outweighs the harm.

Sadly, this argument makes some sense. But I say "sadly" not because it defends dolphin captivity, but because the argument is based on the assumption that there is a depressing absence of intelligence, imagination, sympathy and compassion in *Homo sapiens*. In essence, this defense of captivity argues that human beings are so self-centered and thoughtless that without the direct experience of seeing dolphins in person, many of us will revert to seeing these cetaceans as just clever mammals. Unfortunately, given how poorly humans treat members of our own species, I cannot say that this would not happen. However, if the best defense of captivity is that humans are so lacking in compassion, I trust it is apparent that this is not a defense of the institution of captivity itself. Captivity then becomes just a check against the recklessness of a potentially destructive species.

But what about the benefits of scientific research and education that captivity allows? Scientific research and education are almost sacred enterprises in human culture. Aren't the benefits – to dolphins and humans – so considerable that they provide a strong ethical defense of captivity? I don't think so. More research may, indeed, lead to better treatment of dolphins in the future. The work of future scientists should bolster the picture that dolphin research currently suggests (self-aware individuals with significant cognitive and affective abilities), so the case for protecting them from harm will be even stronger. Future research may even persuade more humans than current research does. Doesn't this make a difference?

As someone who has been a teacher and researcher since 1971, I have to confess to feeling a powerful impulse to label research and education as special factors that can defend certain instances of captivity. I know that the researchers and educators involved in these situations are generally hard working, poorly paid, selfless individuals who are not only dedicated to advancing the welfare of dolphins, but usually at the forefront of campaigns to protect them. Nonetheless, I believe that what current research tells us about dolphins is sufficient to call into question the ethical defensibility of all instances of captivity. We now know enough to realize that we need to change how we treat dolphins. Any argument that contends that the absence of future research will jeopardize the welfare of future dolphins because humans will "backslide" is, again, a claim that humans lack the wit to remember what we have already discovered. And, in my opinion, that is not a strong enough defense of the intrinsic features of captivity to make it ethically acceptable.

Appropriate treatment   One of the central questions from a philosophical perspective is whether the individuals involved are being treated appropriately. That is, do captive facilities treat dolphins in a way that respects their dignity as beings with moral standing? Are they being treated as "persons" not as "property"? It is difficult to see how captivity can pass muster from this ethical perspective.

First, captive dolphins that were forcibly removed from their natural environment are placed in situations that don't realistically allow them the option to leave. Similarly, dolphins that were bred in captivity aren't raised in conditions or ways that give them that option. So their presence can't be construed as "voluntary" – surely one of the first requirements for "appropriate treatment" for a being with moral standing. As we saw above, the best interpretation we're entitled to is probably something like "acceptance of the fact that there's only one realistic option" – something that falls far short of "free choice."

Second, it is difficult to interpret the way that dolphins are treated in captive facilities as any way but largely as objects – whether it is to generate profit, to entertain us, to satisfy our curiosity, to improve humanity's treatment of nonhumans or even to learn something that will let us save the lives of stranded dolphins. That is, no matter what sort of good is achieved, dolphins are being used as *means* to an end that our species chooses. Again, we have a situation in which the dignity of a being with moral standing is not being respected.

Third, from an ethical perspective, the idea that it is appropriate to breed self-aware beings to maximize their utility as economic commodities is fundamentally troubling. It, again, appears to take us to a point where we have no qualms labeling certain "persons" as "property."

Captivity for therapy and military purposes

Although most of the controversy about the captivity of dolphins revolves around entertainment facilities, there are two other uses of captive dolphins that deserve our attention. Dolphins are also used in human therapy and by the military. Are these uses ethically defensible?

Dolphin-assisted therapy and dolphin "healing" "Dolphin-assisted therapy" refers to a variety of practices that aim to facilitate healing of human disorders through direct interaction with dolphins. The approach remains controversial, with no small debate about its effectiveness. One of the more reputable practitioners is psychologist David Nathanson, who has been a pioneer in the field since the late 1970s.[29] Nathanson has worked mainly with individuals

---

[29] D. E. Nathanson, "Dolphins and Kids: A Communication Experiment," in *Congress Proceedings of the XVI World Assembly of the World Organization for Preschool Education* (1980), pp. 447–451; D. E. Nathanson, "Using Atlantic Bottlenose Dolphins to Increase Cognition of Mentally Retarded Children," in P. Lovibond and P. Wilson (eds) *Clinical and Abnormal Psychology* (North Holland: Elsevier, 1989), pp. 233–242; D. E. Nathanson and S. de Faria, "Cognitive Improvement of Children in Water with and without Dolphins," *Anthrozoos*, 6(1) (1993): 17–29; D. E. Nathanson, D. de Castro, H. Friend and M. McMahon, "Effectiveness of Short-term Dolphin Assisted Therapy for Children with Severe Disabilities," *Anthrozoos*, 10(2/3) (1997): 90–100; D. E. Nathanson, "Long Term Effectiveness of Dolphin Assisted Therapy for Children with Severe Disabilities," *Anthrozoos*, 11(1) (1998): 22–32. For a response, see Lori Marino and Scott O. Lilienfeld, "Dolphin-Assisted Therapy: Flawed Data, Flawed – Conclusions," *Anthrozoos*, 11(4) (1998): 194–200.

affected with cerebral palsy, Down syndrome, and autism. He uses interaction with dolphins mainly as a reward for patients' correctly completing
therapeutic work. Nathanson claims that working with dolphins can increase
both the attention span and motivation of afflicted individuals. Nathanson
sees these as important elements in patient improvement.

Despite the therapeutic goal of such programs, from an ethical perspective, they don't overcome the problems of any other captive facility. The mix
of benefits over harm is slightly different. However, the benefits still flow
only in one direction (to the humans) with the costs being borne by the
dolphins. It remains doubtful that the situation is fully voluntary and that
treatment is fully consistent with what's appropriate to the dignity of a
self-aware being.

Even more problematic, however, are programs that are not run by specialists
like Nathanson but that intimate some sort of vague therapeutic or healing
benefit to swimming with dolphins. Such programs increasingly target wild
dolphin populations and are generally not supervised by specialists in dolphin
behavior. The result is that the ignorance and enthusiasm of human swimmers can lead to serious disregard for dolphin welfare. In one instance in the
waters off Oahu, for example, a swimmer who got so close to dolphins that
it risked disrupting mother/baby nursing reportedly defended her actions by
saying that it was perfectly all right for her "to share with the dolphins this
wonderful moment because the dolphins knew I was a mother myself."

Military use of dolphins   Even more controversial than the use of dolphins
in human therapy, however, is their use in human military operations. While,
not surprisingly, all relevant details of these programs are not available,
much is a matter of public record. The US Navy, for example, has had the
Navy Marine Mammal Program for decades. Dolphins are trained: to detect
and mark the location of mines, to identify safe corridors for landing troops
ashore, to serve as underwater sentries and identify unauthorized swimmers.
The Navy dolphins have been used in at least Vietnam and the Persian Gulf.
The Navy also has sponsored research on cetacean health, bioacoustics
and hearing. The United States, however, is not the only country that took
an interest in dolphins. The former Soviet Union also reportedly trained
dolphins for military purposes, ultimately selling some of them to Iran, when
funds for the support of their cetaceans ran low.

The US program trains the dolphins from the start for military life.
Indeed, their captive breeding program has been so successful that they have
not captured a wild dolphin since 1988. As the Navy describes the training:

Early training includes teaching calves how to follow small boats and how to slide out of the water onto beaching trays. It also includes getting the calves accustomed to various things such as boat motors, people in wetsuits, and divers in the water. This is facilitated by the fact that calves tend to mimic adults, especially their mothers. As training progresses, each calf is taught other essentials of the Marine Mammal Systems such as wearing special equipment, leaving the familiar enclosure area to swim for short periods of time in the open water before returning to the enclosure, and beaching into a specially designed boat and going for a ride. They are also provided a chance to socialize with a variety of other dolphins that are in the program, some of which may be their own age and energy level.[30]

As is the case with dolphin-assisted therapy, the military use of dolphins is just as ethically questionable as any other captive program. The military dolphins, like virtually all captive dolphins, are trained to adapt to captivity, and they associate only with other dolphins who are trained in the same skills and dispositions. Accordingly, it is likely that they experience the same lack of development that may be the case in dolphins in captive entertainment facilities. Again, not only are humans the main beneficiaries of this arrangement, but military programs also face the same ethical programs connected with captive breeding and the lack of free choice of a being with moral standing. Therefore, these programs are also ethically questionable.

In short, I do not believe that the captivity of dolphins in any form is ethically defensible.

So What Do We Do?

After everything we've looked at, you may still be unconvinced that our species is doing anything wrong. But remember that the question we're facing isn't, "Can we prove conclusively that dolphins are being harmed?" Instead, it's, "Is it reasonable to think that certain practices *could* harm individual dolphins or treat them inappropriately?" In a questionable situation, our moral responsibility is clear. If there's even a reasonable possibility that dolphins are the kinds of beings I argue that they are, the "benefit of the doubt" requires us to respect a being's dignity and intrinsic worth and refrain from questionable actions.

---

[30]   http://www.spawar.navy.mil/sandiego/technology/mammals/research.html

Because the primary ways that our species interacts with dolphins – fishing practices that harm dolphins and captivity – are at least ethically questionable (and, more likely, ethically unjustifiable), our species faces a dilemma. What do we do now?

First, humanity's most pressing obligation is to find ways to discontinue fishing practices that harm individual dolphins. Whether it be commercial fishing (with purse seine or drift nets) or traditional dolphin hunts, these practices lead to the deaths of nonhumans who share the same basic traits as humans – self-awareness as individuals and sophisticated cognitive and emotional abilities. Purse seiners can operate profitably without fishing "on dolphin." Drift nets can be replaced with other less wasteful methods. And there are other ways to get food and to assert pride in one's culture than to kill cetaceans.

Second, captive facilities should cease all of the current captive breeding programs. Breeding self-aware beings for use in entertainment, research, human therapy or military defense is highly questionable in terms of respecting the dignity of a being with moral standing. However, this does not mean that all theme parks built around dolphins are doomed to close up shop. As anyone who has had contact with dolphins in their natural habitat can attest, dolphins in the wild are far more interesting than dolphins in captivity. Given the entertainment potential (and cost effectiveness) of video technologies like IMAX movies that portray dolphins in the wild, theme parks that begin integrating such technologies into their operation should be able to remain profitable.

Third, we need to recognize that there is no perfect solution for the hundreds of dolphins who currently live in captivity. There is little likelihood that many (if any) could be trained to live in the wild. So, realistically, they should probably remain where they are for the rest of their lives. The current captive generations will then die out over the next 40–50 years. Our responsibility is to make sure they live lives as satisfying as possible under the circumstances and that they are able to contribute as much as possible to research and education that will lead humans to a more enlightened view of dolphins and our relationship with the planet.

In view of the predictable end of a pool of captive dolphins for research, new dolphin researchers should be steered by their mentors into research in the wild. While such research is in many ways more difficult than research on captive dolphins, the work of a variety of scientists shows that it is both possible and leads to important results: Richard Connor and Rachel Smolker (Shark Bay, Australia), Kathleen Dudzinski (Japan and the Bahamas), Denise Herzing (the Bahamas), Ken Norris (Hawaii), Susan Shane (Texas and Florida), Randy Wells (Florida's Sarasota Bay) and Bernd Würsig (Argentina).

Surely, for a species that is as intelligent as we say we are, we can begin to find ways to live peacefully on the planet with another intelligent, even if nonhuman, species.

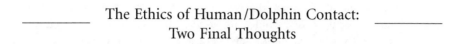

The Ethics of Human/Dolphin Contact: Two Final Thoughts

Before ending this chapter, I feel that I need to address two points: the fact that my discussion has not included any religious considerations, and the fact that the discussion of the ethics of human/dolphin interaction has been one-sided, talking only about human obligations towards dolphins.

The contribution of a religious outlook

I am sure that some readers have found the absence of any discussion of a religious perspective on these issues disconcerting. Religious teachings about right and wrong are probably the main ways that many humans think about ethics, and my conclusion that dolphins deserve the same consideration as humans surely challenges any religious tradition that claims that the natural world is created for human use and that our ethical obligations towards nonhumans amount to no more than "good stewardship." Since I approached this study from scientific and philosophical perspectives, it would not be inappropriate for me simply to say that those were the boundaries of my investigation and leave it at that. However, I believe that there is ultimately no tension between philosophy and religion on this matter. To Eastern religious traditions like Buddhism, the way that humans treat dolphins is clearly offensive. And there is even reason to think that Western religious traditions could agree. One of the most important thinkers to wrestle with the issue of the relationship between God and the natural world is Thomas Aquinas, the Western medieval Christian philosopher and theologian. Deeply influenced by Aristotle's belief in the integrity of the natural world, Aquinas wrote, "To detract from the perfection of creatures is to detract from the perfection of the divine power."[31] In other words, if we refuse to appreciate the wonder,

---

[31] *Summa Contra Gentiles*, Chapter 69: "Of the opinion of those who withdraw from natural things their proper actions."

mystery and beauty of the natural world, we thereby reject the perfection of the Creator who made it. Any reader troubled by the religious implications of my conclusions, then, should meditate on the following thoughts. There is no conflict between the idea that God created the natural world and the idea that it will take us thousands of years to fully understand it. If in the course of that process we discover that God gave dolphins advanced cognitive and affective traits, wouldn't God want them to be treated in a way consistent with those traits? Wouldn't a refusal to do so amount to rejecting the integrity of God's creation and asserting a human view of how the natural world should be (designed for our convenience) over a spiritual view that requires us to recognize that we have more obligations to other living things than human pride might want to recognize?

Dolphin obligations towards humans

While I have said a great deal about our obligations to dolphins, I have said nothing about their obligations towards us. Presumably, if *their* moral standing means that we are required to treat them in certain ways, then *our* moral standing should mean the same in reverse. Some might think that the fact that I have said nothing about their obligations towards us means that I have side-stepped this critical issue because there is no reason to think that dolphins are capable of such sophisticated thinking.

As I have said frequently in this book, it is impossible to know what goes on in the mind of a dolphin. The best we can do is to study their behavior and to infer what their actions might mean about some inner cognitive and/or emotional state. In this case, I think that the most important facts are the ways that dolphins have behaved towards humans for the two thousand years of our recorded contact. Normally, they are nonaggressive – even in the face of provocation. There are even numerous stories of cetacean helpfulness. That is, I'd contend that they already behave in a way that suggests they understand what counts as appropriate and respectful treatment of humans. There is much more of a problem of how we treat them than how they treat us.

Epilogue

I wrote this book in the hope that it will help anyone reading it come to a more accurate understanding of dolphins and of our species' relationship with them. I hope that readers recognize that dolphins are very much like us – they are self-aware individuals with sophisticated cognitive and emotional abilities. At the same time, dolphins are so different from us that the best model for understanding them is probably Diana Reiss's idea that dolphins represent an "alien intelligence" – they have a longer and dramatically different evolutionary history from us; they have a sense that we lack (echolocation) and, hence, they have perceptions unavailable to us; and they are so social that their very sense of self may be fundamentally different from ours. The combination of the similarities and differences means that our species needs to rethink how we appraise the ethical acceptability of how humans treat dolphins. On the basis of 15 years of studying this issue, my conclusion is that all of the following are, in different degrees, ethically indefensible: fishing practices that injure dolphins; the use of captive dolphins in the entertainment industry; and the use of captive dolphins for scientific research, military purposes and therapeutic purposes. The scientific research about dolphins raises enough *reasonable doubt* about the ethical defensibility of these practices that we are morally obligated to stop them. In short, we now know enough about dolphins to realize that they're entitled to be left alone.

At the same time, I recognize the difficulties connected with calling for a change in how humans treat dolphins. Humans do not treat members of our own species terribly well, so I have no illusions that humans are suddenly going to treat members of another species appropriately. Humans murder something on the order of a million and a half other people each year. We kill one another for every imaginable, unjustifiable reason. Tens of millions of humans are held in some form of modern slavery (bonded labor, forced labor, child labor, forced prostitution, sexual exploitation of children, forced marriage, chattel slavery). About one billion people (one-sixth of the world's population) and almost half the world's urban populations live in slums. At present, we don't even operate in a way that guarantees that our species will survive on the planet over the long haul. We have no qualms about making our air, water and land less friendly to supporting life. We regularly fish stocks to the point of depletion. Our species does not act often enough as though we value our own lives. So against this backdrop, I am realistic about how much we will value the lives of dolphins.

A popular slogan points out that "humans aren't the only species on earth; we just act like it." Nonetheless, we humans have repeatedly demonstrated the capacity to recognize as equals beings whom we once saw as inferiors. I believe that humans currently stand in roughly the same relationship with dolphins as white Americans did to black slaves two hundred years ago. During the last two centuries, science and culture were gradually able to transcend the racism that constrained them to see other people only as property. There is, then, reason to be hopeful that, eventually, our species will overcome the cultural, economic and political forces that limit our perspective about other beings with whom we share the planet. It will take patience and persistence, but it is surely not too much to hope of a species that regards itself as so intelligent. Who knows? One day, it may be *Homo sapiens* defining intelligence as "mucking about in the water having a good time."

Index

Note: "n" after a page number refers to a note on that page.